surviving fieldwork

a report of the advisory panel on health and safety in fieldwork american anthropological association

by NANCY HOWELL

a special publication of the American Anthropological Association
number 26

Published by the
American Anthropological Association
1703 New Hampshire Avenue, N.W.
Washington, D.C. 20009

Professional Series Editor
Linda A. Bennett

Library of Congress Cataloging-in-Publication Data
Howell, Nancy.
  Surviving fieldwork : a report of the Advisory Panel on Health and Safety in Fieldwork,
American Anthropological Association / by Nancy Howell.
    p. cm.
  Includes bibliographical references.
  ISBN 0-913167-38-X
  1. Anthropology—Fieldwork. 2. Anthropology—Safety measures. 3. Anthropolo-
gists—Health risk assessment. I. American Anthropological Association. Advisory Panel
on Health and Safety in Fieldwork. II. Title.
GN34.3.F53H68   1990
306'.072—dc20
                                                              90-246
                                                              CIP

ISBN 0-913167-38-X

CONTENTS

                                                        Page

Foreword
Roy A. Rappaport vii

Preface and Acknowledgments ix

1   Studying Health and Safety in Fieldwork 1

2   The Sample of Anthropologists 19

3   Careers and Characteristics of the Respondents 32

4   Fieldworkers and Their Fieldwork 46

5   The Hazards of Exposure 65

6   The Hazards of Animals 79

7   Human Hazards of Fieldwork 89

8   Injury Accidents: Vehicles and Other Causes 101

9   Parasitic Diseases 115

10   Infectious Diseases 128

11   Degenerative Diseases in the Field 142

12   Mental Health and Illness in the Field 152

13   Families in the Field 164

14   Practicing Medicine in the Field 176

15   Making Fieldwork Safer 182

References Cited 194

Bibliography:
Health and Safety Guides Useful for Fieldworkers 198

Appendix: Questionnaire Form 200

Index 208

LIST OF TABLES

		Page
1.1	Percentage of All Deaths, by Causes of Death	12
1.2	Departments of Anthropology, Personnel Changes 1976–86	14
2.1	Professional Anthropologists Listed in the 1976 *Guide to Departments* and the *1976 List of Members of AAA*	20
2.2	Sources of Highest Degrees and Current Employment	24
2.3	Highest Degree, for Total Population and for Sample	25
2.4	Job Position and Sex of the Sample	26
2.5	Highest Degree and Sex of the Sample	26
2.6	Subdisciplinary Speciality and Sex	27
2.7	Rates of Questionnaire Return for the Subdisciplinary Specialities	28
2.8	Disposition of Sample in Participation in the Study	30
2.9	Fieldwork and Response in the Sample	31
3.1	Age and Sex of the Sample	32
3.2	Professional Activities of Respondents	33
3.3	Checklist of Factors that Made It Impossible to Do Desired Professional Activities	34
3.4	Activity Checklist for Training Students to Do Fieldwork	35
4.1	Regions and Countries of Field Trips Reported	52
4.2	Size and Duration of Trips, by Areas	53
4.3	Source of Major Funding of Trips, by Areas	54
4.4	Housing and Sleeping Conditions in the Field	55
4.5	Field Conditions—Water Treatment	56
4.6	Field Conditions—Sanitary Facilities	57
4.7	Food Supplies and Food Preparers	58
4.8	Transportation in the Field	59
4.9	Field Conditions—Access to Medical Care in the Field	60
4.10	Field Conditions—Availability of Safety Equipment in the Field % that Reported Having Each	61
4.11	Medical Precautions Taken Before Going to the Field	62
4.12	Precautions Taken Before Fieldwork: Insurance and Documents	63
4.13	Precautions Taken by Researchers After Arrival in the Country Where the Research Is Being Done	63
5.1	Sunburn Experience	65
5.2	Heatstroke and Heat Exhaustion	68
5.3	Altitude Sickness	70
5.4	Burns from Fire	72
5.5	Frostbite	73
5.6	Cold Stress, Hypothermia	73
5.7	Malnutrition	76
5.8	Weight Loss in the Field	77
6.1	Leeches	79
6.2	Jellyfish and Other Stinging Sea Creatures	80
6.3	Snakebite	81
6.4	Scorpion Stings	83
6.5	Bee and Wasp Stings	84
6.6	Stinging Ants and Black Flies	85
6.7	Disease-transmitting Insects	86
6.8	Bites and Attacks from Mammals	87
7.1	Criminal Interpersonal Hazards, Combined Rate	89
7.2	Robbery	90
7.3	Assault and Physical Violence	92
7.4	Rape and Attempted Rape	93

continued on next page

7.5	Arrests in the Field	96
7.6	Military Attack	97
7.7	Suspicion of Spying	97
7.8	Living through Political Turmoil	98
7.9	Factional Conflict	99
7.10	Hostage-taking Incidents	99
8.1	Car Accidents	101
8.2	Truck Accidents	103
8.3	Injury Accidents from Motorcycles, Motor Scooters, and Bicycles	107
8.4	Injury Accidents from Knives	110
8.5	Injury Accidents from Falls	111
8.6	Injuries from Accidents	113
9.1	Malaria, 24% of Those Exposed	116
9.2	Amebiasis	122
9.3	Amebic Dysentery	122
9.4	Giardiasis	123
9.5	Ascariasis	124
9.6	Tapeworm	124
9.7	Trichinosis	125
9.8	Hookworm	125
9.9	Valley Fever	126
10.1	Colds and Respiratory Infections	130
10.2	Tuberculosis	130
10.3	Pneumonia	131
10.4	Diarrheal Diseases	132
10.5	Bacillary Dysentery—Shigellosis	134
10.6	Hepatitis and Other Infectious Diseases of the Liver	135
10.7	Dengue Fever	137
10.8	Venereal Diseases	139
10.9	Miscellaneous Infectious Diseases	141
11.1	Pregnancy and Termination in the Field	144
11.2	Appendicitis in the Field	145
11.3	Stomach Ulcers	145
11.4	Hemorrhoids	146
11.5	Migraine and Other Headaches in the Field	147
11.6	Toothache in the Field	147
11.7	Allergies in the Field	148
11.8	Arthritis in the Field	149
11.9	Diabetes in the Field	149
11.10	Cancer in the Field	150
11.11	Heart and Circulatory Disease in the Field	151
12.1	Hallucinations in the Field	152
12.2	Manic States in the Field	153
12.3	Depression in the Field	153
12.4	Anxiety in the Field	154
12.5	Culture Shock in the Field	154
12.6	Alcoholism and Drug Abuse in the Field	155
12.7	Repatriation Stress	160
13.1	Percentage of Spouses in the Field	165
13.2	Percent that Has Taken a Spouse to the Field, by Age and Sex	165
13.3	Relationship Problems Caused by Fieldwork	168
13.4	Frequency of Taking Children to the Field	171
14.1	Practicing Medicine in the Field	176
14.2	Proportion Practicing Medicine by Distance to Nearest Doctor	178
14.3	Used Particular Medical Treatments	178
14.4	Success and Failure in Medical Practice in the Field	179
15.1	Level of Hazards Experienced in the Field, by Area	183

LIST OF FIGURES

Page

1.1   Components of the Population of Anthropologists 10
3.1   Age at Starting Graduate School in Anthropology 36
3.2   Age at Finishing Graduate School, for Those Who Earned a Ph.D. 36
3.3   Number of Years to Completion of Ph.D. 37
3.4   Age at First Fieldwork 38
3.5   Age at First Professional Job 38
3.6   Age at which Respondent Feels Career Was Started 39
3.7   Length of Career to Date 40
3.8   Current Health Rating of the Respondents 40
3.9   Rating of Physical Fitness 41
3.10 Rating of Weight Control 41
3.11 Rating of Smoking Behavior 42
3.12 Rating of Caution and Attitude toward Risk 43
3.13 Rating of Organization and Disorganization 43
3.14 Rating of Drinking Behavior 44
3.15 Rating of Cheerfulness versus Depression and Anxiety 44
3.16 Rating of Degree of Sociability 45
4.1   Number of Field Trips 47
4.2   Total Time in the Field 48
4.3   Days of Fieldwork during 1986 50
15.1 Sum of Hazards Reported to Self, by 204 Fieldworkers 183

FOREWORD

Someone—one of our colleagues, I think—once characterized anthropologists as "otherwise sensible people who don't believe in the germ theory of disease": a charge of mild eccentricity that seems designed to delight the accused by validating their mystique. That the preponderance of us are, in fact, firmly convinced of microorganisms' infectious powers but sometimes pretend to act as if we aren't also contributes to the mystique of fieldwork as not mere research but adventure, ordeal, and vision quest as well. Legends and myths, of course, have their uses (or as we used to say, "functions"). Nothing separates anthropologists from rural sociologists more definitively, at least according to our own view of the world, than a nice case of malaria, or the occasional appearance of a crocodile at the boat-landing, or long sojourns alone among radically different "Others." But mystique aside, people do get sick, sometimes seriously, in the field. And they do suffer depression and loneliness, and can and do suffer injury far from medical facilities. It may not be coincidental, however, that at the same time we have treasured the idea of such dangers our systematic knowledge of them has, to put the best possible face on the matter, been slight. As Morris Freilich has pointed out (1977:27), our sources of information have, by and large, been each other, usually one-on-one conversations or discussions in small groups, often late at night over drinks when we have all become too tired to continue more serious talk. What we have had, mostly, are reminiscences, recounted in informal circumstances, sometimes, I suspect, harmlessly embellished to make them a bit more entertaining or to turn them into parables.

Given their nature, it is not surprising (as Freilich and Lévi-Strauss cited by Howell [p. 6] note) that certain elements of field situations and experiences are less likely to enter into such discussions, and thus into public discourse and knowledge, than others. Making the matter even murkier, while some of our colleagues may tend to exaggerate the difficulties and dangers they have seen, others refuse, perhaps for rhetorical, pedagogical, or psychological reasons, to recognize them at all. And so, finally, our knowledge, if it is to be called "knowledge," of the hazards of the field is highly selective and heavily ideologized and, regardless of whatever else it may be good for, it cannot serve us or our students as reasonable grounds for assessing the actual dangers we all may face.

Nancy Howell has given us what is, so far as I know, the first serious attempt to appraise these hazards and difficulties systematically, realistically, and objectively. The results, as readers will discover, could more easily, and perhaps more appropriately, be summarized than weighed, for hazards, including everything from minor cuts to cerebral malaria and homicide, are not all commensurable. The conclusion seems to be that there are some real and substantial dangers, but that there are usually ways to reduce and avoid them. To reduce and avoid them, however, require that we not only recognize them but understand them better than we now do. One of the virtues of this pioneering work is that, in surveying the complete range of fieldwork risks throughout the entire world, it points in the direction of particular areas, geographic, subdisciplinary, and hazard-specific, in which further and more detailed inquiry would be especially useful. Some such inquiries, as for instance into episodes of depression among ethnographers working alone in isolated areas for months at a time (a hazard with which I myself have some familiarity), would, of course, be sensitive: people often would rather not talk about such things. But research concerning such matters might provide us with insights into distressed mental and emotional states, factors in fieldwork generating them, and their effects upon ethnographic accounts, as well as ways to avoid them, alleviate them, and mitigate their effects. In sum, this volume is not only a survey of the hazards of fieldwork and a summary of ways to improve its safety, both of which are reason enough for all anthropologists to read it and consult it. It is also an important contribution to our movement toward greater self-consciousness concerning our own practice. Regardless, if this book contributes to any reduction of field-related injury or illness or death, I think that Nancy Howell, who was at least in part moved to write it by a field tragedy of her own, will count it a success. Anthropologists everywhere are indebted to her.

—Roy A. Rappaport

PREFACE AND ACKNOWLEDGMENTS

My interest in the questions of this report started to develop more than twenty years ago, when I was a sociology student in graduate school at Harvard working with anthropologists as well as other social scientists. I finished my Ph.D. in sociology and married an anthropologist, ethnographer Richard Lee, and went to the Kalahari desert as the demographer on an anthropological expedition, living for two years in one of the most remote locations in the world, working with the !Kung Bushmen.

Typically of new fieldworkers, I had no training or preparation for prevention of illness and accidents, but untypically I, and most of us on the Harvard Kalahari expedition, had taken a six-week course in "barefoot doctor medicine" offered by the Harvard Health Service for anthropologists and others going to remote locations for fieldwork. This course was frequently helpful during the two years of fieldwork I did in association with ten others from Harvard University. I found, during the late 1960s when I was doing my fieldwork, that I was marginally more conservative in my approach to dangers than the other researchers with whom I worked. I took pride in providing a plentiful supply of clean drinking water and nutritious food in what I thought of as "my" kitchen. I even wrote a xeroxed "bush cookbook" to celebrate my sense of mastery of living in the field. But basically I was like many anthropologists in counting upon good luck and an ability to muddle through crises to manage problems.

Over the years, as I taught students preparing to go into the field and heard stories from anthropologists about adventures and scrapes with disaster, it had crossed my mind that someone should make a systematic study of health and safety in anthropological fieldwork. I thought of the project as learning "the costs of anthropology to anthropologists" but that project never came, naturally and gradually, to the top of my own research agenda.

Instead, it came horribly into focus for me in June 1985 when my 14-year-old son, Alex Lee, was suddenly killed and my other son, David, was injured, in a truck accident in Botswana. In the months that followed that accident, many anthropological friends and acquaintances offered information on similar and different fieldwork accidents. I especially heard of many other truck accidents. A few months later, my friend and colleague Glynn Isaac died in Japan, of hepatitis B, acquired during African fieldwork. The news of Dian Fossey's murder in central Africa came to light in December 1985. As many bereaved people do, I began reading obituaries more carefully, especially those in the *Anthropology Newsletter,* and found additional accidents and illnesses of young people. Friends of Melissa Knauer (the young Ph.D. from Toronto who died in the Kalahari in the same accident as my son) organized a symposium in her memory at the American Association of Physical Anthropologists meeting in Albuquerque in April 1986, and

I attended to present a paper. I thought it might be useful to report on training programs in health and field safety in anthropology. Preparing the paper, I found that such programs are few and primitive. At those meetings I learned of a dozen more deaths, and many more accidents and injuries. Although this project has been protracted and energetic, and I now have a list of about 70 deaths to North American anthropologists in the field during the past decade, I still find that I learn of additional field deaths during the past decade when I talk with colleagues about field safety. My list seems to be far from complete.

In spring 1986, I wrote a letter to the *Anthropology Newsletter* about my concerns about the lack of attention to, and policy toward, health and safety in anthropology. I followed that published letter (Howell 1986) with a letter to the Board of Directors of the American Anthropological Association, calling for a study of the problem. The Board responded to my call for research program with an invitation to do it myself, with the moral and financial support of the Association. And that is exactly what I have done.

The Advisory Panel on Health and Safety was formally proposed by (then) President-elect Roy A. Rappaport to the Board of Directors of AAA in May 1986. I was asked to Chair an Advisory Panel, and nominated the following members in accordance with guidelines established by Rappaport:

Jane Buikstra, University of Chicago (physical anthropology)
Maxine Kleindienst, University of Toronto (archaeology)
Melvin Konner, Emory University (physical anthropology)
Robert Netting, University of Arizona (social anthropology)
Renato Rosaldo, Stanford University (social anthropology)
John Yellen, National Science Foundation (archaeology)

Each of these people had expressed independent interest in the issues of field safety, and each agreed to serve as an individual and professional participant, not as an institutional representative of their university or employer. The Board of the Association approved this membership, and allocated several hundred dollars in both 1986 and 1987 to pay costs of data collection and manuscript preparation. The tasks of the Advisory Panel have been: (1) to collate existing data and to collect new data on health and safety, in order to provide an accurate picture to the profession on the state of the problem of occupational health and safety; (2) to raise consciousness of the problem among individuals and units such as departments that might be placed to take remedial action; and (3) to advise and recommend actions for the future if it turns out that the health and safety record should be improved. I would like to thank all of the members of the Advisory Panel for their contributions to the study and their support during the several years it took.

The initial formulation of the problem occurred during a valuable year at the Center for Advanced Study in the Behavioral Sciences, where I had every kind of support for a new project, including the warmth and friendship of the special people, staff and fellows, who were there in 1985–86. The project has continued with support from the Stanford University Department of Sociology, especially Richard Scott and the participants in the Program on Organizations and Aging. I appreciate the critical comments and moral support provided by the fellows in that program too. My own department at the University of Toronto has supported my various decisions to allow this project to take precedence over my ordinary responsibilities of teaching and research. I have particularly benefited from the support of Chairman John Simpson and colleagues Beverly and Barry Wellman and Bonnie Erickson.

Many individuals have contributed to the study while it was being done, with various forms of input and encouragement. Eric A. Roth (Victoria University), Moyra Brackley, and Anne Katzenberg (University of Calgary) helped to conceptualize the problems. Gene Hammel of Berkeley, George Collier of Stanford, Carmel Schrire of Rutgers, Irven DeVore of Harvard, Nick Blurton Jones of UCLA, and Sheryl Horowitz, University of Massachusetts, Amherst, have participated at various stages. Nancy Donovan Segal has provided editorial assistance to advance the project, and Marilyn Davidson, Charles Fidlar, and David Lee helped to produce the manuscript.

The project required the active input of anthropological fieldworkers at every step, and I would like to take this opportunity to thank two groups for making the research possible. First are the small numbers of individuals who have published frank accounts of their fieldwork—its problems as well as its joys—especially Jean Briggs, Napoleon Chagnon, Dian Fossey, Mary and Richard Leakey, David and Pia Maybury-Lewis, Laura Nader, Nancy Sherper-Hughes, Marjorie Shostak, and Mark and Delia Owens. By sharing their experience these researchers have spared us the need to learn everything by trial and error. Additional volunteers of useful materials are cited in the text and implicitly thanked. Hundreds of individuals provided information about their own experiences. All of those mentioned have explicitly given permission to have their names used, and have checked the text of an earlier draft to confirm the accuracy of my accounts.

The second group that provided the raw material of this research are the 311 individuals that ended up, by no fault of their own, in the random sample of the profession. Most of these people spent considerable amounts of time and energy answering questions about their research and the hazards they experienced. The generous contributions of information from the 204 fieldworkers are particularly appreciated. Their names are not used in the text, even when they were very forthcoming about their experiences.

Individuals in the audience at the 1986 AAPA session in memory of Melissa Knauer suggested that a useful task would be to investigate the availability of health manuals, and perhaps write one for the anthropologists to take to the field. Investigation revealed that every year the U.S. Centers for Disease Control (CDC), located in Atlanta, Georgia, publishes a volume entitled *Health Information for International Travel: 1986* (or whatever year is current). This is an exceedingly useful document, one that every department of anthropology should have for consultation by those considering doing fieldwork in various parts of the world. The manual consists of the latest and best advice on vaccination and prophylaxis against disease, and a tabulation of the geographic distribution of potential health hazards to travelers, so that those headed to various parts of the world can anticipate the dangers they will face there, and solid advice in the form of "health hints for the traveler." It would be useless—even dangerous—to attempt to supplant that effort with a volume that would necessarily be less authoritative, and less often brought up to date. Other useful guides to health are listed in the bibliography to this report.

The current volume is a report, primarily, on the hazards that a random sample of anthropologists have encountered in the field, and the consequences of those hazards. The hoped-for outcome of this project is to get anthropologists to debate and discuss and decide for themselves, individually and collectively, whether health and safety training and preparation is adequate where they work. Where it is not, departments and individuals may need to organize to provide opportunities for training and equipping students and faculty when they go to the field. I would like to thank the chairmen of the departments who provided information on the training situation to date, and hope that these people will continue to participate in the process of guiding training.

Current and future graduate students are invited to use the materials collected here to decide whether their training in health and safety procedures has been adequate for the research that they plan to do. I hope that graduate students will play a leading role in evaluating and improving the training procedures of their departments, but I also hope that they will not wait for leadership from their department. Students, like other anthropologists, need to accept that it is their own responsibility to acquire the information and skills that they will need to be safe in the field.

If this report warns anyone, anywhere, of specific dangers that await them in the field, and consequently they are prepared when the time comes, I am sure that all those who contributed to it, most especially me, will feel it has been worth the trouble.

CHAPTER 1   STUDYING HEALTH AND SAFETY IN FIELDWORK

This is a study about anthropologists, and specifically, about the fieldwork of anthropology, the risks that are taken, and the prices that are paid for doing fieldwork in the ways we do.

The Roots of Anthropology

Most of the professional (as opposed to amateur) anthropologists who ever lived are alive today, and we can trace the recent career moves and location of most of the North American anthropologists who ever lived through the successive *Guides to Departments of Anthropology* produced by the American Anthropological Association each year since 1961.

Anthropology grew as a form of natural history from the genre of travel literature, during the 19th century. All the initial participants were amateurs, as I suppose is necessarily true of all professions in their earliest stages. Physicians, missionaries, explorers, and colonial administrators traveled to exotic locales or stayed at home and studied exotics in books, observed the local people in more or less systematic ways, and reported on their observations to others interested in the topics. In the 19th century, amateur anthropological societies were formed in many cities of Europe and North America for the purposes of corresponding on anthropological topics, meeting to read papers, and talking informally about method. In Europe, these amateurs were mostly concerned with African and Pacific societies. In North America, most of the attention was naturally focused on the still plentiful and available aboriginal "Indian" societies of North and South America.

Records of anthropological societies survive from as early as 1830. The first national arena of anthropological concerns was the formation of Section H of the American Association for the Advancement of Science in 1875—a section of that wide-ranging society that immediately attracted the largest audiences of any section at the annual meetings. Section H still preserves the special status of anthropology in that organization, reflecting the amateur interest that many scientists have in the study of unfamiliar varieties of mankind, while all the other social sciences are lumped together in Section K.

Goldenweiser (1941:155) dates the origin of scientific anthropology in America at 1851, with the publication of Morgan's *League of the Iroquois*. The Archeological Institute of America was founded in 1879, the American Ethnological Society in 1842, the American Folklore Society in 1888, and the Anthropological Society of Washington in 1879. The American Anthropological Association (AAA) evolved out of the Anthropological Society of Washington, in 1902, and the Proceedings of the local society were retitled and renumbered to form the first volumes of the *American Anthropologist,* the journal that is still the leading general publication in anthropology.

It is fascinating to look back at the early issues of this journal. Practically all the names mentioned are now well known to contemporary anthropologists as the pioneers of the field. The titles of articles, reporting on esoteric aspects of the physical measurements, linguistics, ethnography, and archeology of remote and usually nonliterate peoples have not changed drastically over the nearly one hundred years of anthropological history. Other professional associations (43 were listed in the AAA's 1976 *Annual Report*) were formed later, and to varying extents their membership overlaps that of the American Anthropological Association. Amateur associations will be neglected in this account of professional organizations, although it is striking that they exist and play a substantial part in sponsoring and carrying out research, especially in local archaeology. None of the other social sciences have any remotely similar set of amateur organizations.

The first paid positions in anthropology in North America were established in the early days of the 20th century, starting with investigative positions for the federal government, and followed by the appointment of Franz Boas at Columbia University. A study of the departments teaching anthropology in the 1920s has been found (MacCurdy 1919) and the details of formation of major individual departments can generally be read in their graduate catalogues. Historical studies of anthropology have primarily focused thus far on intellectual achievements and the contents of anthropological theory (Harris 1968; Silverman 1981; Stocking 1974, 1983). Institutional history, except on the level of departmental pamphlets, has yet to be written.

In Britain, there were originally three centers of anthropology—at the London School of Economics, at Oxford, and at Cambridge (Kuper 1983). These were the only universities in Great Britain where anthropologists were employed until the 1950s. The intellectual contributions of British anthropology have been mightier than their numbers. There were only a few tens of anthropologists in Britain until 1960, and only a few hundred afterward. The growth in anthropology and anthropologists apparently stopped in Britain in the early 1970s, and the system has been contracting since then, with frozen positions and loss of research support and salaries.

In Europe and in other countries around the world, anthropology has taken various and distinctive historical paths. Due to lack of knowledge and lack of resources for gathering it, no attempt will be made to present the facts for anthropology outside North America (the United States and Canada), except for an occasional reference to Britain or the rest of the world. I apologize for the provincialism of this approach to understanding such a cosmopolitan science.

In the United States, anthropology began at Columbia, with Franz Boas and his famous students Margaret Mead, Edward Sapir, and Ruth Benedict, and in Chicago and Berkeley with Alfred Kroeber and Robert Lowie and their students. The scale of the U.S. anthropological enterprise has been larger than that of Britain from the beginning, as the movement grew from one university to another. Typically anthropologists shared a department with sociology at first, admitting graduate students in addition to undergraduates, and then moving off into a separate department. Only a few institutions have split the enterprise of anthropology into separate departments of archaeology and general anthropology, although the methods and skills of each are sufficiently different to be almost nonoverlapping; but many departments contain internal sections with somewhat different required courses and degree requirements. Other early departments that were important include those at Harvard, Yale, Chicago, and the University of California at Berkeley. These are still the leaders, although some more recently established departments have joined them in the front ranks of the field.

It is striking that when we focus on the formation of actual departments during recent decades, it is meaningless to ask how anthropology organized teaching, research, and recruitment of graduate students, since by and large anthropology did not respond as a unit to any of those issues. Rather, universities responded to their own perceived needs by starting up anthropology programs. It is still a structural feature of the organization of anthropology that the jobs and the money to pay for anthropological activities come from universities, and the money for research comes from foundations and the federal government (and, as we will see, from the anthropologists themselves), while the perspective of the anthropological profession as a whole, the spokespeople for the distinctive problems and insights of anthropology come from the professional associations—both the American Anthropological Association and the many regional and subdisciplinary associations.

The problem of the formal organization of anthropology was seen, albeit in an excessively optimistic way, by the father of American anthropology, Franz Boas, who (according to Hinsley) perceived that

As an institutional form, the university department of anthropology . . . was intended to retain the virtues of both patron and bureaucracy, permitting the imaginative genius to flower in a disciplined environment of reliable financial and moral support. [Stocking 1983:68]

Departments and their surrounding universities no doubt frustrate and aggravate anthropologists more often than they appear in the guise of a flower bed, but it cannot be denied that the growth and spread of departments has been the mechanism that has created some ten thousand paid jobs for persons who might be forced to pursue their anthropological interests as an expensive hobby if they were not paid for doing it.

Departments teach undergraduate courses in anthropology and in multidisciplinary studies that include anthropology. In 1986, 14,221 undergraduates, majoring or concentrating in anthropology, were taught in 479 departments, by faculty numbering from one member in the smallest department (a joint department with other academic specialities) to about 60 in the largest. Faculty employed in academic departments in 1986 numbered 4,908. If we assume that one in seven is on sabbatical leave during any particular year, that leaves 4,207 to teach the 14,221 undergraduates—an average of only 3.4 students per faculty member. That sounds like a very light teaching load, but we have to remember that each student may take several courses per year in the subject, that some faculty who are not on leave nevertheless do more research or administration and less teaching than average, and that this calculation includes only undergraduates, not graduate students. In addition, faculty teach large numbers of students, for instance in the introductory courses, who are not majors or concentrators in anthropology. I suspect, nevertheless, that some anthropologists reading this will be convinced that they bear far more than their share of the teaching load, and no doubt many will be correct.

During the same year, 1986, the departments reported having taught 6,946 graduate students, candidates for master's or doctorate degrees in 152 departments with graduate programs. In 1985–86, departments awarded 3,490 B.A. (or B.S.) degrees, and 839 master's degrees. They also awarded 420 Ph.D.'s, about half to women and half to men. These numbers suggest that roughly 25% of the undergraduates who major or concentrate in anthropology go on to get a master's degree in the subject, and that about half of those who get a master's degree go on to earn a Ph.D. These proportions are only a rough indicator, since we do not know that these are the same people who continue on to higher degrees, nor do we know what trends over time may complicate the calculations.

Ninety-nine departments were listed in the *Guide to Departments of Anthropology* as entitled to award Ph.D. degrees in anthropology in 1986–87, 84 of them in the United States. Generally speaking, it is the largest and the oldest of the departments that produce most of the Ph.D. degrees. The most productive department in 1985–86 was the University of Michigan at Ann Arbor (with 23 Ph.D.'s awarded), followed by University of California at Los Angeles (19), University of California at Berkeley (17), University of Chicago (13), and the University of Illinois, Champaign-Urbana (10). By any accounting, these are leading departments. Other departments produced less than ten new Ph.D.s in the year, and quite a large proportion of the 99 produced 0, 1, or 2. Clearly the proportion of the faculty work load that consists of supervision of Ph.D.'s varies widely between departments, and clearly the degree of connectedness of new Ph.D.'s to the world of North American anthropology departments depends very heavily on their initial choice of a graduate school.

This departmental split between the production of anthropologists and their employment has produced a considerable over-supply of Ph.D.'s since the 1960s, in excess of the jobs available, in anthropology as in many of the social sciences and humanities. Only about 60% of the last cohort of anthropologists (1986) has found jobs in the standard departments and museums, while others are employed in unconventional arenas for anthropologists or have left anthropology altogether (approximately 15%).

Many of the features of the organization of anthropology can best be understood as the result of recent historical accidents and partial planning—decisions taken recently by identifiable people for (no doubt) good reasons, but for limited purposes and to reach local goals. Stinchcombe (1986) suggests that the characteristics of the period in which an organization is formed leaves lasting traces on it, and it should be easy to check this hypothesis on departments formed between 1910 and 1970.

The Centrality of Fieldwork in Anthropology

Fieldwork *is* the central activity of anthropology. It is fieldwork, more than common theories or substantive issues, that distinguishes anthropology from psychology, sociology, political science, and economics. It is fieldwork, more than the distinctive content of the material, that produces the uniqueness of anthropology and that entitles the anthropologist to professional status. It is the anthropologist who goes to the subjects of study and lives with them, collecting information, impressions, and the physical objects that reflect the subjects of study, and who reports what has been learned from the experience.

Morris Freilich (1977:16) has been one of the most thoughtful commentators on fieldwork and helpful in his role as an editor in getting colleagues to discuss the realities of fieldwork concretely. He introduces his discussions of fieldwork with Trinidadian peasants and with Mohawk steel workers by observing:

> For the young graduate students preparing for the first field trip, field work represents mystery, opportunity, and excitement. Field work is also a trial through battle in a war for which the novice has little preparation. The student knows that this is a challenge he will have to face, a major *rite de passage* that will provide him with the opportunity to prove his ability, courage, and tempera mental suitability for the profession. He knows that, in doing field work and in working with the ethnographic data he will collect, a number of transformations will occur. . . . Much like the *rites of passage* of many primitive societies, success in field work is more a function of personal ability than of previous training in specific techniques. Success in field work proclaims manhood and generates a major transformation: a student of culture becomes an anthropologist.

Anthropologists even tend to look like people who do fieldwork. Fieldworkers can frequently be identified by a "uniform" that reminds others of fieldwork for the rest of their lives. Men may wear beards, reminding one of the difficulties of shaving in the bush. Both sexes tend to wear khaki clothing or other "bush gear" and jewelry or cloth made by or worn by the subjects of their studies. Sometimes there are additional marks of distinction that are physical—a deep tan, the dried skin that results from years of exposure to sun and wind, the extreme thinness of chronic diarrheal disease, a limp that recalls a serious accident, or the yellow hue of jaundice, from bouts of hepatitis. We can sometimes use these cues to pick out the anthropologists in a mixed group of social scientists, which encourages the belief that the anthropologist is basically a different kind of person. But is this true? Or are we at risk of overgeneralizing from a handful of colorful people to the whole group of thousands of scholars and scientists who share professional training, a pool of jobs and research support, and a series of professional associations, including, prominently, the American Anthropological Association?

The "prototypical" anthropologist may be imagined as someone like Napoleon Chagnon, traveling in a motorboat down a remote river in the Amazon in central South America, landing near a hostile tribe to stay for weeks or months. Others, like Skip Rappaport, may envision trekking on foot for days into a remote village in the mountains of New Guinea. Students of Hal Movius may imagine arriving at a three-star inn in the French Pyrenees for a summer of digging in the caves and rock shelters at LesEyzies. Alan Beals may picture returning to a dusty peasant village in India. Jean Briggs recalls the sights and sounds of arrival at a small collection of igloos in the Arctic. Raising these prototypes of fieldwork experience reminds us that we need a technique to establish reliable information on the role that each kind of fieldwork plays in the whole. This study will provide that technique.

We may imagine the prototypical anthropologist as going alone and staying for several years, in order to develop language fluency and intense rapport with the people, but we will see from our studies that many anthropologists travel in groups or teams of specialists. They may complete their task and move on within a few weeks of arrival. These specialists are equally anthropologists, equally a part of the picture we seek to understand.

We may expect the prototypical anthropologist to struggle with the elements of survival on a daily basis, boiling water, digging latrines, suffering major and minor injuries and the inconveniences of the life, living with hardship on a regular basis. It is more prestigious to work in an exotic setting than a domesticated one, more characteristic of anthropology to work far from home rather than close by, and more laudatory to work for a long time than for a short time, more admirable to work under dangerous conditions than under unchallenging conditions. Laura Nader put into words what many anthropologists feel:

> Anthropological rank is achieved through field work, and at times the rougher the field situation, the greater the rank. Supposedly one grows under stress, and the greater the stress, the more we grow. . . . Sleeping on a wooden bench is more anthropological than sleeping on a comfortable double bed in the hinterlands of Mexico—the argument being that a comfortable bed would only accentuate the differences between the anthropologist and the people he is living with. This positive attitude toward roughing it (which we use as a way of distinguishing ourselves from our social-science brethren) has until recently also molded our philosophy of training anthropologists. The student is thrown into the ethnographic ocean, and nature takes its course. If he is worth his salt, he will return from the field an anthropologist. [Golde 1986:114]

And yet ethnographic research on the tribe of lawyers located downtown in a major U.S. city permits at least one anthropologist to have lunch in a fine restaurant each day. A well-respected colleague does her fieldwork among aging matrons in suburban America, and some anthropologists go into the high schools, community centers, mental health clinics, drug detoxification programs, and other interesting corners of North American society. Learning how many anthropologists do how much fieldwork under what kinds of conditions will be a product of this study.

Pervasive Silence on the Details of How Fieldwork Is Done

Given the centrality of fieldwork to the lives and to the image of anthropologists, it is astonishing how little is written about it in the voluminous papers and books on the results of anthropological research and how little is taught about it to students. If you were to do a literature search on the topic of fieldwork methods you would find only a handful of texts. If you confine your search to health and safety in fieldwork, or accidents in fieldwork, you would find nothing at all except for occasional tales of particular fieldwork crises. Many monographs that provide great detail on the mythology or the kinship patterns of a people do not even provide information on where the people live or how the researcher came to work among them.

Morris Freilich (1977:31, n. 19) offers the suggestion that

> Learning a native culture is still, for many anthropologists, a procedure not unlike seducing a woman. Success is made more probable if one knows the language, if he is passionately attached to the goal, if he has the charm and style to gain good rapport, if effective use is made of special informants, and if the project is vigorously pursued with a high investment of time and energy. Questions concerning very specific techniques, operationally described, are rather indecent.

Claude Lévi-Strauss (1984:39) proposes a more devious motive for the silence:

> The means of approach to the tribe are carefully glossed over, so as not to reveal the presence of the mission station which has been consistently in touch with the natives for the past twenty years, or of the local motorboat service reaching into the heart of the territory.

Even if Lévi-Strauss is correct about the motive for silence in some cases, the silence goes further than that, almost as though talking about the realities of how the fieldworker does his or her work is shameful.

The details of survival during the day-to-day activities of fieldwork are rarely discussed in teaching or in formal settings, but are interesting and emotive topics to many anthropologists who like nothing more than telling "bush" stories over drinks with intimate friends. Freilich (1977:27) comments:

> An institution that probably contributes to the lengthening of the delays (in writing up the results of fieldwork) is the "bull session" on field work that often takes place at anthropological conferences. After a day of listening to and presenting scholarly papers, anthropologists generally get together at little parties where the talk frequently turns to field work. In an atmosphere made cheerful by alcohol, and often in the presence of envious graduate students yet without field experiences, these discussions of life in the field almost invariably omit certain kinds of information. . . . Considerable time is spent recalling the "joys" of fieldwork, but it is rare indeed to hear a speaker describe the emotional pains . . . by maintaining and developing the fiction of the pure joys of field work, the anthropologist conveniently represses some of the misinterpretations he has often made of his own fieldwork performance.

Some enjoy fantasies of survival without technological civilization, pouring over guidebooks that teach one to chip stone tools, trap small animals, and disinfect drinking water for emergency conditions (Wiseman 1986). A few take the challenges of bush living very seriously, and try to master all the skills—mechanical, medical, linguistic, self-defense—that might someday be required in an emergency. Some others are offended when such topics are discussed in anthropological circles, disliking either the romantic or the grubby aspects of this subject. "This is not a Boy Scout camp," I overheard one professor comment gruffly when graduate students were discussing techniques of fire-building in my presence in their departmental offices. He feels that the essence of anthropology is social theory, not backwoods survival, and that the enterprise is demeaned by spending time and attention on the skills of field living.

For other reasons, some anthropologists have strongly protested at focusing attention on the dangers of fieldwork. There are at least two strains of motivation involved in these protests. One is that there seems to be a streak of "dependency phobia" among some anthropologists. Somehow the verb "coddle" frequently seems to creep into the indignant discussion that follows a mention of the needs of students and employees in the field. Dian Fossey referred in her diary to "changing nappies for six kids at Kabara" (Mowat 1987:106) when she was obliged to help six census takers get started on professional work that she needed and had requested, under her direction. Ruth Tringham described working with students, especially at the beginning of the field season, as "babysitting," and didn't hesitate to admit (at a public meeting to discuss the special problems of women's fieldwork) her resentment at being cast in the role of the all-providing mother in the field. The more usual strategy of anthropologists is to ignore and object to demands for help and reassurance rather than to meet or even acknowledge those demands. This behavior is difficult to document, but many anthropologists admit that they have observed it, in others if not in themselves. And many may recall encountering that attitude during their own graduate student days, from their own professors.

Another reason for objecting to an attempt to document the dangers and difficulties of fieldwork may be a fear that fieldwork will be spoiled. Partly this fear may be focused on practical aspects of the process of fieldwork. If universities, and insurance companies, the families of anthropologists, or even students were to become aware of the facts of the dangers of anthropology, it might be more difficult to raise money, get permission to work in remote areas, recruit students to do difficult work, and so on. Anthropologists value their ability to carry out fieldwork according to their best judgment from day to day. Some fear bureau-

cratic interference by foundations, universities, and governments with the sensitive process of fieldwork. Others fear that they will be compelled to take on more
responsibility for students and employees.

A consequence of this negative attitude toward awareness of the difficulties and
dangers of fieldwork has been that—until this study—virtually nothing has been
known about how often and where a cross section of current anthropologists do
fieldwork. There have been only scattered accounts of the basic facts of fieldwork:
where they go, and how they do it in the sense of day-to-day activities.

In 1968 Napoleon Chagnon wrote an informative and unromantic account of his
fieldwork experience. It stands today as a vivid introduction to what fieldwork
may actually be like under extreme conditions. Though the conditions of his work
with the Yanomamö may have been some of the most difficult and unpleasant in
the world, he points out:

> What I say about some of my experiences is probably equally true of the experiences of many other
> fieldworkers. I wrote about my own experiences because there is a conspicuous lack of fieldwork
> descriptions available to potential fieldworkers. I think I could have profited by reading about the
> private misfortunes of my own teachers; at least I might have been able to avoid some of the more
> stupid errors I made. [Chagnon 1968:iv]

We want to know how anthropologists travel to and in the field, where they
sleep, what they sleep on, whom they sleep with, how they get their food, who
prepares it, and how they get their water. Do anthropologists get medical checkups before they go to the field? Do they take out special insurance policies? Do
they read books or take courses to learn first-aid? Do they get sick in the field? Do
they have medical emergencies, toothaches, appendicitis? What about snakebite,
vehicle accidents, natural disasters? How often do anthropologists become temporarily incapacitated, disabled, permanently handicapped, or even die from their
field experiences?

Is Anthropology a Dangerous Profession?

This study started with that last group of questions, asking what the risks of
mortality—death—and morbidity—disability, handicap, acute illness—are for
anthropologists as a whole. It is plausible that anthropology is much more dangerous than other occupations, especially other scholarly occupations. Individual
cases of death and disability can be cited, with names and corroborating details,
that could only happen under the circumstances of fieldwork. But how can we
know that we are not falling victim to the fallacy of the striking individual case,
ignoring the hundreds of less colorful cases of people who do their jobs and do
not suffer any major illness or accident?

Anthropology is not, of course, the only dangerous branch of science or even
the only science that does fieldwork. Geologists, geographers, botanists, zoolo-
gists, and oceanographers also go to the field and run risks in the process of doing
so. Recently newspapers have reported the death of Mark T. Macmillan, a 22-
year-old research assistant from San Jose, California, in a diving accident while
on a National Science Foundation Antarctic research project. A geographer died
in 1986 in Central America from anaphylactic shock resulting from bee stings.
British traveler and travel writer Richard Mason was ambushed and killed by a
hunting party of Kreen Ahrore peoples in Brazil in 1970. Biologist Joanna Copley

of St. Andrews University in Scotland was killed by a charging rhinoceros in a game park near Durban, South Africa, in 1988 while observing baboon behavior.

Occupational health and safety is a well-known field of investigation, with bodies of data and techniques of analysis that have been honed on the study of many occupations. A response to the questions raised here is to go to the literature of occupational health and safety, to see how anthropology rates as a safe or dangerous occupation. Is anthropology a high-risk occupation, like mining or construction, with a rate of 25–30 deaths per 100,000 workers per year, an average-risk occupation with a rate of about 10 per 100,000 workers per year, or one of the low-risk occupations, like the professorial occupations as a whole, with a rate of 2–3 deaths per 100,000 workers per year? The result, as of 1986 when this study was started, was clear-cut but frustrating: no one knows. There was no established literature on anthropology as a group, either because it is too small, or too specialized, or just because no one had taken the trouble to carry out a study of its hazards.

On logical grounds, generalizing from the isolated position of many anthropologists working in remote locations among risks such as wild animals, snakes, parasites, fevers, unpredictable peoples and their politics, from isolated cases of harm and even death to particular anthropologists, and from colorful symbols of the anthropological mystique such as novels and movies, it appears that anthropology *is* a dangerous business. Its romance and adventure depend upon it being dangerous. But perhaps the dangers are exaggerated; perhaps anthropologists only have a notable number of field accidents and illnesses because they spend a lot of their time in the field; perhaps most anthropologists take few or no risks that exceed those they would run at home. Indeed, perhaps anthropologists do not go to the field as often as we might guess, or stay as long as we might suppose.

In order to ascertain how dangerous anthropology is compared to other occupations we need to know how many anthropologists there are, what fieldwork they have done, and what consequences for their health and safety they have experienced. Since we look for the basic studies of this behavior and find there are none known to the librarians, to the specialists in occupational health and safety, or to the officers of the anthropological association, we conclude that if we are going to solve these problems by reference to solid research, it is going to be necessary as a first step to do that research.

What Is an Anthropologist, and How Many Are There?

To determine how many anthropologists there are depends on what we mean by *anthropologist*. Figure 1.1 diagrams some of the greater and less inclusive groups for which this term might be used. Outside the widest circle lies the vast public, with very little idea of what anthropology is about, and whose image of an anthropologist might be based on Indiana Jones in *The Raiders of the Lost Ark*, or on the mad scientist who shows up in a movie on late-night TV.

The broadest circle contains those educated persons who are "interested" in anthropology; who are aware that it uses scientific methods; that it is concerned with exploring the range of human patterns and human nature, past and present; and that conservation of artifacts, peoples, and knowledge is central to the enterprise. These are people who may have had some courses in college, who know the names of Margaret Mead or Louis Leakey, who read *National Geographic* or

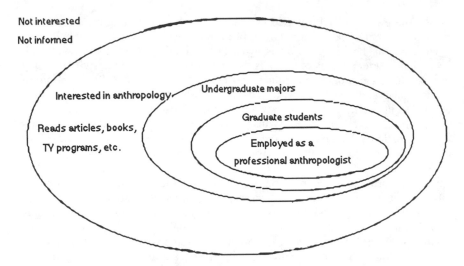

Figure 1.1. Components of the Population of Anthropologists

watch TV documentaries with some pleasure. In the United States at the present time, this circle probably contains some 20 to 50 million people—a substantial pool from which support for anthropology and its activities is drawn. But these people are not who we mean when we call someone an anthropologist.

Moving inward on our diagram, we see that the concentric circles each contain a narrower circle of people more concentrated on the more professionally advanced activities of anthropology. If we look at those currently involved in any anthropological activity, including those who are teachers and students in courses in anthropology, the circle narrows to something like a hundred thousand people spread among the several thousand schools, colleges, and universities where anthropology is taught.

When we get to the level of undergraduate majors in anthropology, and those more closely involved in professional activity—graduate students and professors—we find that the major professional association for North America, the American Anthropological Association, provides an annual count. For example, in 1986 there were some 14,220 undergraduate majors and fewer than 7,000 graduate students enrolled in degree programs at the 372 universities and colleges listed in the *Guide to Departments of Anthropology*. About 6,000 individuals are listed as employed in the 479 departments (including 65 museums, 33 research organizations, and 9 federal government departments, in addition to the universities and colleges). All these numbers, of course, change from one year to another, and there has been a general increase over the 50 years or so that anthropology has been a distinct academic speciality in North America.

Not including students, then, or retired members, there must have been between 17,000 and 20,000 anthropologists (or people with some substantial claim to be considered an anthropologist) in North America in the 1970–80 period. We know that students, including graduate students and undergraduate majors, total about 15,000, so the maximum number of individuals personally involved with anthropology each year is in the neighborhood of 35,000.

Collection of Information

In order to find out what these anthropologists do and what happens to them in the course of doing it, a number of data collection strategies have been used, and these are reviewed below. Most of this report is derived from a random sample survey of anthropologists. Where the results of other means of data collection can be summarized quickly, it will be done in this section.

Obituaries

As is typical in anthropological research, data have been collected by a number of different methods from a number of different sources. Perhaps the first systematic source of information has been the obituaries printed in the *Anthropology Newsletter,* the *American Anthropologist,* the *American Journal of Physical Anthropology, American Antiquity,* and many other topical and regional journals. The period of time systematically examined has been the past decade, 1976–87. Obituaries of anthropologists have been found for 487 people in that period. Two hundred six of these were deaths of persons under age 65, which might be considered premature deaths—that is, deaths of persons of working age. These deaths are of particular interest because we can compare them to the rates of deaths to people in other occupations, where the rates are interpreted as saying something about the relative dangers of the occupation. The deaths of older persons are disregarded for these purposes because we cannot compare them to other occupational groups.

If we attempt to calculate an occupational death rate on the basis of these data, we are on shaky ground. The calculation is simple enough: 206 deaths divided by the person-years lived and worked over the ten years that the deaths were collected from the obituary. Since we estimated a maximum of 35,000 people who have some claim to be called anthropologists, the occupational death rate is 139 per 100,000 workers. But this is spuriously accurate: the obituaries do not include all the deaths among that population, but mostly those of the more senior and well-known anthropologists. The calculation may be biased by including many of the long since retired anthropologists in the deaths but not in the calculation of the population at risk. The obituaries also include some relatively famous people from outside North America—in Europe and Japan, for instance. If we had confidence in its accuracy, we would say that the occupational death rate seems to be high compared to that of other occupations (construction, for instance, has about 20–30 deaths per 100,000 workers, and manufacturing has about 5 per 100,000), but we need to find a better data base before we can take such a calculation seriously.

Looking just at the 206 premature deaths of anthropologists found in the obituaries, Table 1.1 classifies them by cause of death. Disregarding the 42 for whom the cause of death was not specified, we see the three largest categories are cancer, heart disease, and vehicle accidents, just as they would be in a tabulation of the total U.S. population of deaths. It is difficult to find comparable data for other groups, because the age composition of the anthropologists should be matched for a close comparison. But if we look at the causes of death for the U.S. population as a whole aged 30 to 65, for 1964 (which happens to be the latest year for which data on deaths by cause are conveniently available [Preston, Keyfitz, and Schoen 1972:769]) we can get a rough idea of the ways in which anthropologists are different in their causes of death from others.

Table 1.1. Percentage of All Deaths, by Causes of Death

	U.S. Males, 1964 N = 343,934	Anthropologists, under 65, 1976–88 N = 164
Cancer, all types	19.4%	29.9%
Cardiovascular diseases	50.6%	22.0%
Motor vehicle	3.5%	20.1%
Other violence	7.6%	28.2%
All other and unknown cause	19.0%	10.3%

Compares the premature deaths in the obituary collection for anthropologists, 1976 to 1988, to Preston's 1964 data for U.S. males, age 30–64 (Preston, Keyfitz, and Schoen 1972:769).

Looking at the percentages of deaths due to various causes, Table 1.1 seems to alert us to some unusual features of deaths among anthropologists. There seems to be considerable excess in the categories of motor vehicle and, especially, in the category of "other violent deaths." The table seems to show a lower than expected proportion of cardiovascular disease. Differences may be due to the way that data were collected, or attributed to the different age structures of the two groups. Anthropology has a "young" age distribution (despite the fact that no one becomes an anthropologist much before age 30). But we don't want to overinterpret these data, especially before we have a better sense of the causes of death that are producing them.

Other Library Resources

The library was searched for research directly on this topic, but it was found that to an astonishing extent the collections are silent on the problems of maintaining health and safety in anthropological fieldwork, and equally silent on the extent of the problems of failing to do so. There is no registry of accidents and illnesses, and until now not even a systematic registry of deaths associated with fieldwork. While there are rich collections of data, methods, and analysis on occupational health and safety in other fields, the heading of anthropology is missing from that collection.

In the texts on doing fieldwork, there is much written on establishing rapport and learning the language, but little on the subject of how to get food in the field. Similarly there is little written on the topic of providing a safe and pleasant supply of water at minimum cost in time and energy. Yet many anthropologists encounter unpalatable or unsafe water, and large numbers contract diseases, infectious and parasitic, from unpurified sources. Little is written in the anthropological literature about providing latrines or using those that exist, of sleeping on beds or on the ground, of providing shelter from the elements and protection from insects and animals. Almost nothing is said about problems of hostility or assault by local people, sane or crazy, drunk or sober—so that reading anthropological literature one might conclude that being an anthropologist guarantees the love and esteem of the local community members. All these practical aspects of life in the field have enormous impact on individual comfort and safety, and contribute to the quality of the intellectual work that gets done, yet are ignored by practitioners in their written work as if they were totally unproblematic. In fact, as we will see, these practical aspects of fieldwork *do* cause problems for anthropologists, and failure to solve these problems satisfactorily does lead to sickness, injury, and death. (The Bibliography [pages 198–199] cites a few texts that provide concrete information on health and safety.)

Exploratory Interviewing in Departments

Several departments agreed to serve as "guinea pigs" as I oriented myself to the problems of health and safety. On two occasions, I tried going down the halls of a department, knocking on each door, attempting to speak with every member of the department about his or her experiences with accidents and illnesses in the field. What I heard convinced me more than ever that health problems in the field are common, serious, and rarely discussed. My contacts were frequently forthcoming about the details of their crises and disasters in the field, although it was striking that many were reluctant to think about the general problems of anthropological field safety or to consider what might be done systematically to reduce such problems. These interviews contributed to my files of instances of sickness and accidents, although most of these communications must be kept confidential due to the wishes of those who told me the stories. Nevertheless, what I learned helped me decide that the topic was worth further research, even if some of the detailed stories could not be told.

A Survey of Departments

Thinking about departments as a framework within which most of the business of anthropology is done, and as a source for learning more about the events in which particular anthropologists died or were seriously hurt in the field, led to a preliminary data collection from department chairmen. In the obituaries that I was gradually collecting, almost all gave the departmental affiliation of the deceased. That fact suggested working backwards: to take a list of the departmental membership at a time in the past (1976–77 was selected for the starting point, and the AAA *Guide to Departments of Anthropology* for that year was taken as the official list) and to trace the members of each department to the present, where they should either be listed in the 1986–87 *Guide* or be in my file of obituaries. Comparisons of the departmental lists for the two dates revealed that many or most departments had a few people who had "disappeared" over the decade—people who might have retired, quit anthropology, moved to other work places or another department of the university, changed their names, or died. There was no way to find out which except to write to each department.

Individual letters were sent to the current chairman of each department asking what had happened to each of the named individuals who were present in 1976–77 and absent in 1986–87. Since this represented a fair amount of work (even with a personal computer to minimize the clerical task), two other questions of importance to this study were appended to the request: (1) Are there any cases of sickness or accidents that occurred to members of the department during the past decade that this study should be aware of? and (2) If the department has a procedure to train students in health and safety in fieldwork, what is that method? Responses to the former question contributed to my general education and to my file on striking examples.

Table 1.2 shows the results of the survey. There were 317 departments listed in the 1976 *Guide*, 24 of which (7.5%) were no longer listed in 1986 and were

Table 1.2. Departments of Anthropology, Personnel Changes 1976–86

	Department	Anthropologists	
Departments listed in *Guide* in 1976	317		
Omitted from mail survey (not listed in 1986)	24		
Departments in survey	293		
Departments that responded	223	3,844	
Stayed at same dept, 1976–86		2,470	(65%)
Moved to another department		530	(14%)
Retired		100	(3%)
Deceased		154	(4%)
Left anthropology, known to hold another kind of job		236	(6%)
Lost to observation, chair doesn't know		354	(9%)
Totals		3,844	(101%)

dropped from further study, leaving 293. Most of those omitted were joint departments, in which anthropologists cooperated with sociologists, political scientists, social workers, or others to provide a social science program to undergraduates, and of these joint departments, most were in very small colleges and universities, so that relatively little information was lost by dropping them.

Among the 293 departments surveyed, only about 54% (158) of the chairmen of departments had responded to a personally addressed letter of inquiry after two months, and a second round of letters was sent to the chairs of departments that had not responded. An additional 65 (22% of the total) responded to the second letter, leaving about 24% that seem to have ignored the request.

Only one departmental chairman among the 223 who answered refused to provide information on the grounds that he believed it to be unethical to provide information about individuals. Another chairman answered the questions about past members of the department, but expressed unwillingness to pass on information about injuries and illnesses that current department members had suffered, feeling that such information is confidential. Many other chairmen simply ignored that request, or provided information in the most general manner ("Several of our faculty report having had malaria in the field"): it is difficult to say whether these chairmen were motivated to save time and energy or were primarily concerned about issues of privacy. It is likely that many chairmen truly did not know the answers to questions about accidents and injuries, and it is understandable that a busy chairperson would not want to take the time and effort to investigate the questions from individual members. Denial of dangers may also play some role. It was striking that in a department in which I know of a recent very dramatic death in the field to a junior faculty member, the chairman blandly reported, "we have had no problems."

Despite these difficulties in obtaining information, a substantial number of additional deaths to department members (including some fieldwork deaths) were discovered from the chairmen's responses, along with valuable information about retirements, and people who dropped out of the field prior to retirement age, an input that considerably changes our assessment of the occupational health and safety of anthropology.

The data in Table 1.2 provide us our first opportunity to calculate any kind of a measure of the frequency of death in anthropology. The calculation is a simple one: 3,100 people (those found in the same or another department, and those who retired but are still alive) were exposed to ten years of risk, and 390 (those who died and those who left anthropology) were exposed to an average of five years apiece, a total of 32,950 person-years at risk. There were 154 deaths to that group, so the rate of death for these people is 4.7 per 1,000 years at risk. Note that we omit those who were lost to observation since we do not know if they have died or not. A death rate of 4.7/1000 (or 470 per 100,000 years, as such rates are usually presented) is very high as an occupational death rate, but difficult to interpret without controlling for the age distribution of the population. [Note that these are deaths to the employed population but not necessarily deaths "on the job," so it is not appropriate to compare this number with those who die (primarily of accidents and heart attacks) while at work.]

While the systematic study of departments provided one kind of framework for evaluating the safety of anthropology in a comparative way, and while the collection of case studies and instances of problems was illuminating of the range of problems to look for, a direct confidential data collection from a random sample of the members of the profession was essential to clarify the problem fully. The directories and the chairs of departments could not tell us how much fieldwork the individual anthropologists in their departments do per year, under what conditions they do it, and how much and what kind of trouble they get into in the course of doing it. Only the individuals directly involved know the answers to those questions, and only if we know the answers to those questions can we really make sense of the scattered facts of accidents and injuries.

Are there too many accidents and injuries, fatal and otherwise, in anthropology? The answer depends not only on how many accidents there are, but on how many anthropologists there are, how much fieldwork they do, and whether some dangers are avoidable. If the deaths in anthropology are proportional to the size of the population, controlled perhaps for age and sex, or if the proportion of all deaths that occur in the field is proportional to the amount of time that anthropologists spend in the field, then the particular deaths that occur may be deeply regretted and regrettable but they are not excessive. We have to establish many facts about the population and the deaths that occur before we can answer the question of whether deaths are excessive in anthropology.

The Random Sample Survey of Employed Anthropologists

The methods of random sampling are more characteristic of sociology than of anthropology, as it is frequently difficult or impossible to apply sample methods in anthropology, owing to the lack of population lists or the inability to obtain information from the selected informants. I suppose it is predictable that the method is used when a sociologist studies anthropologists, but there were some ways in which it was difficult to apply. A few of those who were sent a questionnaire, for instance, either sent it back unanswered or ignored it until telephoned many months later, explaining that they did not want to ruin the study by including their experience, which was not typical. The random sample approach was needed in this instance, as it is frequently needed, to obtain data, typical and atypical, which are not otherwise documented about a population.

Two aspects of our definition of the population may require clarification. First, "the anthropologists" are operationally defined here as those employed as professional anthropologists according to the *Guide to Departments of Anthropology, 1986–87,* of the American Anthropological Association. Once we have a list of this population, drawing a sample so that all members are equally likely to be part of it is a well-understood matter, and the statistics of generalizing to the population from the random sample are also well understood (although complicated by matters such as nonresponse of some part of the sample, biases in response rates, and occasional deception in answering questions).

The second part of the definition concerns the nondocumented facts about the members of the sample. There are many facts that we would like to have about the sample of anthropologists, but there are practical considerations about which facts we can obtain accurately, reliably, in a reasonable period of time for the respondents, and without alienating them so that they refuse to participate. Generally speaking, the questionnaire is a mixture of questions with answers that can also be established elsewhere, in order to test the characteristics of the sample that has been drawn, and questions with unknown answers, such as those that concern attitudes, intentions, experiences, or factual knowledge.

Essentially, we need a random sample to study a question like health and safety in fieldwork in order to go beyond our own perspective, from the point of view of our colleagues, our graduate school fellow students, our special friends, to that of the whole population. No one in the field is in a position to know the experiences of all anthropologists. Those who know large numbers of others tend to know the elite—the most central, most active, most well-known others—so that there is always the suspicion that there may be large numbers of unknown anthropologists on the periphery who are very different, perhaps do not do much fieldwork at all, or perhaps do it more (or less) cautiously. We need a random sample in order to transcend our guesses and turn them into solid observations of the whole group. In the next chapter, we will look at the features of the random sample that was drawn.

The Strategy of Reporting

The random sample is going to provide us with a framework of individuals and events—a descriptive account of what anthropologists were really like in the 1980s. Because of the bargain explicitly made with those in the random sample, their individual identities will be concealed, and the vivid details of their experiences will not be provided, even when the person in the sample volunteered such a description.

These accounts will provide us with a descriptively accurate framework within which we can tell the stories of other individuals who have published accounts of their adventures, those whose stories became public in obituaries, and those survivors who have told their stories and have given explicit permission for their stories to be told. Wherever possible, we will name the individuals who died, who were injured, who suffered mishaps, who had narrow escapes from danger, or who made observations on sets of potential problems. When names are provided, you can be sure that the account did not come from the survey sample, but from a published or a volunteered account.

Anthropology is a small profession, one in which many of the people know each other face-to-face. Field accidents and illnesses are events that interest all of us, and it may already be the case that dozens or hundreds of others know that a particular anthropologist experienced a certain kind of field problem. In some cases, the circumstances of the events are so vivid that the identity of the individual will be obvious to his or her many friends and friends-of-friends, and only unknown to those who are distant in the professional structure from the central person—the outsiders, and especially the students. If one of the goals of the research is to raise consciousness of the issues of health and safety in fieldwork, it seems particularly important to allow these peripheral people to know the names of central anthropologists' field problems.

It would, of course, be unethical to reveal events inaccurately or without the permission of the people involved. At least initially, until it is widely realized that virtually all anthropologists suffer mishaps in the field, some may fear that being identified as having suffered in the field will mark them in the eyes of others as incompetent or unskilled. Indeed, anthropologists who do not have tenure could conceivably lose a job or a promotion in this way. So the method used to handle identification is to avoid detailed case material that might be identifiable as pertaining to students and junior members of the profession whose job security could be affected. For those who volunteered case material, the pages of the draft report recounting the events have been sent, with a request to give permission to publish and to double-check the facts. Published sources, however, are simply cited, as is usual in scholarly writing.

Aside from the question of identification, the strategy of presentation in this report will be one of simple description of procedure and results, with the goal of making it possible for others to replicate this study if they choose to do so. If that seems like an old-fashioned positivistic method, in an era of hermeneutics and self-reflective texts, so be it. Even though the random sample strategy is central to this study design, the immediate goal is not so much hypothesis testing and model-building as description and exploration of the basic facts of the case. And since a major goal of the research is to raise consciousness among individuals of problems that can potentially be solved or reduced, we do not want to alienate readers by using unfamiliar statistics.

The strategy of this document is to introduce the members of the random sample in Chapter 2 to give an overview of the members of the profession at the present time. The fieldwork that these people have done will be presented in Chapter 3, giving the areas of the world, the duration of the fieldwork, the composition of the work group, and the length of time per expedition and per year that various kinds of anthropologists spend in the field. This information is essential for finding out the population at risk for fieldwork accidents and illnesses. Conditions of fieldwork, hard and easy, will be specified.

Then we will go through the types of hazards reported by the sample in Chapters 5–12, providing information on the frequency and duration of exposure to that risk and the proportion who experienced it. The discussions will be illustrated with case materials from other, often named, individuals who have provided detailed information. If there is solid medical advice on treatment, or good nonobvious advice on prevention, it will be presented or cited in the discussion.

Data on the problems and features of taking families to the field will be discussed in Chapter 13. Practicing medicine in the field on oneself, one's family, students, employees, and local people will be discussed in Chapter 14.

The observant reader will note that we never get to the question of whether it is all worthwhile—whether the value of the information, the insight, the theories of human nature and culture and societies produced by anthropological efforts justify all the risks and injuries and deaths. In this study we will be attempting to understand part of the activities of thousands of complicated persons and projects, leaving out of our consideration almost entirely the product of their work, and the value of that product. It is as if we were studying the activities of painters as applying pigments to canvas, without looking at the images created, or studying the activities of brain surgeons without bothering to notice whether the patients lived or died. Admittedly, this is a narrow focus, and ultimately both the profession and the society must weigh the product in with the costs of the process of production. But first, let us meet the anthropologists in our random sample and see what they do, and what their activities have cost them in health and safety.

CHAPTER 2   THE SAMPLE OF ANTHROPOLOGISTS

How Many Anthropologists Are There?

To count the anthropologists at a point of time implies defining them. As an anthropological demographer, I frequently tell students that the counting is easy—it is knowing when to start and when to stop that is difficult. Thus, to count the anthropologists we must specify a time and place, and criteria for who counts as an anthropologist.

Rather than attempt to count the personnel continually since the birth of anthropology as a field, we will confine our serious attempts at counting to the past decade or so. If we can account for the numbers of anthropologists at risk from 1976 to 1988, we will be doing well. These numbers can then provide the basis for more accurate calculations of the numbers of anthropologists at risk for events such as accidents and death.

Second, we will define our task as obtaining the numbers per year of professional anthropologists, including all those post-Ph.D. persons employed in universities and museums with the title of anthropologist (as the core population), but also including persons with advanced training and interests in anthropology, even if such a person is employed in another academic department, another kind of educational institution (for instance, a high school or community college, a publishing company or journal), or even employed outside professional anthropology (as in a family business). Such a person must have an advanced degree in anthropology (at least a master's), and will be identified by membership in one or more professional associations. Persons lacking the Ph.D. will be included if they are employed in professional anthropology, do fieldwork or other professional activities of anthropology, or publish in a professional way. Operationally, we will depend upon directories of employment and professional associations to find out how many professional anthropologists there are at a point in time.

We regret our inability to estimate for this same time period the numbers of students of anthropology. To the extent to which these people participate in the activities of anthropology, they are at risk of its hazards, and we need to include them in our consideration. But they are hard to find while still working on their research, and the listings of Ph.D.'s do not include those who do not finish their studies. Omitting them here reflects the limits of resources, and is not an assessment of their importance to the problem.

Counting Professional Anthropologists, 1976

We start with the 1976–77 academic year—a year ten years prior to the start of this study and one for which, as it happened, I had both the *Annual Report* (including a membership list) and the *Guide to Departments of Anthropology* (including a list of faculty for the departments) on my personal shelf of reference works.

Table 2.1 presents the summary numbers of anthropologists from these two sources, and their overlap. The table requires a little explanation.

The 1976 *Guide* gives an annual total of 4,285 and the *Annual Report* gives a total for the year of 10,120 members. These proportions of individuals listed as both or as only in one source or the other comes from a comparison of the sources for a sample of individuals. The sample was drawn by selecting every sixth page of the alphabetical index of individuals in the *Guide to Departments of Anthropology* 1976–77, which turned out to represent 17.3% of those listed. The corresponding portion of the alphabetized list of members of the American Anthropological Association was then checked to see if each person in the *Guide* was also in the *Annual Report*. This comparison produces the proportions given in the cells. The fourth cell of the table, those anthropologists not listed in either source, is calculated from the probabilities of not being listed in each source, on the assumption that the probabilities are independent. We infer the existence of 986 anthropologists from the proportions of members who are not in the *Guide,* and those in the *Guide* who are not members. From this calculation we estimate that in 1976, 32.4% of the potential anthropologists were not found on either of these two major sources of information on anthropologists. To estimate the size of the whole population we multiply the numbers in the sample by 5.78, because the sample turned out to consist of 17.3% of the total in the *Guide to Departments of Anthropology*.

The *Guide* lists the professional staff of 372 academic departments, 65 museums, 33 research organizations, and 9 federal government departments. The coverage of employers of anthropologists is very good for the United States, almost complete for Canada, but only sparsely representative of employers of anthropologists outside North America: American University in Cairo is listed, the Chinese University of Hong Kong, the University of Guam, the University of Puerto Rico, and University College, London. The random sample survey includes only those departments listed in the AAA *Guide* for 1986–87, and each member of any department listed had an equal chance of being included in the survey.

Table 2.1. Professional Anthropologists Listed in the 1976 *Guide to Departments* and the *1976 List of Members of AAA*

Sources	1976 Guide to Departments		
Annual Report, 1976 List	In *Guide*	Not in *Guide*	Total
Listed as member (proportion)	.571/.249	.751	
N	436	1,315	1,751
Not listed as member (proportion)	.429	(.324)	
N	327	(986)[a]	1,313[a]
Totals in the sample	763	2,301[a]	3,064[a]

[a]These numbers are inferred from their proportions in the two data sources. Other numbers were observed in the sample.

The 1986 *Guide* includes 6,135 individuals employed in these departments: this is the target population of our study. As we have noted, the approximately 21,000 students (graduate and undergraduate) enrolled in these departments are not included.

Drawing the Sample

The *Guide to Departments of Anthropology* gives us a list of anthropologists, and some of their characteristics, such as position and area of expertise. In order to find out additional characteristics of the people listed there—even simple characteristics such as age and fieldwork experience in 1986, for example—we have to draw a sample of that population and ask them to answer questions.

How large a sample to aim for is always a problem in survey research. We want to keep the sample as small as possible, to minimize the work of collecting the data and analyzing it. The point of taking a sample of the total, of course, is to spare the trouble of collecting data from all the members of the population, so the smaller the sample the better, as long as it tells us what we want to know.

In any study, there is a ceiling on how large the sample can be, given the resources for processing entries. For this study, the ceiling was fixed by the costs of obtaining responses, entering them into the personal computer that has been used for all the work of this study, and tabulating the results. Knowing my own limitations of time and energy, I knew that I would not be able to work with more than about 500 responses, preferably less.

At the same time, in this study as in others, there is a floor of sample size, below which it is hardly worthwhile bothering to collect any data at all. When one respondent is a substantial portion of the sample, small differences of opinion or fact threaten to drown out the meaningful findings of the study. As it happens, my own research over the years has made me something of an expert on methods of analysis of small population data. I often recommend to others that it is hardly worth conducting a statistical analysis of a body of data of less than 100 members, unless one is very sure that it represents a total population of some meaningful category, and/or that the usual biases and sources of random error are small and predictable. In the present case, where we could be sure that the studied group did not represent a total population, but were rather a random sample of a list, I wanted to aim for a sample that would provide a minimum of 200 valid responses, to avoid the worst of the small numbers problems.

That number of 200 is arbitrary, of course, but it is arrived at with the realization that we want to be able to describe significant differences between the kinds of anthropology—physical or biological, archaeological, social-cultural (ethnographic), and linguistic anthropology. We want to have at least some representation for all the major areas of the world where North American anthropologists do fieldwork (North America, Europe, Africa, Latin America, the Indian subcontinent, Asia, and the Pacific). We could not, of course, ensure that we would have at least some representation of finer categories, such as those who study the Yanomamö or those who work in East African prehistory, without making our sample so large as to be coextensive with the total population of anthropologists. The point is that categories that make up a small proportion of the total are not likely to be represented in the sample, or (just as troublesome) are likely to be represented by one or a few people, so that idiosyncratic features of those individuals swamp the information available on the group. If the purpose is to ask a finely detailed question, the answer to which will involve a small number of identifiable people (for example, "Has Yanomamö research been more dangerous than !Kung research during the past decade?") random samples are not the right method for pursuing the answer.

The target number to aim for when you know the minimum number of responses needed depends in part, of course, on the rate of returns that can be expected. And the rate of returns depends, in turn, on the characteristics of the population (in general, a well-educated population provides high return rates), on the motivation of the sample (being asked to participate in a survey of health and safety by a representative of one's professional association is probably an exceptionally positive situation for expecting a high-level of motivation from the sample, but of course we worry about those who do not consider it good for the profession to know the problems). The return rate also depends on what the sample is being asked to do and how the task is presented to them. Short questionnaires, well prepared, with few or no ambiguous questions or questions requiring long answers will produce the best return rates, whereas difficult questionnaires will drive off all but the most hardy and well-motivated.

Unfortunately, the desire for a short questionnaire to increase the response rate conflicts with the desire to obtain a large amount of information from each of the respondents. The only way to improve on this situation is to engage in elaborate pretesting of the questionnaire, working to produce a form that will elicit the most information at the lowest cost to the respondents. The present questionnaire went through thirteen pretests, each absorbing the patience and good will of friends and colleagues who served as guinea pigs for the questionnaire design, until the form to be seen as the Appendix was achieved on the fourteenth attempt.

That questionnaire, like all such, is the result of compromises between legal requirements (see the elaborate instructions in the cover sheet, inserted for protection of human subjects, which clearly invite the recipients not to respond), the advice of experts (especially Dillman 1978, but also those who served in the pretest), common sense, input from previous drafts, and a feel for what respondents are willing to put up with. The remaining errors of spacing and spelling to be seen in the Appendix are not put there on purpose—they are just errors that were not detected before printing. With that questionnaire, a target population size of just over 6,000, and a minimal requirement of 200 valid questionnaires, it was decided to draw a sample of 1:20, which produces a random sample of 311.

The mechanics of drawing the sample proved to be another compromise between convenience and scientific rigor. If I had a numbered list of the target population in my computer I would simply have drawn four-digit random numbers between 1 and 6,135 (discarding all those over 6,135) until I had 311. Instead the most convenient list was the alphabetized "Index of Individuals" at the back of the *Guide to Departments of Anthropology*. A nice feature of the Index is that it eliminates the potential problem that some individuals hold more than one job listed in the *Guide*. In the Index, individuals are listed only once. Using the *Guide* to trace individuals over the ten-year period from 1976 to 1986 demonstrated that the Index was accurately compiled, in that individuals listed in Departments were reliably listed, with few errors of names or institutions.

Rather than number that list, I divided the Index into segments, each consisting of 20 names. A list of random numbers was consulted, and divided into two-digit segments. All the even numbers in the tens digit were treated as zeroes, and odd numbers were treated as ones, except that 00 was translated into 20. The number of the person selected was then found in the list (i.e., 06 means count to the sixth name in the group of twenty), and that person's name was found in the directory. If the person was marked as on leave during the 1987 winter or spring quarter, the next random number was selected for that block of names: 13 of the 311 were found to be on leave and were replaced by other names. In one case the second person selected was also on leave, and a third name was selected from that block of 20. Two additional members of the first-drawn sample were eliminated on the grounds that they had participated in the planning and pretesting of the questionnaire, and were replaced by others selected randomly from the same segment of names. Persons were not removed from the sample on the basis of their jobs, their locations, their interests, or any professional criteria. In this way, everyone listed in the Index had an equal probability of being drawn (except those on leave and those who had helped with the pretest).

The bias that is introduced into the sample by using blocks of 20 names arranged in alphabetical order rather than drawing anywhere from a numbered list is that it prevents anthropologists with the same or very similar names from both being included in the sample. If it were important, for instance, to allow for the inclusion of both partners of married couples in the sample proportional to their presence in the population, this would not be a good method to use. Although the marital status of the anthropologists in our sample is of interest, we do not need to include both members of pairs, an event that would occur at very low probability even if the sample were fully randomly selected.

Anthropologists who were noted in the directory as being on leave were excluded from the sample in order to avoid a bias closer to the central concerns of this research—the bias of including those who stayed at home to answer their mail during a leave and systematically omitting those who went to the field. Being on leave is a fairly high probability status for anthropologists (although we would expect to find about 44 on leave if the whole field went on leave one year in seven, whereas we actually found only 13), and it is better to eliminate all those on leave than to bias the sample against fieldworkers, the very group of greatest interest to this study. As we will see, despite this precaution we failed to obtain responses from some people in the field who had not been listed as "on leave" in the *Guide*—but at least we did not systematically eliminate them from the sample.

Characteristics of the Sample

Sampling is like dipping a net into the ocean. Each sample drawn will be a little different from others, and each tells us about what is in the depths of the water below. In the sample that we happened to draw, we find the characteristics of a cross section of those listed in the *Guide*, plus or minus sampling error.

Some of the individuals drawn in this particular sample are famous anthropologists—people whose research is widely read and well cited, who have held office in the AAA, and whose names would be known to many of the others listed in the *Guide*. I found that I knew the name and at least something of the work of about 50 of the 311 drawn in the sample, but that is perhaps more a statement about me than about them. No doubt there are many people in the field who would recognize more of the names than I did, but probably no one would know them all, as anthropology is not organized on that kind of face-to-face, personal acquaintance basis. A few of the people in the sample would have to be considered world-famous—well-known outside anthropology as well as inside.

Looking up each of the 311 drawn in the sample from the directory, we learn more about their current and past positions. We find that the vast majority—282—live and are employed in the continental United States, while 23 are living and working in Canada. The other six are in places outside North America, such as Guam, Puerto Rico, Australia, Hong Kong, and Egypt.

Highest Degrees of the Sample

The individuals in our sample obtained their Ph.D. degrees from a distinguished group of universities. The University of Chicago leads the list, with 19 alumni among our 311 sample members, followed by the University of California at Berkeley with 17, and Harvard University with 15. Other substantial contributors include University of Arizona (11), University of Pennsylvania (9), University of California at Los Angeles (9), Columbia University (9), University of Michigan (8), Indiana University (7), and University of Wisconsin and the University of New Mexico (6 each). The largest group from a non-U.S. university come from the University of Alberta (5), and there are a few each from universities in England, Canada, and Australia. Twenty-six other U.S. universities contributed four or fewer graduates each to the sample. It is striking that the members of such a small occupation are trained at such a large number of institutions: the 6,135 individuals listed in the *Guide* list 209 colleges and universities in North America as the sources of their degrees, plus 81 universities overseas.

Table 2.2 provides data on two characteristics of the sample members that may be of interest: (1) where they earned their highest degree, and (2) where they are currently employed. We cannot provide the detailed list of universities, either as sources of highest degree or as employer, because the individuals would be identifiable from that data. Instead we classify universities into (1) a "top ten" group, (2) into a group that includes all other universities that offer the Ph.D., and (3) a category for current employment at the non-Ph.D. granting schools. In addition, some are employed in museums and research organizations such as the Bureau of Land Management and the National Park Service.

Table 2.2 shows some important features of the social structure of anthropology. A large proportion of the students are trained in the best and biggest departments, but only a small minority manage to hold jobs in those departments at any point in time. Indeed, only about 60% of those who hold Ph.D.'s are currently teaching in a Ph.D.-granting institution. The sad truth (sad from the point of view

Table 2.2. Sources of Highest Degrees and Current Employment

Place of Employment	Source of Highest Degree			
	Ph.D. (Top Ten)	Ph.D. (Other)	Not Ph.D.	Total
Top-ten University	14	9	4	27
Another Ph.D. University	52	64	15	131
College or Other Non-Ph.D. Institution	28	37	9	74
Museums, Research Organizations	11	26	42	79
Total	105	136	70	311

of ambitious entering graduate students) is that most anthropological careers will be marked by at least apparent downward mobility, as students are trained in the centers of excellence and then spread out to teach undergraduates as well as graduates, in easily accessible as well as elite institutions, and in all parts of the country, not just the frequently preferred Northeast and the California coast. Movement from one institution to another over the course of the career and adjustment to appreciation of the charms of peripheral institutions and localities take the sting from that observation for many, if not most, professionals. Incidentally, only 18 people, 6% of the total, were found teaching in the same university as they had earned their Ph.D., although many are working in the same state or region where they studied for their highest degree.

Before we start an exploration of other characteristics of the sample, we will present one comparison of the same variables—the highest degree reported for the individuals listed in the directory—for the total population of 6,135 and for the sample of 311 that we drew (Table 2.3).

We note that the percentage distributions between the degrees are similar, but not identical, for the total population and for the sample. In this particular sample out of all the possible samples we could have drawn, we captured seven more people with B.A.'s as their highest degree than we expected, five fewer Ph.D.'s, and one each fewer in the categories of M.A.'s and no degree. These small deviations from the population are expected to be found in all samples, on all variables. The sample allows us to learn a great deal about the population and to have solid confidence that what we are learning is accurate within the range of statistical bounds, but it requires us to maintain continual uncertainty about the boundaries of the categories we examine.

Job Positions of the Sample

What else does the sample tell us about the population? Table 2.4 shows the sex distribution for the whole sample of 311 along with the job titles listed for them in the *Guide*.

Table 2.4 shows the distribution of the sample in job categories, by sex. Overall about 70% of our sample are in university teaching positions. We note that men heavily dominate the full professor category (87%), with less in the associate professor category (68%), while women are almost equally represented in the two lower levels, a finding that has been noted before (D'Andrade et al. 1975). Women are well represented among those who work in museums, which make up

Table 2.3. Highest Degree, for Total Population and for Sample

	Total Population		Sample	
	N	%	N	%
Ph.D. and other doctorates	4,717	76.9	234	75.2
M.A. and other Master's Degrees	793	12.9	39	12.5
B.A., other Bachelor's Degrees	361	5.9	26	8.4
No higher degree, other technical	264	4.3	12[a]	3.9
Total	6,135		311	

[a]Includes seven who have a Ph.D. in another field, such as chemistry, geology, or sociology.

Table 2.4. Job Position and Sex of the Sample

	Male		Female		Both Sexes
	N	%	N	%	N
Full professor	81	37%	12	13%	93
Associate professor	45	21	21	23	66
Assistant professor	21	10	16	17	37
Lecturer, Other academic	14	6	13	14	27
Museum	28	13	24	26	52
Archaeology, Nonuniversity	23	11	4	4	27
Nonprofessional, Other	6	3	3	3	9
Total	218	70%	93	30%	311

Table 2.5. Highest Degree and Sex of the Sample

	Male		Female		Both Sexes
	N	%	N	%	N
Ph.D.	171	78%	63	68%	234
M.A.	23	10	16	17	39
B.A.	15	7	11	12	26
Other, or none	9	4	3	3	12
Total	218	70%	93	30%	311

together about 17% of the sample. People who describe themselves as professional archaeologists, not employed in university teaching, are almost entirely men. This group, about 9% of our sample (and about 25% of those who identify themselves as archaeologists overall) are employed in government agencies (National Park Service, Bureau of Land Management, state highway agencies) and private research contracting companies. Only a few of the women in our sample are employed in one of these jobs. Finally, there is a miscellaneous category, making up about 3% of the total, including university administrators with no professional or scholarly position, librarians, and so on.

Table 2.5 shows the cross-tabulation of highest degree listed in the *Guide* for the individuals in our sample, by sex. We note that women are somewhat underrepresented in the Ph.D. category, overrepresented among those with M.A.'s and B.A.'s, and underrepresented among those with no higher degree listed. The source of the difference seems to be that there are more lower-level jobs for women in museums, whereas the men listed as ''Other, or none'' are more likely to be Ph.D.'s from other departments who are cross-listed.

As we might have expected, a very high proportion of those in professorial positions have a Ph.D. (or equivalent), while an M.A. or even a B.A. is adequate for museum jobs and archaeological specialties (outside the university). Some of those who list M.A. or B.A. as their highest degree are probably graduate students who are working on a Ph.D.

What Kind of Anthropologist? Subdisciplines in the Sample

As anthropologists are acutely aware, but others may not be, the field of anthropology is subdivided into the discipline of archaeology, physical (or biological) anthropology, linguistics, and social-cultural anthropology. Some anthropologists would subdivide the profession along somewhat different lines, but all would agree that there are important differences in training and activities for specialist groups. Most university departments of anthropology strive to offer expertise in all four subdivisions, and since the professional requirements and skills of subdisciplines are rather different, this can sometimes mean substantial cleavages within departments.

Members of the sample who returned the questionnaire classified themselves into one of the four subdivisions of anthropology, and most seemed to have no problem doing so. For the 75 people who did not return a questionnaire, this classification is somewhat more arbitrary, because I had to make the judgment on the basis of the statements in the *Guide to Departments of Anthropology* listing the special topics and geographical areas of interest of each person. Usually the listing made the classification easy.

Table 2.6 shows the distribution of types of anthropologists represented in our sample, by sex. The largest group is that of social-cultural anthropologists—46% of the people listed in the *Guide*. Next is archaeology, with about 30% of the population. Much smaller are physical anthropology (about 10%) and linguistics (about 5%). About 9% of those listed are "none of the above"—sociologists, chemists, museum textile preservers, administrators, secretaries, and librarians who, although listed as members of anthropology departments, museums, or research organizations, are in some ways not "real" anthropologists at all.

We note that the following are women: about 45% of physical anthropologists; about 60% of the "other" category; about 28% of social-cultural anthropologists; about 22% of archaeologists; and 19% of the linguists. It is interesting to think about the selective factors that have led to this rather different gender distribution for the subdivisions. We particularly want to be sensitive to any tendency for the women to be clustered in the nonfieldworking areas of the professions.

If we compare the proportions in the subdisciplines with the proportions in various kinds of jobs (see Table 2.4), we note that archaeologists have a higher proportion of jobs outside university employment, both in museums and in archaeology for government. And if we look at the highest degree for the members of the subdisciplines, we note that very high proportions of linguistic and social-cultural anthropologists have a Ph.D., while the M.A. is the highest degree of something like 15% of the archaeologists and physical anthropologists—again reflecting the nonuniversity employment in these fields. It is not possible to tell

Table 2.6. Subdisciplinary Speciality and Sex

	Male		Female		Both Sexes	
	N	%	N	%	N	%
Archaeology	74	34%	21	23%	95	30%
Biological-physical	16	7	13	14	29	9
Linguistics	13	6	3	3	16	5
Social-cultural (ethnology)	104	48	40	43	144	46
Museology, other	11	5	16	17	27	9
Total	218	70%	93	30%	311	100%

from the listing in the *Guide* whether these non-Ph.D. people are currently graduate students or whether they have ended their formal education.

Response Success Rates

Table 2.7 shows us the rates of returns of questionnaires for the different types
of anthropologists. We note that about half the returns are from social-cultural
anthropologists, with archaeologists the other large category. Later we will combine the category of archaeology with the relatively few biological-physical anthropologists who do fieldwork, and combine the linguists with the social-cultural
anthropologists.

Overall we have data from 236 respondents—76% of the random sample selected. The social-cultural and the physical anthropologists both have the best return rate (80%), and the linguists have the worst (56%). We will examine some
of the other characteristics of those who did and did not respond, in order to provide information on how seriously the results of this study are biased by the non-
responses of nearly a quarter of the sample.

The response rate is somewhat better from those who hold university positions
than those employed outside the university, and somewhat better at the higher
levels than at the lower. But the trends are not strong.

Women were slightly more likely (80%) to return their questionnaires than men
(74%), but the difference is not so large as to skew the overall impression of the
population. If we depended only upon those who returned the questionnaires, we
would guess that the proportion of the total population that is women is 32% rather
than the 30% that our sample gives us, an estimate within the bounds of the sampling error we expect. We cannot learn the differences in response rates for the
age groups in the sample, because we only have age data from those who returned
the questionnaire.

The response rate was better for the U.S. residents in the sample (77.3%) than
for the Canadians (60.9%) and those from other countries (66.7%). It was striking
that colleagues in the French language Canadian universities did not respond to
the (English language) questionnaire, and did not return phone calls (messages
left in English). Overseas colleagues who did not respond to the written requests
were not phoned.

How Well Did We Do Getting Respondents?

How should we evaluate a return rate of 76% of the sample? Is that a lot or a
little by the standards of survey research?

Table 2.7. Rates of Questionnaire Return for the Subdisciplinary Specialities

	Total	Returned	% Returned
Archaeology	95	68	72%
Biological-physical	29	23	79
Linguistics	9	4	56
Social-cultural (ethnology)	14	116	81
Museology, Other	27	20	74
Total	311	236	76%

No large survey succeeds in obtaining 100% returns. Some losses are always expected from people who are involved in work or personal crises at the time of the survey—who move away, die, give birth, go on an alcoholic binge, or fall in love just when the researcher would like to have their undivided attention. It is an unfortunate feature of real human beings, as all social scientists know, that they don't necessarily sit still to be studied. So a certain "failure rate" is to be expected in survey research.

On the other hand, it doesn't do to be too accepting of nonresponse. Recently, I received a copy of the report of a survey done by an archaeologist as a professional service to obtain information from colleagues, which reported a 4% return rate. The designer of the survey nonchalantly asserted that "these kinds of response rates are accepted in survey research and do not invalidate the study." Well, perhaps, but one wonders about the differences between them and the 96% who did not respond.

Similarly we have to wonder about the differences between the 76% who did respond to this survey and the 24% who did not. If we could be sure that nonrespondents were just the same as all the other members of the sample in their answers to the questions, nonresponse would be no problem at all. Indeed, under those circumstances it would be no different than the question of the size of the sample drawn—just another way of obtaining lower numbers, but with the correct distributions. Unfortunately, nonrespondents are (sometimes, often, frequently) different from respondents, in ways that may matter a great deal. For the purposes of our study, we worry that nonrespondents may do much more (or less) fieldwork than other anthropologists, may do more (or less) dangerous fieldwork than others, and may have been more (or less) successful than others in avoiding accidents and illnesses as a result of problems.

For all these reasons the characteristics of the nonrespondents must concern us deeply. Why didn't they respond? Was the study not salient to them? Were they even aware that a study was going on? Or were they troubled at the prospect of reporting their experience and reluctant to do so? We can understand the reasons of some of the nonrespondents by knowing their circumstances, and by knowing how this study appeared to them.

The procedure used to contact members of the sample was to send the questionnaire, which included an individually addressed and signed covering letter, to the person's office address, with a stamped return envelope. Following the tested suggestions of Dillman (1978), after ten days a follow-up postcard was sent thanking those who had responded and reminding the rest. About 50% responded to the first mailing. Thirty days after the postcard, a second questionnaire, a return envelope, and a personalized letter were sent to those who had not yet responded, which produced another 47 questionnaires.

In June 1987, I started phoning the 109 who had not yet responded, at their offices, and succeeded in reaching 72 of them. Each was reminded of the study, and their right to refuse to participate was acknowledged. They were told that in case they wanted to participate, they should know that the data collection would be closed on July 1. Of these, 47 promised to send the questionnaire, and 34 actually did so. Thirty-eight were reached but did not send a questionnaire, and many of them gave some idea of why they had not responded, including the very important group of 18 nonfieldworkers. Thirty-seven were not reached at all.

Of the 37 who were not reached, eight were not available by telephone. Two of these worked in overseas departments, and six were said by someone in the department to be in the field in remote locations for long periods of time (despite my rule about not including anyone who was marked in the *Guide* as being "on leave"). It is not clear whether those in the field ever received the request to participate. Another six probably never received the request: one young woman who worked for a museum quit suddenly before the questionnaires were sent and left no forwarding address. A junior professor listed in one department changed jobs just before the start of the year and never appeared at the department where I wrote to him. The departmental secretary didn't know what the policy was on forwarding mail to him, and found no address posted for him on her list of routinely forwarded mail. Two retired professors of considerable age were described by departmental secretaries as no longer responding to mail. And two professors had died in the time between when the *Guide* was compiled and the time I wrote to them (one of cancer and one of heart disease).

Another ten potential respondents were lost to the survey by being gone away for the summer, either to the field or to a summer home, when I phoned. These people had presumably received the three mailings earlier in the year without responding. When the department had a forwarding continental U.S. phone number to give out, I attempted to use it, but these ten did not have forwarding numbers. I am embarrassed to admit that I located one faculty member at the out-of-state phone number given by his department, only to find that I had pursued him to his mother's funeral. He accepted my apologies and sent in his questionnaire when he returned to his university.

The largest group of nonrespondents, 13, exercised their decision not to participate by not being available when I called and by not returning messages (usually I reached the departmental office and left a message twice before giving up). Presumably these people knew why I was calling and were passively refusing to take part, or to answer any questions at all.

Thirty-eight potential respondents were reached by telephone but did not agree to participate. Eighteen of these told me that they never did fieldwork, and did not feel that participation in the survey was appropriate for them. Of course, once I knew that they did not do fieldwork, it was as good as having a full questionnaire. The phone calls were worthwhile to learn about these 18 nonfieldworkers, who cannot be considered respondents, but for whom we know the relevant facts for this study.

The other 20 had done fieldwork but would not participate. One was very sick and could not concentrate upon the details of the questionnaire. Another was re-

Table 2.8. Disposition of Sample in Participation in the Study

	N	*N*	%
Returned questionnaires (respondents)		236	75.9%
Nonrespondents		75	24.1%
Nonfieldworkers, felt to be inappropriate	18		(5.7)
Circumstances, away from university, sick	26		(8.4)
Refusal, active or passive	31		(10.0)
Total		311	100.0

Table 2.9. Fieldwork and Response in the Sample (Returned Questionnaire)

Fieldwork, ever:	No	Yes	Total
Yes	58	205[a]	262
No	18	31	49
Total	75	236	311

[a]One fieldworker who returned the questionnaire gave no further usable details and had to be eliminated from the analysis.

covering from surgery following an automobile accident, which was not a field-work-related accident, and couldn't take part.

Thirteen fieldworkers in this group of 20 promised to complete the question-naire and send it in, but did not do so in the month or so following the phone call. I consider these cases to be passive refusals to participate, inasmuch as the person was clearly aware of the study and must have made a decision not to take part. The decision is not necessarily hostile to the goals of the study, but these people may have found when they sat down to the task that it required more time and energy than they wanted to give to the job. It may also be the case, of course, that the task made the person anxious and uncomfortable, perhaps because of personal experiences that have been traumatic, and this is the kind of consideration that causes us to regret losing the nonrespondents. They may have had very different experiences than those of the respondents.

Finally, five people in the sample actively refused to take part, although of course the right to do so was reiterated with every mailing and phone call. Four of these cited competing pressures of work and other projects, and one refused on principle, stating that he did not approve of attempting to study personal events. "I'm not interested in participating," he said, "This is a delicate problem and I'd rather have nothing to do with it."

Table 2.8 sums up the responses of those contacted. We have 81.7% success, in that we have full information on the 236 that returned the questionnaire plus the 18 who said on the phone that they do not do fieldwork. We have a 10% refusal ($N = 31$) rate (apparently entirely among fieldworkers, but we can't be sure), and a loss of 8.4% of the sample to a variety of circumstances such as death, sickness and travel.

Table 2.8 summarizes the information on the relation of returns to fieldwork. Overall 49 of the 311 (15.7%) chosen for the sample do not do fieldwork, and never did. The jobs reported by those respondents (or listed in the *Guide* for non-respondents) include art historian, chemist, museum technician, professor of psy-chology, secretary, sociologist, textile conservator, urban ethnohistorian, and professor of urban studies. Presumably many of them do research, but not field-work.

We note that the rate of doing fieldwork (87%) is higher among those who re-turned the questionnaires than the rate (76%) among those who did not return the questionnaires (Table 2.9).

In this chapter we have seen the characteristics of the sample as a reflection of the population from which it was drawn, and we have considered the degree of success in getting responses from those in the sample. In Chapter 3, we will look more closely at the respondents, focusing upon the fieldworkers among them, and consider their careers, their health, and particularly the research they do.

CHAPTER 3 CAREERS AND CHARACTERISTICS OF THE RESPONDENTS

In this section, we will take a closer look at the 236 members of the sample who returned the questionnaires. We will be exploring the answers to the questions they sent in, rather than merely depending on the listings in the *Guide,* asking what kinds of careers these people have had, and at what stage of their careers they are at when they answer these questions. We will see something of their participation in the training of new students. We will also ask what kinds of people they are, or how they see themselves as compared to others, especially in the area of health and personal habits. We will look at the kinds of research they do, focusing particularly upon the fieldworkers among them.

Age and Sex Composition of the Respondents

We start with the age-sex distribution of the respondents. Because the *Guide* doesn't give age or year of birth, we have to consult the sample for this information. Table 3.1 shows the sex and ages of respondents in 1987, divided into ten-year age groups.

The age distribution of anthropologists reflects not only the birth and death rates of the population over the past century, but more important, the rates of recruitment to and retention in anthropology over the years. Anthropology was a small profession before World War II, but grew rapidly thereafter until the early 1970s, when the rate of unemployment signaled problems for new Ph.D.'s. The small number of anthropologists in their twenties, however, is not so much due to slowing of growth in the field as it is a reflection of the long training period and generally late age at which anthropologists complete it and take a professional job.

Table 3.1. Age and Sex of the Sample

Age	Male		Female		Total
	N	%	*N*	%	*N*
20–29	3	2%	1	1%	4
30–39	35	22	25	34	60
40–49	62	39	32	43	94
50–59	29	18	12	16	41
60–69	22	14	3	4	25
70+	9	6	1	1	10
Total	160		74		234[a]

[a]Two respondents did not answer the question of the year of their birth.

Large numbers of persons in their twenties are a part of the field, in the role of student, but they are rarely listed in the *Guide*.

Ages of respondents range between a minimum of 27 and a maximum of 85, with a mean of 47.13 (standard deviation 11.04). The standard error of that distribution is 0.722, so we expect to see the mean age of the population in the range $\pm$ 1.415 years (the 95% confidence interval) around the sample mean, 95% of the time if we repeatedly estimate a population mean from a sample of this size.

Among those who returned the questionnaire, we have about 32% females to 68% males—a substantial, even if not equal, representation of women in anthropology. In general, Table 3.1 shows that the proportion of women is less at older ages, reflecting changes over time in the recruitment of women into anthropology. While there were some very famous women like Margaret Mead and Ruth Benedict in the oldest generation of anthropologists, overall the field recruited few women in those days.

Professional Activities of Respondents

In the last chapter, we saw the kinds of professional jobs and educational achievements that the population has reached. Table 3.2 provides some information on the kinds of professional activities that the respondents report they have been engaged in as a "substantial" part of their work. "Substantial" was defined in the questionnaire as taking up about ten hours a week for a year, or equivalent. We see that research, teaching, and writing are checked as major activities by most respondents. Museum work and consulting or applied anthropology seem to be specialized niches that do not necessarily combine with research and publication. Only a few report that they have been unemployed for a substantial period of time, although we might have found a greater proportion unemployed if we had sampled from the directory of members rather than from the *Guide to Departments of Anthropology*.

Teaching, of both graduates and undergraduates, is central to the employment of most of the sample, but the most frequently cited activity is that of fieldwork. Anthropologists are distinguished by their use of fieldwork in their research, although we note too that a substantial proportion of the scholars also do the kind of research that is better characterized as library or laboratory research. Incidentally, a few (5) of the people who described their fieldwork in a later part of the

Table 3.2. Professional Activities of Respondents. [Checked that the component has ever been a substantial part of his or her work. (In order of frequency) N = 236]

Fieldwork—off-campus, excavation, survey, ethnography	199	84%[a]
Teaching, graduate and undergraduate	194	82
Publications, editing	156	66
Research on campus, laboratory, library	153	65
Administration, of university or business	112	47
Consulting, government, applied work	99	42
Museum work, curator	65	27
Unemployment, retirement	19	8
Sick leave (including maternity leave)	13	6%[a]

[a]Note that percentages do not sum to 100 since individuals checked more than one activity.

questionnaire did not check fieldwork in this list of activities—a minor discrepancy that is not being "corrected."

Anthropology tends to be a job in which those who do it have a wide range of control over their activities. When individuals do more or less of the various components of the job, we generally assume it is because the individual enjoys particular aspects of the job more than others, or because that task fits into the research agenda that the individual has created. But sometimes outside forces influence what is possible for an individual. Table 3.3 presents the checklist of answers to the question, "Have you ever wanted to do any of the preceding career activities (teaching, etc.), but been unable to because of . . ."

We note in Table 3.3 that there are some recurrent problems that prevent anthropologists from doing what they want to do with some frequency. Inability to get a grant—whether the person applies and is turned down or merely doesn't apply because he or she knows that the chances are not good in the current granting climate for a certain project—is the most commonly cited problem, especially for not doing certain fieldwork. We will see later that the funding available for fieldwork is frequently marginal, and it often happens that fieldworkers supplement funds from grants out of their own pockets.

Political instability in other countries is another major obstacle to doing fieldwork. Quite commonly a project is started in the field, and the necessary language learning, establishment of rapport, and other high-investment, low-payoff activities are performed. But then a change of government, a civil war, a revolution, or a military takeover makes continued work in the area—even nonpolitical work—difficult or impossible. Scholars have been denied access to their field sites for months, years, or even decades. It is a major risk of doing fieldwork abroad.

The third major obstacle to doing one's work comes from family responsibilities. Frequently, the anthropologist has children, but works in an area where it is difficult or impossible to take them, at least at certain stages of their lives. We will look at this set of problems in more detail in Chapter 14, where we discuss families in the field. Note that only a few scholars list "family objections" as an obstacle to doing desired work: it is their sense of their own responsibilities, not the views of the family members, that interferes with work, especially fieldwork.

**Table 3.3. Checklist of Factors that Made It Impossible to Do
Desired Professional Activities**

	Any Activity (N = 236)		Fieldwork Only (N = 204)	
	N	%	N	%
1. Inability to get a grant	52	22%	33	16%
2. Family responsibilities	39	16	20	10
3. Political instability in other countries	31	13	18	9
4. Financial need	29	12	10	5
5. No jobs available	29	12	5	3
6. Lack of skills	13	5	5	3
7. Personal problems	11	5	1	—
8. Too dangerous	10	4	6	3
9. Poor health	6	3	2	1
10. Family objections	5	2	2	1

Other family responsibilities that have been discussed are those to a spouse whose work does not permit going to the field, or the need to care for aged parents.

Table 3.3 also shows us that financial problems and lack of jobs sometimes interfere with scholars who want to follow their own agendas. The table also demonstrates how rarely anyone reports interference from poor health, an evaluation of danger, a lack of needed skills for carrying out the work, or personal problems. It will be useful to recall these observations later in the report, when we look more closely at the dangers and problems that fieldworkers tell us they have encountered, and the lack of specialized skills for dealing with them that the workers sometimes report.

Training Students for Fieldwork

Because fieldwork preparation is so central to anthropological research, the respondents were asked to specify whether training students to do fieldwork had been a part of their duties. Table 3.4 presents their answers to this series of questions. Again, they are checking whether they have ever at any time taken part in this activity.

We note in Table 3.4 that only a minority of the professionals report taking a very active role in the training of students for fieldwork. Only 17% have ever accompanied a student to the field to start fieldwork, while about a quarter have visited one or more students in the field while fieldwork was going on. Forty percent of the professors report that they have had students come to their own field sites, perhaps because the students were working as assistants on the professor's project as well as obtaining training. Most of the professors report more distant forms of training students for fieldwork, such as offering advice, writing letters of encouragement while the student is in the field, and writing letters of recommendation to help the student get a grant or research permission.

Careers of Respondents

On the average, the respondents who started graduate school (206) did so at age 24.8, with a standard deviation of about 4 years. The range goes from 17 (apparently someone thought we were asking for age at starting college) to age 46 (Figure 3.1). Graduate students are not, by any stretch of the imagination, children, and it is important to note this observation in considering the degree of training and supervision that is needed for their training in fieldwork.

Table 3.4. Activity Checklist for Training Students to Do Fieldwork [$N = 236$]

1. Advising students before they go to the field.	59%
2. Providing moral support and advice in letters, while the student is in the field.	47%
3. Writing letters of recommendation to colleagues, for grants, etc.	41%
4. Taking students with you to *your* research sites.	39%
5. Reading and commenting on students' field notes.	38%
6. Teaching a course on fieldwork preparation.	31%
7. Visiting a student at his or her field site.	28%
8. Teaching or administering at a field school.	25%
9. Letting the student work entirely alone.	21%
10. Taking the student to his/her own site.	17%

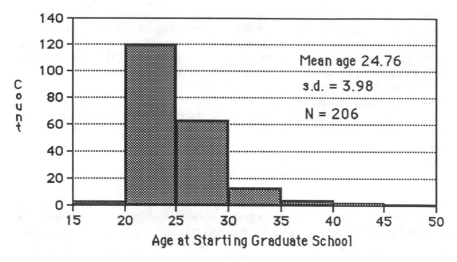

Figure 3.1. Age at Starting Graduate School in Anthropology

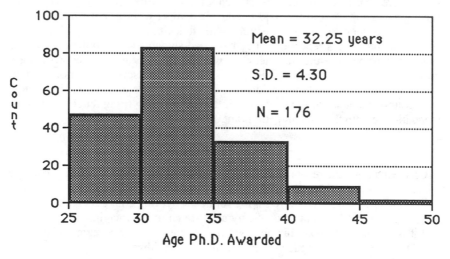

Figure 3.2. Age at Finishing Graduate School, for Those Who Earned a Ph.D.

There is some ambiguity about whether starting graduate school means starting on a master's degree or starting on a Ph.D. Many anthropologists do not get a master's degree before starting the Ph.D., and others may not have considered it significant.

For those 176 who earned a Ph.D., the average age at finishing graduate school is 32.2, and the standard deviation is about 4.3 years. Figure 3.2 shows the histogram, and we see that there are substantial proportions of the group who earned the Ph.D. at ages 25–29, at 30–34, and even at 35–39. Partly this is because people start the degree at various ages: in some cases the decision to start is delayed by military service or false starts in other career lines. But often it is due to differences in the number of years it takes to get a Ph.D. For this sample, the average time to Ph.D. from start to finish is almost eight years (mean = 7.96; s.d. 3.4) but the range goes from 3 years (which must be close to the minimum possible) to as much as 29 years—a period that implies starts and stops. Figure 3.3 shows the histogram for the range of four to 13 years, the central part of the distribution.

Anthropologists have a clear definition of what fieldwork is, and rarely asked for guidance or clarification of what was meant by the term in interviews or in questionnaires. As we will see later, however, fieldwork varies by subdiscipline and in different areas of the world. Fieldwork is central to their professional identity, and anthropologists are sometimes indignant if forced to recognize that others may mean something different by the same term.

The 206 respondents who answered this question report that they were, on the average, 24.9 when they started—in other words, about the same as their age at starting graduate school. The question here is not about the first fieldwork under their own direction, but about the first fieldwork of any kind. The minimum age reported is that of one year, reported with great pride by a senior anthropologist who was taken to the field as a baby by his parents, pioneers of ethnography. The oldest age at starting fieldwork is 57, reported by an informant who had a substantial career in business overseas before becoming so interested in anthropology that he took professional training, and he has spent the last decade working as an anthropologist in the same field area where he was a businessman so many years.

Figure 3.4 gives the histogram of the age of starting fieldwork. Those who report starting as teen-agers, generally speaking, are archaeologists or physical anthropologists who began their career by being a volunteer or a summer worker on a dig. The age group 20–24 is the modal class, and a substantial proportion are over age 25 when they start.

Respondents were also asked for their age at the time they held their first professional job, and the results are shown in Figure 3.5. The first professional job, like first fieldwork, is difficult to define for the whole group, but no one seemed to

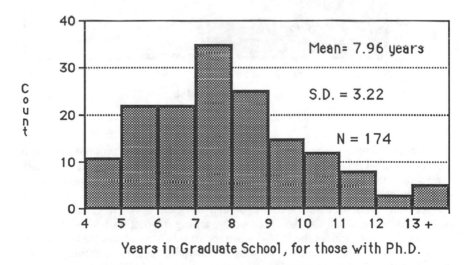

Figure 3.3. Number of Years to Completion of Ph.D.

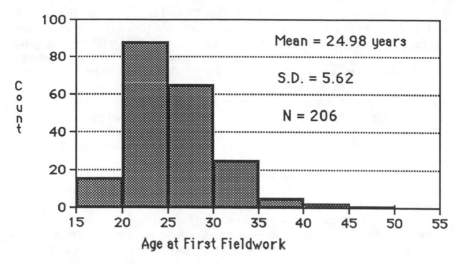

Figure 3.4. Age at First Fieldwork

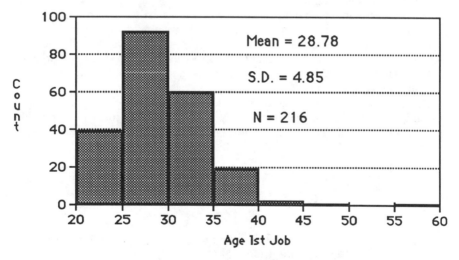

Figure 3.5. Age at First Professional Job

have difficulty in applying the concept. The mean age at first professional job is
28.78—in other words, it corresponds to a time in the career after starting graduate school but before being awarded the Ph.D. Until the 1970s, it was usual for
people to obtain an assistant professorship after completing the fieldwork for the
degree, but before the dissertation was actually written. In recent years, with jobs
scarce, more seem to finish the Ph.D. before taking the first professional job.

Since the job crunch of the 1970s, when the supply of graduate students finally
exceeded the number of entry level jobs in anthropology, fewer anthropologists
have had their first professional job before finishing the Ph.D. Indeed, a survey
in 1981 (National Academy of Sciences 1982) indicated that 40% of the recent

cohort of awarded Ph.D.'s in anthropology had no professional job of the kind listed in the AAA *Guide to Departments of Anthropology*. This was the highest rate of unemployment of new Ph.D.'s among the scholarly occupations studied. Figure 3.6 shows the age at starting the career given by the respondents. The concept, however, is a flexible one, subject to some retrospective redefinition, so that a person in their twenties asked this question might think of the first job that had anything to do with anthropology, while an older person might think of the first professorial job.

In order to obtain some insight into which events—the start of graduate school, the initiation of fieldwork, first professional job, or the awarding of the degree— is the most significant for anthropologists, respondents were asked to give the date when they consider that their career was started. Results suggest that the first professional job is most closely correlated with the start of the career. The answer to this question allows us to calculate how many years the respondents feel that they have had a career in anthropology (by subtracting the answer to this question from 1987, the date of the data collection). Figure 3.7 shows that the respondents have a great deal of experience among them, with an average length of career of almost twenty years, a modal length of 15–19 years, and a total among them of over 4,200 years! Even a small sample is reporting on a great deal of experience in professional anthropology.

The 204 respondents who have done fieldwork report an average of somewhat more than 22 years since they started their first fieldwork, so that they are reporting, collectively, on something more than 4,500 years as fieldworkers, in some of which they actually did fieldwork and in others not. In the next chapter, we will look more closely at the actual amounts and kinds of fieldwork that the members of this group have done.

Health Status and Habits of the Respondents

To complete this introduction to the respondents, we will look at their answers to a series of questions on their current health and health habits. Each was asked

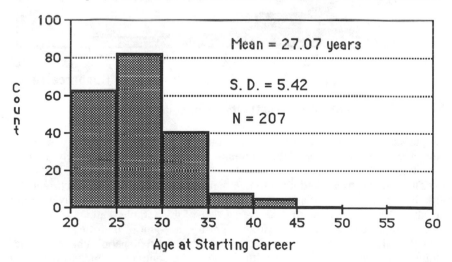

Figure 3.6. Age at which Respondent Feels Career Was Started

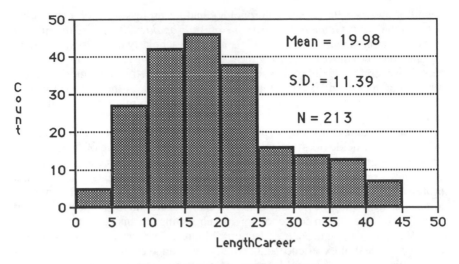

Figure 3.7. Length of Career to Date

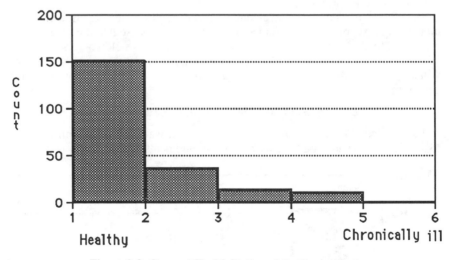

Figure 3.8. Current Health Rating of the Respondents

to put a check mark on a blank line indicating that they were closer to one end or the other, or in the middle of the continuum of two concepts "compared to others you know."

The first question asked them to rate themselves as healthy versus chronically ill. Figure 3.8 shows that the members of the sample find themselves pretty healthy. Keeping in mind that the average age of this sample is about 48, and that some respondents are advanced in old age, this account of their health suggests that they are a hardy bunch. Figure 3.8 shows that about 50 people checked something other than the extreme "healthy" end of the continuum, and we will learn more about their health problems later in this report.

Closely correlated with the answers to the question on general health, but some-what less positive, is the continuum "fit and athletic" to "limited in physical activity," shown in Figure 3.9. Only people extremely limited in physical activity (on crutches, recovering from surgery, etc.) seem to rate themselves a "5," but many are not as fit as they might be.

The next question asks about that perennial obsession of Americans, satisfaction with weight. Note that Figure 3.10 reverses the direction of the "good" end of the continuum from those of the first two questions, to avoid the notion of right and wrong answers to these questions. About half the respondents indicate that they are satisfied that their weight is "normal," while almost half suggest some degree of dissatisfaction or "overweight." We don't know that those who scored themselves "1" are actually much heavier than those with a "5"—perhaps they

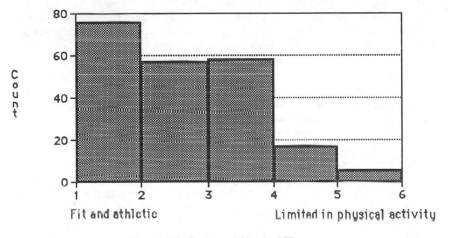

Figure 3.9. Rating of Physical Fitness

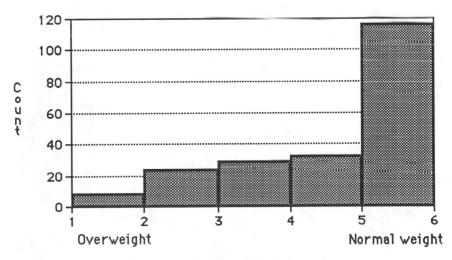

Figure 3.10. Rating of Weight Control

are just more unhappy about it. One wrote in the margins "What about under-weight?" and we will see later that severe weight loss in the field was reported as a health problem, whereas weight gain was never mentioned as a field hazard. One woman volunteered that if it were not for the weight loss that she regularly experiences in the field she wouldn't know what to do about controlling her obesity.

Figure 3.11 surprises me with the overwhelming majority of anthropologists who report themselves as nonsmokers in 1987. Only about 40 admit to any use of tobacco at all, and only 15 report heavy smoking. Having complained over the years of the heavy pall of smoke that hangs over anthropology conferences (as opposed to demography conferences, for instance), I would have guessed that more were smokers—but perhaps it is merely that the individualistic tendency in anthropology leads to reluctance of nonsmokers to curb the smokers. Or perhaps it is a matter of perceptions (mine) lagging behind changes in behavior (theirs).

Figure 3.12 reports the respondents' answers to the question, "Are you a cautious and careful person, or do you enjoy taking some risks?" A few respondents commented that this is not a true dichotomy, and that is true. The item was included to induce the respondents to think about these dimensions of their behavior, and encourage them to make comments about the relationship of their personality to the risks they take in the field. In any case, the answers they gave are interesting. Figure 3.12 shows a symmetrical distribution in which the largest group, about half, indicated that both ends of the continuum applied to them, while others report themselves closer to one extreme or the other.

The degree of organization is a personality trait that might well be correlated with ability to run a safe and smooth field trip. Most anthropologists admit to some degree of disorganization as a habitual trait, but only a few report it to be extreme (Figure 3.13).

Extremes of drinking behavior are part of the folklore of anthropology. Senior anthropologist Bernice Kaplan recalled in a *Anthropology Newsletter* "Commentary" that in the postwar expansion of anthropology

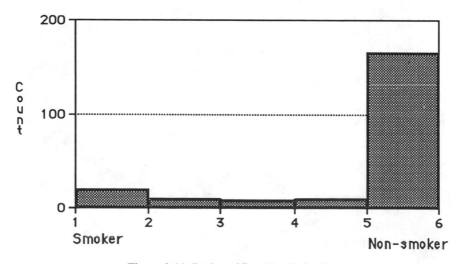

Figure 3.11. Rating of Smoking Behavior

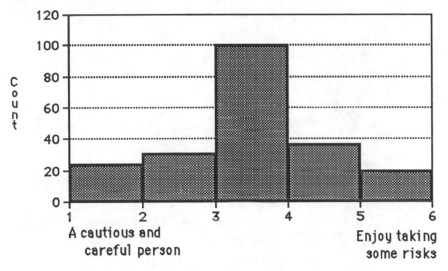

Figure 3.12. Rating of Caution and Attitude toward Risk

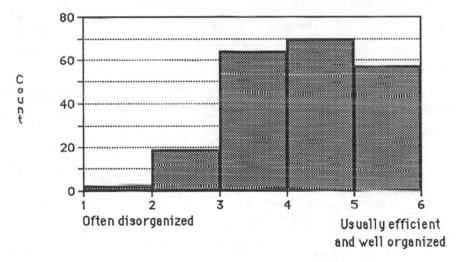

Figure 3.13. Rating of Organization and Disorganization

At our annual meetings a local version of "potlatching" began as departments vied to give the largest, most lively party to attract new students. A "successful" party had a police bust; the "best" had revelers taken from the hotel to the cooler for the night. [Kaplan 1986:28]

Anthropologists seem to enjoy believing that the Association has been thrown out of some of the best hotels in America for drunken destruction (and others assert that the Association is courted by hotels because of the size of the bar profits during the meetings). Whatever the truth of these claims, Figure 3.14 shows that about half the respondents in this study consider themselves "moderate or non-drinkers," while others admit to varying degrees of "sometimes drink too much

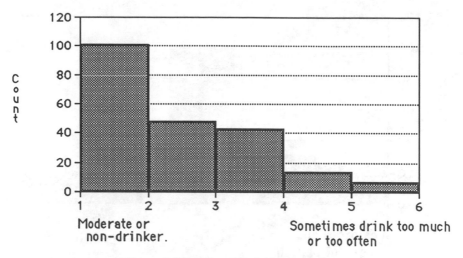

Figure 3.14. Rating of Drinking Behavior

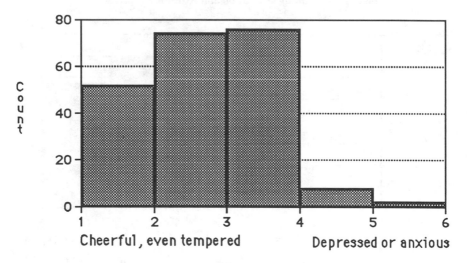

Figure 3.15. Rating of Cheerfulness versus Depression and Anxiety

or too often,'' with only a few at the extreme. In general, the data do not support the idea of an epidemic of heavy drinking among the professionals.

The next trait is another of those that refer to personality more than behavior. Respondents were asked to rate themselves as ''cheerful, even-tempered'' on one extreme, or as ''depressed or anxious'' on the other (Figure 3.15). The vast majority placed themselves on the cheerful, even-tempered side of the dichotomy, although not in the extremely ''cheerful'' category. One respondent phoned to emphasize that she is chronically depressed and anxious, and we discussed this trait in relation to fieldwork. Later we will look at the frequency of reported depression and anxiety in the field.

Finally, respondents rated themselves on the dimension of sociability, from "a loner, need time to yourself" to "sociable, have many friends" (Figure 3.16). Again, this dimension is not strictly dichotomous, as one can simultaneously be both. As in the case of risk-taking, most respondents report themselves as balanced between these extremes, with both a solitary and a sociable side to their personality. One can easily imagine that this flexibility is crucial to the success of some kinds of anthropology, where the investigator must establish good relations with local people but must not become totally dependent upon their good opinion.

In this chapter, we have learned something about the careers and the attributes of the men and women who will be reporting in the following chapters on the fieldwork they have done, and the sicknesses and injuries they have experienced in the course of doing it.

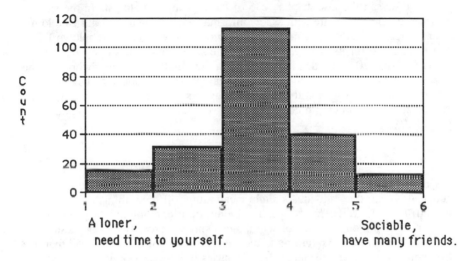

Figure 3.16. Rating of Degree of Sociability

CHAPTER 4 FIELDWORKERS AND THEIR FIELDWORK

History of Fieldwork

As we saw in the last chapter, 236 of the 311 anthropologists in the sample returned the questionnaire with usable information, and an additional 18 told me over the telephone that they never did fieldwork. So we know the fieldwork history of 254 informants. We see that 205 of the anthropologists surveyed had done fieldwork, and 204 provided information on the conditions of fieldwork and the hazards experienced as a part of it. In this chapter we will look at that experience, and from section to section the number of events counted will change from the 254 or 204 fieldworkers, to counts of field trips for which information has been provided.

How Many Trips?

On the question of the number of distinct "field trips" that our informants tell about, it is clear that individuals might mean rather different things. Let us imagine a trip to Africa, where one spends a month in orientation and language learning, and then a month in each of six villages, spread across two sides of an international border, before returning to the starting point. Some would call that one trip, some would count the number of countries in which work was done and call it two, and some would count the number of different sites where a base camp was established and call it seven field trips. There is not really a right answer to the question, but we need to be aware of differences in definition. For the purposes of this study, we let the respondent define what is meant by a trip, and we just report the numbers provided (Figure 4.1). In a few cases, respondents who had agreed in advance to allow it were phoned to clarify their responses.

The full distribution of the number of field trips mentioned in response to the question, "To summarize the history of fieldwork, how many distinct field trips have you gone on" has a mode at four field trips (25 persons), a median at nine (half the 204 informants who had done any fieldwork did more than nine trips, and half nine or less), and a mean at 18.8 trips. This is a very skewed distribution, with a long tail at the higher end. Only 30 people report more than 25 field trips, but these account for a large proportion of the trips mentioned. Twelve report 100 or more trips. The maximum number cited is 200, reported by two senior researchers (clearly such a large number is an estimate).

The sample shows us that virtually all professional anthropologists (or at least those listed in the *Guide to Departments of Anthropology*) do some fieldwork. Fifty of the 254 whose fieldwork history we know report none, and among them are department chairmen who happen to be sociologists rather than anthropolo-

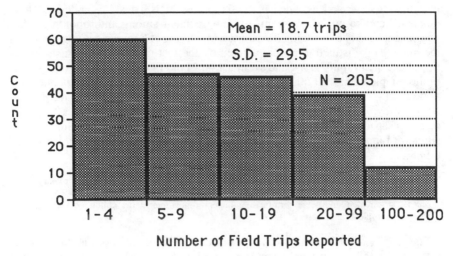

Figure 4.1. Number of Field Trips (note unequal categories)

gists, cross-appointed chemists or art historians, and an occasional librarian or secretary. Among the physical anthropologists, about half the informants characterize their work as laboratory (or forensic) rather than field-related. In each of the other specialities of anthropology—archaeology, linguistics, and social-cultural studies—no fieldwork at all is rare. Overall, more than 80% of the kinds of anthropologists listed in the *Guide* are fieldworkers.

Figure 4.1 shows that the pattern of anthropologists who go to the field for their dissertation research but never go again is rare among those listed in the *Guide to Departments of Anthropology*. Only 2% of the fieldworkers had gone to the field only once, and some of these are young people just getting started on their careers who will no doubt go again. Freilich (1977:16) comments on the need to go to the field repeatedly:

> Much like the knights of old who periodically had to legitimize their status by yet another involvement in mortal combat, the anthropologist must periodically return to the "combat" of field work, so as to demonstrate that he is still an effective professional. The first field trip provides membership in the anthropological fraternity, but those who rest on the laurels of the *rite de passage* research become marginal members of this fellowship. . . . Field trips subsequent to the initial trip are thus *status-maintenance rites* and, I would claim, purification rites.

The Duration of Fieldwork

The duration of a field trip may be an "accordion" concept, one which honest people may use rather differently at different stages of their careers. New workers and those who have done little fieldwork may report as one of a few expeditions a stint of fieldwork that would be forgotten by those who do much more. A "field trip" may last several years or as little as a week or so, may involve travel for weeks around the world before arrival to start the fieldwork or may only require a few minutes' travel from a university to a location not very different from the usual one.

The coding of the length of fieldwork was based on rounding up to whole months: a trip described as lasting two weeks (or two days) is coded as "one month," "five weeks" is coded as "two months," "100 days" is coded as "four months," and so on. There seems to be agreement among anthropologists that one cannot be said to be doing fieldwork while living at home and going home for the night. This distinction is complicated by the fact that anthropologists sometimes take their family along and set up a household in the field. Only one person in the sample counts all the time since he became an anthropologist as one continuous ten-year ("one hundred twenty month") field trip, and he is justified in doing so by virtue of living on an Indian reservation, employed in a full-time research capacity. A volunteer informant, Thomas Headland, of the Summer Institute of Linguistics, illustrates this extreme of fieldwork experience. He writes (1988):

> My family and I had our share of health problems in the field. My wife and I spent twenty of the last twenty-four years (1962–86) living with an Agta Negrito hunter-gatherer group in the Philippines. Our three children were born there and spent almost their entire childhood years in Agta camps in a tropical rain forest.

Figure 4.2 shows the responses to the question of the number of months of fieldwork performed by our respondents, summing over all their trips. The median is 35 months—half the sample have done more, and half have done less than 35 months. The mean is 41.6 months per person, implying that a minority have done a great deal of fieldwork. The total, summed over all 204 fieldworkers with their average of 18.8 trips apiece, is 8,528 months in the field, an average of 2.22 months per trip (or somewhat less, since we rounded up to whole months).

One naturally wonders about the relationship between these two ways of measuring exposure to fieldwork—number of trips and number of months. In particular, it seems possible that such patterns might be associated with different subdisciplines of anthropology—with archaeology and physical anthropology characterized by many short field trips, and social-cultural and linguistic research characterized by longer and fewer trips. Are length and frequency of trips two

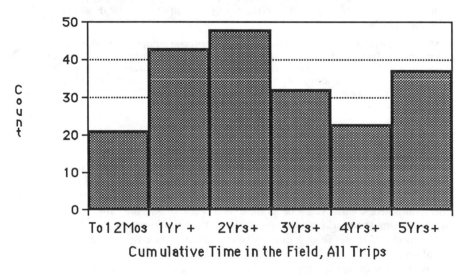

Figure 4.2. Total Time in the Field ($N = 204$ with any fieldwork)

ways of looking at the same thing—a commitment to fieldwork—or are they compensatory?

Briefly, the answer to this question is that the correlation between the number of trips and the total number of months spent doing fieldwork is not high ($r = .3$, less than 10% of the variance accounted for), but if we calculate the mean length of field trip per person (number of months total divided by number of trips), we get an individual characteristic that is related to several individual properties.

Not surprisingly, older people (or, more accurately, those with longer careers) have done more fieldwork and have taken more field trips, but report only slightly longer average field trips. The younger people may not yet have had time to go on all the extremely long field trips (say, more than 24 months) that they will eventually undertake. There is no evidence here for a strong trend in longer or shorter field trips over time.

Women report somewhat fewer and shorter field trips than men, but when we divide them into older and younger, the difference almost entirely disappears. Since women make up a larger proportion of the younger anthropologists than they do the older, the age (or length of career) variable is particularly important for them.

Stereotypes lead us to expect that archaeologists and physical anthropologists would have more and shorter field trips, and social-cultural anthropologists (including the linguists) would have fewer but longer field trips, because they have to spend a great deal of time and energy learning a language, establishing rapport with the locals, and so on. The data, however, do not support that expectation very strongly. A few more social-cultural anthropologists than expected are in the one-to-four-trip category, and a few more archaeologists than expected are in the 20–99 category, but overall the differences are small.

There is no significant difference in number of trips, average duration of trips, or total number of months spent in the field between the two types of anthropologists. Their activities in the field no doubt differ, but the external variables of frequency and duration do not differ—at least not enough to be detectable in a sample of this size.

Fieldwork in 1986

Figure 4.3 shows the answers to the question of how many days during 1986 the respondent spent in the field. This question is meant to provide a higher level of accuracy of reporting on behavior than the more general questions that ask for lifetime fieldwork history, which might be distorted by poor memory or exaggeration. The year 1986 had ended three months before when the question was asked, so there should have been relatively good recall. This question bothered some respondents who feared that the researcher would get an entirely wrong impression from the answer, especially if 1986 happened to be a year of much more (or less) fieldwork than usual.

In fact, however, Figure 4.3 shows that 1986 was a less than "typical" year for fieldwork among American anthropologists, although in it, as in all years, some individuals did more or less than their average. In the group as a whole, although 130 of the 205 fieldworkers did no fieldwork at all, the average reported 33.9 days in the field. The distribution is J-shaped, sharply declining at the longer durations, with the relatively few who did more than 90 days contributing consid-

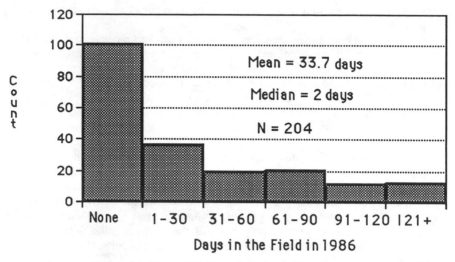

Figure 4.3. Days of Fieldwork during 1986 (*N* = 204)

erably to the total. Note that we are seeing the effects of the usual academic year, whereby a large proportion of the total take advantage of the summer vacation to do fieldwork of something less than 90 days. Overall, about 50% did no fieldwork in 1986; about 19% were in the field less than 30 days; 20% were in the field 30–90 days; and 12% were in the field more than 3 months.

To check the internal consistency of these sets of findings, we compare the distribution of days in the field reported for 1986, a count made by individuals on their own recent activities, with a cruder calculated measure of average time spent in the field per year by the fieldworkers. The numerator is the answer to the question "To summarize your experience, roughly how many months (or weeks or days) have you spent doing fieldwork, all together?" The denominator is the difference between 1986 and the year listed as "first fieldwork experience," the number of years in which any fieldwork could possibly be done. The resulting calculations have an average of 63.63 days per year, about twice as long as the amount claimed for 1986.

Perhaps some of the difference is due to the lower level of specificity requested, perhaps some is due to an exaggerated sense of the amount of fieldwork done, corresponding to its importance in their life; and some to a decline in the amount of fieldwork being done in recent years. A major factor may be that few of the people listed were involved in Ph.D. dissertation fieldwork during 1986, whereas their career average of days of fieldwork per year includes their (usually more extensive) dissertation fieldwork experience. Without a baseline, it is impossible to separate these possible causes, but we can conclude with some confidence that the 80% of professional anthropologists who do any fieldwork average between 30 and 60 days a year over the course of their professional lives.

Our preliminary summary of the extent of fieldwork for anthropologists, then, is that about 20% never do any fieldwork at all, and about 40% do some during each year. Seventy-five percent of those who do fieldwork in a year carry it out in three months or less while the other quarter (who are only 10% of the professional anthropologists) do more than three months' worth in any particular year.

Features of the Field Trips

We have been generalizing about groups of individuals up to this point. Now we shift our focus to the unit of the field trip. Each of the 204 fieldworkers was asked to provide information on the place (country and site), date, size of the research group, and the funding source for each of up to ten field trips. The maximum number of trips they should tell about was not actually specified, but only ten lines were provided on the questionnaire. Some informants sent a printed list of field trips, typically a xeroxed page (or pages) from their curriculum vitae. The questionnaire form acknowledged that this is a difficult and time-consuming question to answer, and asked for the patience of the informant. For each individual, then, some details were obtained about one to ten field trips—an average of 5.3 apiece.

For the next series of tables, we will use this group of 1,094 field trips as the base of calculations. These field trips represent only about 28% of all the field trips mentioned in the summary question, and probably overrepresent the longer, more exotic, and more important field trips. Table 4.1 summarizes a great deal of what was told to us about these field trips, and allows us to relate the number of people to the number of field trips.

Overall, 45% of field trips reported were to destinations within the United States, and 70% of the fieldworkers reported at least one field trip to a North American location. U.S. fieldwork tends to be the least exotic and least expensive, and most frequently omitted in the accounts that follow. We must remember that North American fieldwork is a large proportion of the total. The amount of that fieldwork that was done in Canada, 13%, is about proportional to the population, although not, of course, to the territory in that country.

About 8% of the field trips were to European destinations, with a few trips reported to each of virtually all the European countries. Only the United Kingdom and France have any concentration of investigators and investigations.

After North America, Latin America is the most common area for field trips for this group. Overall, 22% of the field trips reported were to Mexico, the Caribbean, Central America, or South America. Mexico accounted for 79 trips, making it second only to the United States as a country of fieldwork. Other frequently visited countries are Peru, Brazil, and Guatemala.

Sixty-three field trips were to locations in South Asia, including India, Pakistan, Bangladesh, Afghanistan, and Ceylon. Only India shows more than four trips, with an impressive total of 55.

Africa is represented by 103 field trips, spread across the continent and including the Near Eastern countries of Israel, Egypt, Iran, and Iraq. East Africa, especially Kenya and Tanzania, forms one focus for fieldwork on the continent, and South Africa forms another.

Finally, there are 88 field trips reported to Asia and the Pacific area, again with the distribution spread widely and thinly across the territory. Only China, Papua New Guinea, the Philippines, and Thailand represent concentrations of research.

These continentwide classifications will prove useful in exploring the different kinds of fieldwork conditions reported and the hazards associated with them.

Expedition Size, by Continent

An important determinant of safety and the conditions of daily life is the size of the research group. In some ways it is no doubt easier to work entirely alone,

Table 4.1. Regions and Countries of Field Trips Reported

Region	Trips	Persons	Months
	(% of 1094)	(% of 236)	(Average per trip)
I. North America	492	145	3,655
Canada (66)	(45%)	(61%)	(7.4 mos)
United States (428)			
II. Europe	106	45	811
England (G.B.) (18)	(10%)	(19%)	(7.8 mos)
France (20)			
Italy (5)			
Norway (5)			
Yugoslavia (6)			
III. Latin America	242	71	1,578
Argentina (8)	(22%)	(30%)	(6.5 mos)
Brazil (15)			
Chile (6)			
Colombia (6)			
Costa Rica (8)			
Ecuador (7)			
Guatemala (12)			
Mexico (79)			
Peru (46)			
Puerto Rico (9)			
Venezuela (7)			
IV. Indian Subcontinent	63	23	698
India (55)	(6%)	(10%)	(11.0 mos)
V. Africa	103	29	871
Kenya (10)	(9%)	(12%)	(8.5 mos)
South Africa (6)			
Tanzania (8)			
Egypt (7)			
Iran (9)			
VI. Pacific and Asia	88	31	869
China (8)	(9%)	(13%)	(8.6 mos)
New Guinea (18)			
Philippines (11)			
Thailand (14)			

in that one does not take on responsibility for others, but solitary workers have no one to help with domestic chores, cooking, nursing, or responding to emergencies. We will see later that fieldworkers tend to have strong opinions about the pros and cons of taking others with them to the field. Those who go to the field with others may be with their families (we will look at their answers to questions about the presence of families in Chapter 13), or may go with a few or many coworkers, students, or research colleagues.

Table 4.2 shows the percentage of the field trips reported in which the investigator was alone, and the cumulative percentage that were with a small group (one to four others, making a group size of five or fewer). We note that many

Table 4.2. Size and Duration of Trips, by Areas (based upon 1094 trips)

	N. America	Europe	L. America	India	Africa	Asia
Number of Field Trips	492	106	242	63	103	88
Investigator worked alone (%)	22	21	25	46	25	51
Investigator had 1–4 companions (%)	28	31	38	44	40	35
Investigator had 5+ companions (%)	50	48	37	10	35	14
Average Number in Group	9.4	8.8	7.8	2.7	5.3	3.1
Average Months in Field	7.4	7.8	6.5	11.0	8.5	8.6
Person-Months in the field per trip[a]	68.9	63.0	66.3	27.44	48.7	61.8

[a]Person-months in the field per trip was calculated from the exact numbers of persons and months given in the individual responses, not from the averages for the continents.

more investigators who work in India and in Asia and the Pacific go alone (nearly 50%) while only about 25% of those who work in North and South America, Europe and Africa go alone. Similarly, around 90% of the trips to India and to Asia and the Pacific are staffed by a group of five or fewer, while about 60% of those working in Latin America and Africa go alone or in a small group, as do about 50% of those working in North America and Europe. The easier field conditions seem to be associated with larger groups.

These areas differ, too, in the number of people who go on the expedition, and whether the others are family members, colleagues, or students. North America and Europe are alike in that 21–22% of trips there were made by only the anthropologist-respondent, with an average of about 9 to a group. Latin American and African trips had about 25% anthropologists going alone, with an average of about eight to a group in Latin America, and about five in African groups. Indian and Pacific-Asian trips were quite different, in that approximately 70% of the anthropologists went alone, and the average group size was only about three. These percentages and averages reflect differences in the costs and difficulties of taking along additional personnel, as well as differences in the purely scientific issues of the research.

Sources of Funding for Field Research

Not only are the costs of fieldwork quite different for various regions, but the sources of funding available are also different. It was not possible to collect detailed data on the amounts of grants or the adequacy of the funding, as the topic is a very complex one, and respondents would often need to consult documents to reconstruct the amounts of grants and their sources. But at least the major source of funding for each of the 1,094 expeditions was ascertained from the respondents (who were not always the principal investigators of the projects). Table 4.3 shows the results.

This table tells us that the U.S. government-funded agencies (National Science Foundation and the various National Institutes of Health) are the major source of funding for 35% of all research trips reported here; 60% of the groups funded worked in North or South America.

Other governments funded about 4% of the trips, and the North American region was the site of the largest share of these, which reflects Canadian government support for primarily Canadian research. Other governments were rarely cited as

Table 4.3. Source of Major Funding of Trips, by Areas
(Table entries are number of trips, total = 1,094)

	N. America	Europe	L. America	India	Africa	Asia	Total
Number of Field Trips	492	106	242	63	103	88	1094
Source of Major Funding							
1. U.S. federal grants—NSF, NIH	173	34	71	33	40	33	35%
2. Grants from other countries	12	8	5	4	7	9	4%
3. U.S. national foundations (Ford, etc.)	20	6	20	12	6	6	6%
4. State contracts	47	0	1	0	0	0	4%
5. Universities	11	29	62	5	20	17	23%
6. Museums	10	5	9	1	1	1	2%
7. Private sources	77	12	56	1	10	14	16%
8. Self-funded (unfunded)	24	6	15	2	11	8	6%
9. Don't know, blank, refused to say	14	6	3	5	8	0	3%

sources of funding. Private foundations (Ford, Rockefeller, Carnegie, Wenner-Gren, etc.) funded another 6% of the expeditions, spread quite evenly around the world. Probably these sources (government and foundation) provide more generously for research than the other sources we will be considering. Even in this category, interviews revealed that the major source of funding only rarely covered all of the expenses of the research. More often, the researcher had to seek additional funding, or, very frequently, supplement the grant with his or her own resources.

Another 5% of groups were supported by state governments and contracts: virtually all of these were U.S. archaeology projects. Overall, 23% of trips were reported to have been funded primarily by universities—a resource that informants stated could be meager. Frequently university financing of research covered only part of the expenses. (One wonders how often researchers refer to the funding as coming from a university, when actually the university was only administering a grant derived from a government agency or a foundation.) In any case, 46% of these field trips said to have been supported by universities were in North America and another 25% in Latin America, with a small percentage of the trips to other parts of the world. Museums provided for only 2% of all expeditions, not heavily concentrated in any one region.

Perhaps the most interesting and mysterious source is that referred to by informants as "private funding." One imagines patrons, sponsors, corporations, or rich parents, friends or relatives providing for the more than 15% of trips reported under this heading. Private funding is frequently mentioned for Latin American research (23%), and both North American and Asian research is supported for about 15% of the total trips, with other regions 10% or below.

Finally, the source most surprising to those outside anthropology is "self": overall, 6% of trips; the major source of funding for 10% of trips to Africa, Asia and the Pacific, and about 5% of the rest. The great advantage of self-funding of research is that one doesn't have to bother about applications or about accounting for how the money was spent, which are great advantages to many bureaucracy-hating anthropologists. But of course few anthropologists have the resources to provide for large expeditions to distant parts from their own bank accounts, and the research done often seems to be a compromise between what proposals can be funded and what the anthropologists would like to do, if money were no object.

Living Conditions for Fieldworkers
at Sites in Different Parts of the World

The living conditions of fieldworkers as they carry out their observations determine in large part the health, safety, and comfort of the anthropologist and the field team. Some anthropologists are anxious to see that the standards for field conditions should not become excessively comfortable or "soft" (Nader 1969:114). Others may be concerned that if it were known how comfortably they had arranged their lives in the field, they would be considered unprofessional. For whatever reason, no one has documented the physical conditions of fieldwork before this study. Hence the information in Tables 4.4 to 4.10 has special interest.

These tables are based on 528 field trips that were described in more detail by our 204 fieldworkers. After listing up to ten field trips, the informants were asked to select up to three sites that have been most important to their own research. Analysis of the data shows that the single most important and interesting dimension of fieldwork along which these variables vary is that of the region of the world in which the fieldwork was done. Hence in all the tables to follow, we will use the categories of regions to present the data, and only discuss other variables, such as subdisciplinary differences, age, or sex of the anthropologists, when these are striking.

Housing in the Field

One dimension of field conditions is housing, or the absence of housing. All of the combinations of shelter and sleeping arrangements found have been grouped into three categories. The fieldworkers reported that in about 40% of their expeditions they lived in a house and slept in a bed. Another 20% were living with and like the peasants and villagers they studied, and lived in a structure they described as a hut, sleeping on a rope bed, a mattress on the floor, or a cot. Another 40% report that they slept in a tent, the back of a truck, or outside without shelter, typically on an air mattress or on the ground. Table 4.4 gives the degree of comfort in housing and sleeping arrangements by continent: European research seems to be the most comfortable along this dimension, with African research and Pacific-Asian research the most "rough."

Source and Treatment of Drinking Water

A second element of living conditions in the field is the source of water and the treatment of it before drinking. Water that arrives piped and treated by competent

Table 4.4. Housing and Sleeping Conditions in the Field (based upon 528 field sites)

	N. America	Europe	L. America	India	Africa	Asia	Total
Number of Field Trips	216	51	131	39	45	46	528
Living-Sleeping Conditions							
House—sleep on a bed	45%	63	35	41	24	26	41%
Hut—sleep on a cot, mattress	13	10	26	23	29	35	20%
Tent—sleep on ground, camping	42	27	39	36	47	39	39%

water authorities is available almost everywhere in North America and Europe. In Table 4.5 it is referred to simply as "safe," and fieldworkers do not boil or otherwise treat it.

In other parts of the world, drinking water is obtained from a well, a stream, a river, a lake, or is collected from rain water. Some of it may be quite free of bacteria and parasites, but it is hard to tell without elaborate testing equipment. Under these circumstances, some fieldworkers boil or filter or chemically treat their water before drinking (or instruct a member of their staff to do so), while others just drink the water and take a chance. In Table 4.5, the expeditions are counted as "treated" or "risky" for the water they drink. Of course, there may be daily or other variation in what is done, but the classification in Table 4.5 is based on the self-reports of fieldworkers about their water at a particular site. No doubt the objective degree of riskiness varies. We note, for example, that 36% of expeditions in North America are described as "risky," but the water may nevertheless be pure or purified. It is interesting to see the substantial rates of water treatment reported by those who work in the underdeveloped areas of the world (whether or not their treatment is entirely efficacious).

We note that few of the field sites outside North America and Europe can rely upon a public water purification system. The majority of research groups have to take responsibility for providing safe water or taking the risk to drink untreated water. The majority of the reports on work in Latin America, the Indian subcontinent, and Africa say that they make the effort to treat the water. Methods reported are boiling it (which is most frequently reported for well water, typically from those who work in villages and towns), or filtering it (which is reported most often by those who work in cities or towns in the Third World). Chemical treatment (with iodine or chlorine) is a rather cumbersome method to use over a long period of time, and is most useful to those who work in sparsely settled parts of the world, or for short periods of time, while travelling or getting settled in other areas.

Untreated water is used at 31% of the research sites, by 50% of those who drink well water, 39% of those who get their drinking water from a stream or river, and 31% of those who depend on lake or pond water. Later, when we look at the frequency of intestinal tract infections, we will remember this large group of researchers who take their chances with the local water supply.

Sanitary Facilities

Similarly we inquire, at the risk of being thought improperly curious, into the toilet facilities of the researchers (Table 4.6). Overall, 42% of the expeditions had flush toilets (or chemical toilets), while another almost 40% had latrines, either

Table 4.5. Field Conditions—Water Treatment (% of Field Trips, by Major Areas)

	N. America	Europe	L. America	India	Africa	Asia	Total
Number of Field Trips	216	51	131	39	45	46	528
Water Source and Treatment							
Safe—piped purified water	46	63	12	5	11	7	30
Treated—natural, then boiled	18	8	63	85	62	48	39
Risky—natural, untreated	36	29	25	10	27	46	31

Table 4.6. Field Conditions—Sanitary Facilities (% of Column)

	N. America	Europe	L. America	India	Africa	Asia	Total
Number of Field Trips	216	51	131	39	45	46	528
Sanitary Disposal							
Toilets, flush or chemical	51	55	36	44	13	30	42
Latrines, new or existing	32	39	33	41	60	52	38
No removal, burial, woods	16	6	31	15	27	17	20

existing ones or ones that the researchers dug. About 20% of the research groups had neither, at least for a substantial proportion of the time, and used "woods and fields," burial or scattering of urine and feces, or "followed local custom," which might mean eliminating into running water, or into the ocean. Of course, the facilities vary by parts of the world, with modern plumbing usually available in North America and Europe, and latrines usually available in Africa and the Pacific. Absence of any facilities is most common in Latin America and in Africa, and no doubt this absence complicates the entire health and safety picture for fieldworkers in those areas.

Generally, the availability of toilet facilities varies with density of population—with toilets typically available in cities, latrines available in villages and farming communities, and scattering of urine and feces most frequently used in sparsely settled regions. The danger of scattering excrement is that of infection of locals or researchers by microorganisms or parasites.

Fecal contamination of water and food can produce serious illness, and later we will see that anthropologists often suffer from such illnesses. Whether the illness was produced by insufficient care in disposal of their own urine and feces, or whether the problem was caused by others cannot be told in any particular case. Researchers report digging latrines for about 15% of sites.

Food in the Field

Health in the field, as anywhere, depends in part on the diet available. Researchers typically have to balance their desire for a supply of fresh and attractive foods of the kinds they enjoy with their desire to avoid spending a large portion of their time cooking, shopping, or even growing food or hunting and gathering it. Table 4.7 shows the reports of the researchers on the source of their food and who usually prepared it.

There are several observations to make about the information in Table 4.7. We note that the single most frequently mentioned arrangement for food preparation is to hire a local cook and have that person do the cooking (and usually the shopping as well). Presumably this means something rather different when the cook is hired from a local village in France and shops at the *boulangerie* and the *charcuterie* than when the cook is hired from a New Guinea village and gets the food from the local farmers. But nevertheless the problem of how to arrange meals without spending the whole day at it is often solved by hiring a cook, and generations of anthropologists have in addition used such employees as supplementary research informants. Other arrangements consist of cooking for oneself, sharing the task with research team members (who may be subordinates, but need not be),

Table 4.7. Food Supplies and Food Preparers (% of Column)

	N. America	Europe	L. America	India	Africa	Asia	Total
Number of Field Trips	216	51	131	39	45	46	528
Who Prepares Food?							
Researcher alone	18	20	14	0	7	9	14
Research team members	26	14	19	3	11	9	19
Family members	19	20	13	15	22	16	17
Local cook	18	18	31	64	44	36	28
Inn or restaurant	16	28	13	10	7	11	15
Fed by local people (not hired)	4	2	11	8	9	20	7
Source of Food							
Modern supermarket	53	51	15	10	2	11	32
Local market (self or cook)	17	27	40	79	54	38	36
Locally grown (not sold)	1	2	19	5	9	20	8
Grown by self or team	3	4	6	5	7	16	5
Hunted or gathered locally	1	0	1	0	2	7	2
Hauled in by researchers	20	2	14	0	27	13	15

or having someone in the family, usually the researcher's spouse, do the cooking. In all these arrangements the cultural framework of food selection and preparation is that of the researcher rather than the locals, which may simplify the tasks of protecting health and safety in the kitchen but complicate the problems of learning the new culture. We see that researchers say that they never fed themselves in the Indian subcontinent, but instead depended heavily on a locally hired cook. Note particularly how rarely researchers in all areas report that local people fed them, not in a formally commercial arrangement, but as part of the stay in the community, although this arrangement is a kind of prototypical ideal for the anthropologist in the field.

We also see in Table 4.7 that researchers in North America and Europe most often report buying their food in what they describe as a modern supermarket, restaurant, or hotel. Buying food in a local market is more commonly reported for Latin America, India, Africa, and Asia and the Pacific. We see that it is relatively rare for researchers to be dependent on gifts of food from the local people, or to be dependent on food grown or hunted and gathered locally. Acquiring food locally outside the marketplace is too time-consuming and difficult to be compatible with research, and researchers avoid that arrangement when they can.

Transportation in the Field

The means of transportation used on expeditions can be a source of danger— vehicle accidents are a frequent source of injury and death, as we will see—and at the same time, a source of safety during illness and accident (Table 4.8). Research groups with cars, trucks, airplanes, and helicopters can more quickly reach medical care when it is needed than those who have to depend upon public buses, hitchhiking, or walking.

Research teams may use many kinds of transport in the course of carrying out their investigations. The choice of vehicle depends in part on the work that is being done (whether research materials must be carried, whether there are roads

Table 4.8. Transportation in the Field (% of Column)

	N. America	Europe	L. America	India	Africa	Asia	Total
Number of Field Trips	216	51	131	39	45	46	528
Transportation in the Field							
High tech—trucks, planes	61	36	55	36	76	33	54
Medium—cars, cycles	34	46	24	18	13	26	29
Low tech—walking, buses	4	18	21	46	11	41	17

available) and also depends in part upon the financial resources available. Groups may use many kinds of transport in the field. We have classified the means of transport in Table 4.8 by the highest level of technology reported.

Table 4.8 shows that the "high tech" means of transportation—trucks, helicopters, and planes—are most frequently used in North America, Latin America, and Africa. In these areas, research may require traveling substantial distances, and roads may not exist or may be unsuitable for motorized transport. The "medium tech" category includes cars, motorcycles, motorboats, snowmobiles, and other motorized vehicles that are relatively easy to learn to drive, and require a relatively low investment of money. They dominate transport among European field projects, and are commonly used in North America. "Low tech" solutions may reflect the availability of public transport, the absence of a need to haul a lot of equipment and material to the field, lack of roads, or the scarcity of funds of the researcher. In this category we include using buses and other public transport, bicycles, walking and hiking, and animal transport such as use of horseback riding or dog sleds. As we will see later, transportation is the source of many of the serious accidents that occur during fieldwork.

Availability of Medical Care

Doctors or the local hospital provide any medical care needed during fieldwork for most fieldworkers in North America, Europe, and India, while fieldworkers tend to rely on their own skills (or those of fellow research group members) in Latin America, Africa, and the Pacific. The accessibility of the local hospital or doctor varies between almost immediate availability to situations in which the researcher estimates it might take a week to evacuate someone in an emergency (from an island, for instance, where one might have to wait until the next boat stops, or in situations where a message must be sent on foot to call for air transport.)

Accessibility is coded as "easy" if the researcher estimates it would take two hours or less to get to a hospital (up to about 100 miles for those who have a truck or car), as "an effort" if the estimated time is two hours to about eight hours, and as "remote" for those who estimate more than eight hours, up to a day or several days. Overall, 45% report that they have easy access and would go to a local hospital or doctor for medical help in the field. Another 9% would go, although it would be an effort; and 5% would go even though the access is remote. About 15% would treat medical needs themselves, even though access to a doctor or hospital is easy; and another 15% would rely on their group for medical care in situations where access is difficult. Table 4.9 summarizes all these responses.

Table 4.9. Field Conditions—Access to Medical Care in the Field (% of Column)

	N. America	Europe	L. America	India	Africa	Asia	Total
Number of Field Trips	216	51	131	39	45	46	528
Medical Care in the Field							
Local doctor, hospital	70	76	42	82	34	43	59
Self, other group members	25	17	47	18	55	50	34
Accessibility to Nearest Hospital or Doctor							
Easy—2 hours or less	78	84	49	66	40	53	65
Effort required—2–8 hrs	15	7	23	16	36	26	19
Remote—8 hrs to weeks	6	4	28	8	22	19	14

Table 4.9 indicates that most of the researchers in North America, Europe, and the Indian subcontinent depend on local physicians and hospitals for medical care in the field, and that most can reach a physician or hospital with relatively little difficulty. A substantial portion of those who work in Latin America, Africa, and Asia, however, do not depend on physicians in case of need but try to treat the problem themselves, either personally or looking to another member of the research team. Substantial proportions of those who work in Latin America, Africa, and Asia and the Pacific report that it takes them at least eight hours to reach medical care, or, in some cases, days or weeks.

Safety Equipment Carried in the Field

Finally, researchers were asked whether they usually had a list of safety equipment with them in the field at the sites they reported on. This equipment is not equally appropriate for all sites or all field conditions: there is little call for spare parts for vehicles if the research is being done on foot or with public transportation, and no need for a two-way radio in a city where telephones are readily available. Some of the items may not contribute to safety: the presence of a gun may contribute more to danger than safety (although some researchers would strongly disagree), and the snakebite kit, as we will see later, may be of doubtful value. Nevertheless, the checklist response is interesting for what it tells of the researchers' habits.

Table 4.10 shows that carrying safety equipment is not necessarily standard procedure on anthropological expeditions. Only "a serious first-aid kit'" is reported for a majority of sites ("serious" is intended to convey something more than Band-Aids and aspirin). Other kinds of equipment seem to be specific to areas of work. In Europe, researchers carry little safety equipment, while in Latin America (and generally in Africa, and Asia and the Pacific) they take more. Africa and North America seem to be the places where extra vehicles and spare parts for vehicles are needed and carried, while India and Asia are like Europe, in that few researchers report that they back up their vehicles for safety. We see that injectable antibiotics are carried by some researchers in Latin America, Africa, and Asia, but rarely taken elsewhere, and we recall that the places where they are carried tend to be the areas with poorer access to physicians and hospitals. Guns are carried by a minority of researchers everywhere, but more frequently in North America, Latin America, and Asia and the Pacific (especially New Guinea). Re-

Table 4.10. Field Conditions—Availability of Safety Equipment in the Field % that Reported Having Each (Note: %s do not sum to 100)

	N. America	Europe	L. America	India	Africa	Asia	Total
Number of Field Trips	216	51	131	39	45	46	528
Two-way radio	12	2	10	0	4	4	8
A serious first-aid kit	59	41	90	31	42	54	51
A gun or guns	10	4	12	0	9	13	9
Extra vehicle in case of breakdown	30	14	9	0	18	0	17
Spare parts for vehicles	13	6	21	8	33	6	15
Injectable antibiotics	1	2	19	3	11	13	8
Snakebite kit	27	4	37	13	29	17	26
Water purification equipment	12	10	42	23	38	9	22

searchers who carry guns for safety are sometimes quick to defend their usefulness, especially to respond to or prevent human violence, rather than to respond to animal attack or to provide food. Two-way radios are rarely reported as safety equipment carried, although we will see later that, in many parts of the world, they could contribute considerably to health and safety.

Individuals Classified by Region of Research, Precautions Taken

Note that when we classify *people* (as opposed to trips) by area, as we did in one of the columns of Table 4.1, we are referring to the bulk of the fieldwork they report, not all of it. Most of our respondents have done at least some fieldwork in North America, but only 61 of the 204 (30%) report that all or their most important work has been in North America. (In the *Guide to Departments of Anthropology,* 45% of our respondents listed North American areas as their first area of research, which presumably reflects current research and teaching interests.) The next most frequently claimed field area, as classified from the questionnaires, is Latin America:63 (31%) are classified as primarily Latin Americanists. Europe and the Indian subcontinent (including Pakistan and Bangladesh, as well as India) each are reported by 17 (8%); and Africa and Asia (including the Pacific) each are reported by 23 (11%), a total of 204 fieldworkers.

In the next chapters we will be looking at the experiences these people had and the kinds of hazards encountered during fieldwork. But before we leave these issues of preparation for the field, let us look at the precautions that fieldworkers report they have taken before setting out. After the respondents had gone through the checklist of hazards they encountered, and had reported on their worst and most difficult problems in the field, they were asked to check "Which of the following precautions have you taken before going to the field?" In the following tables, they are classified by the area of the world in which they most often (or currently) do fieldwork. The precautions checked are not necessarily associated with the research in that area, but probably are.

Table 4.11 shows us that a majority of fieldworkers at least sometimes consult a physician for a medical checkup before going to the field, and many of them get inoculations at that time (or regularly). Some of these inoculations are required for overseas travel, in order to obtain visas or to reenter the United States after

Table 4.11. Medical Precautions Taken Before Going to the Field (% of Column)

	N. America	Europe	L. America	India	Africa	Pacific	Total
Number of Field Trips	61	17	63	17	23	23	204
Precautions							
First aid course	33	18	25	18	17	17	25[a]
Medical check-up	60	65	81	76	83	61	71
Inoculations	46	65	83	53	91	69	67
Dental check-up	36	65	54	59	65	69	53

[a]Note that percentages do not sum to 100, as individuals may take several precautions.

travel in areas of exposure to contagious diseases. Others are merely recommended to reduce the probability of hazards, from rabies and tetanus, for instance.

The table provides us information on the percentage of fieldworkers who report that they do take precautions, and the obverse is the percentage who do not take these precautions. But of course those who do not may be subdivided into rather different groups—those who have no need for the precaution because they are not exposed to the risk of that hazard, and those who are exposed, but who do not take the precaution because they do not think of it in advance, because they prefer to run the same risks as the local people, or because they just like to take risks. Those subgroups cannot be easily separated, but we will keep this underlying distinction in mind as we examine the percentages of workers who suffer from the risks that precautions are intended to prevent.

Note that only about a quarter of the fieldworkers report taking a first aid course to prepare for fieldwork, despite the fact that many will be working far from adequate medical care and may be responsible not only for themselves but also for less experienced fieldworkers, family members, and employees and other local people. Interviews with some of the people who do prepare for fieldwork by taking first-aid courses indicate that they perceive the available North American courses as not very useful in other parts of the world and, in any case, insufficiently serious to be of help in a crisis. The simplest courses available from the Red Cross are indeed likely to be insufficient for fieldworkers, who need more detailed and ambitious training, but seldom get it in any formal way. One volunteer suggested that the most appropriate training course for fieldworkers among those offered in his community was that intended for ambulance workers. Note that the highest percentages of those who report having taken a first-aid course are those who work in North America, apparently a result of the fact that the U.S. government agencies that employ anthropologists often require such courses as part of job training, and those so employed most often work in the United States as well. Where the need for training to cope with medical emergencies is most acute, fieldworkers least often get it. We will look at this problem of medical knowledge in more detail in Chapter 14.

Table 4.11 shows that a majority of fieldworkers have a dental checkup before going to the field, and no doubt sometimes avoid the uncomfortable and sometimes expensive crisis of toothache in the field, which we will see later is commonly reported.

Table 4.12 presents the data on the precautionary paperwork that fieldworkers do before setting off. An injury or accident in the field can be extremely expen-

Table 4.12. Precautions Taken Before Fieldwork: Insurance and Documents (% of Column)

	N. America	Europe	L. America	India	Africa	Pacific	Total
Number of Field Trips	61	17	63	17	23	23	204
Precautions							
Checking your health insurance	43	41	40	53	52	48	44[a]
Checking others' health insurance	18	18	13	12	26	13	16
Buying or checking life insurance	18	12	14	12	17	13	15
Making a will	20	29	16	29	13	17	19
Obtaining manuals for vehicles	21	18	20	12	22	9	19

[a]Note that percentages do not sum to 100.

Table 4.13. Precautions Taken by Researchers After Arrival in the Country Where the Research Is Being Done (% of Column)

	N. America	Europe	L. America	India	Africa	Pacific	Total
Number of Field Trips	61	17	63	17	23	23	204
Precautions							
Visiting scholars for advice	28	24	36	41	26	43	33
Visiting local physicians for advice	24	24	27	24	22	26	25
Registering at consulate	18	47	41	41	43	48	36
Planning emergency evacuation	11	12	9	12	9	13	10

sive, in money as well as in suffering. As a precaution, workers often check up on and frequently buy health and life insurance, for themselves and for those accompanying them on the expedition. Some universities provide this insurance coverage to their employees and students, but it is a good idea for the researcher to be familiar with the coverage and procedures before departure. Research foundations rarely look sympathetically upon spending research dollars for insurance.

Making a will and buying life insurance imply recognition of the possibility of death in the field. Table 4.12 shows two interesting facts: first, that only a minority of researchers apparently take these steps, and second, that the proportion who do make a will or buy (or check) their life insurance before going to the field are those who work in the safest environments, those of North America and Europe. India is not, as we shall see later, a safe environment in many of the health dimensions, although it does have a plentiful supply of physicians, and researchers there are seldom far from medical care. Yet 29% of Indianists report making a will, whereas those who work in Latin America, Africa, and Asia and the Pacific, where the probability of death is much greater per unit of time in the field, less often make a will or express concern about life insurance. Perhaps this is evidence for the fatalism or risk-taking orientation of those fieldworkers.

In any case, one might expect that fieldworkers would routinely obtain the manuals for the vehicles they drive from the manufacturer, since it is rarely possible to pick up the phone and call the garage in a field emergency, but few (less than 20% overall) report doing so.

Finally, Table 4.13 reports on the frequency of use of precautions that researchers can take after arrival in the country where their work will be done, but before actually starting the fieldwork. These precautions focus on obtaining information—from local scholars, local doctors, the consulate of the home country, and from local transport services—which might very much be needed during the field-work to maintain health and safety, and which is unlikely to be readily available far from the field site.

Only minorities of fieldworkers report taking these precautions as they go to the field. Interviews with scholars who are nationals of other countries elicited the suggestion several times that North American fieldworkers on the way to work in their country should call upon local scholars before starting fieldwork, as a cour-tesy, for scientific reasons, and to obtain the kinds of detailed useful information that prevent ''learning the hard way.'' (Many North American anthropologists may call upon local scholars, of course, but they did not report here that they see such calls as a precaution relevant to health and safety in the field.)

Similarly, it could be useful to consult the closest physicians before beginning fieldwork—those who would be the sources of emergency help if needed. Such local physicians can often warn about special features of the local scene, medi-cations that are particularly useful, strains of disease organisms that have unusual features, and so on. Apparently only about a quarter of fieldworkers attempt to use such resources in advance of a medical crisis: we cannot tell from these data whether the majority consider it unnecessary, or have no such resources to draw upon.

Note that outside North America, many researchers register at the nearest U.S. or Canadian consulate. Such registration is sometimes required and is often rec-ommended by the U.S. consulate staffs, in order to alert them to the presence of nationals in case the emergency services of the consulate are ever needed. It has sometimes happened on anthropological expeditions that the first contact with the consulate in the country where research was being done has been after the death of a national, when help is needed to obtain the documents that permit returning a body for burial.

Finally, we note that only 10% of respondents overall report having made a plan for emergency evacuation from the country in the case of crisis. Later we will see that political crises are common among fieldworkers in some parts of the world. It would be useful to know the fastest route out of the country in case of political crisis, or the quickest way to reach medical care, but few researchers explicitly plan for these contingencies during their fieldwork. Many of those who report suffering from accidents, illness, death of a member of the research group, or the effects of political turmoil during fieldwork also tell poignant stories of the additional suffering caused by the difficulties they encountered when trying to arrange transportation, money, documents, and other necessities of life in a crisis.

In the chapters that follow, we will review the information that the 204 respon-dents provided about their experiences in the field with a wide range of threats to health and safety.

CHAPTER 5 THE HAZARDS OF EXPOSURE

In the following chapters we are going to look at the experience of hazards of fieldwork reported by the sample of 204 fieldworkers. In some cases we will illustrate the hazards with accounts from additional volunteer informants, who can be more informative precisely because they are not part of the sample whose privacy must be protected. The hazards will be grouped into the three major classifications of causes of death: (1) trauma (Chapters 5–8), (2) infectious and parasitic diseases (Chapters 9–10), and (3) degenerative disease (Chapter 11). Here we will start our accounts of traumatic hazards with those that come from exposure to the elements, cold and heat, wetness and dryness, and altitude.

Hazards of Exposure

We have already seen that most (but not all) anthropologists do a substantial amount of fieldwork during their professional life (an average of 22 months done to date for this sample of workers in midcareer). We have also seen that the field conditions vary quite widely, from the veranda of a palatial accommodation, a mud hut in a village, a tent, an abandoned schoolhouse, an igloo, or out of the back of a car or truck. Whatever the accommodations, in whatever the climate and environment, certain risks come directly from the environment—risks of heat and cold, sun, lightning, or water.

Before we start, let us take a moment to observe the form of the tables in this and subsequent chapters by examining Table 5.1. Using a standard format helps to make the data readily available and quick to find. The column headings are the areas of the world where the fieldworkers have done most of their fieldwork, or their most recent fieldwork. Many of them have, in addition, done fieldwork elsewhere, so that characteristics they report do not necessarily reflect conditions in their area of specialty, but probably do.

The first line of the table gives the totals in each area. Subsequent lines give the numbers (standard text numbers) and/or percentages (italic numbers) of the

Table 5.1. Sunburn Experience

	N. America	Europe	L. America	India	Africa	Pacific	Total
Total	61	17	63	17	23	23	204
Had condition, self	34	3	28	2	11	8	86
	56%	*18%*	*47%*	*12%*	*48%*	*35%*	*42%*
Others in group had it	8	4	8	2	2	1	25
	69%	*41%*	*57%*	*24%*	*57%*	*39%*	*54%*

column total. Generally the first line gives the number or percent that reported the hazard to self: the second line gives the percentage that reported it for others in the field group in addition to themselves. Percentages are cumulative: the percentage for "others" includes those who reported the hazard for themselves, so it can be interpreted as a measure of experience with the hazard by any of the members of the research group. These conventions will be used throughout the rest of this report.

Most anthropologists—66% overall—report some suffering caused by exposure to the elements. By and large, those who work in cities report the fewest and least severe problems in dealing with the elements, and those who work in rural areas, especially in remote rural areas, report the most problems.

Hazards of Heat and Sunburn

More than half the respondents report problems with sunburn. The problem is most frequent among those who work primarily in North America, Latin America, and Africa, and least frequent among those who work primarily in Europe and South Asia, but it is common everywhere. It may be that the proportion that have had a notable sunburn during fieldwork is even higher than half, as some people may consider the risk so routine that it is not worth reporting. Only six people explicitly stated that sunburn was never a problem in their fieldwork.

Sunburn is so frequent an experience that we have all witnessed the unattractive and uncomfortable consequences of it from time to time, on field trips or on vacation. Acute sunburn causes reddening and swelling of the skin, and pain. The degree of response depends both on the degree of exposure and/or protection, and also on genetic predispositions and habituation to sunlight.

Severe acute sunburn may cause blistering, and could produce serious dehydration due to fluid loss through the skin. Severe sunburn can also produce permanent scars on the skin, usually in the form of depigmented spots in the burned areas.

Chronic sunburn can produce thickening of the skin and a tendency to wrinkles over time, effects that can be readily witnessed in any group of anthropologists over 30. A more serious long-term consequence is the contribution that sunburn makes to the probability of skin cancer, a condition that is highly correlated to the kind of thickening and wrinkling of the skin that we frequently see. The most frequent form of skin cancer is the basal cell cancer, which usually grows so slowly that it can be noticed and removed without serious threat to life. The more dangerous form of skin cancer is melanoma, known to have affected several anthropologists. It is not possible to say that the rate of melanoma among anthropologists is higher than among other occupational groups, because the number of cases is so small.

Almost all light-skinned people who are working in an area where the local people are dark-skinned are at risk of serious problems with overexposure, and denial of that possibility or the desire to minimize attention to one's light skin by refusing to cover up or apply sunblocking lotions is ill-advised.

The first line of protection from sunburn involves clothing, especially hats, and staying out of direct sunlight, under trees or tarpaulin. According to Jeremy Sabloff, of the University of Pittsburgh, Mesoamerican archaeologists have become much more attuned to the problems of sun exposure for workers and students during the past decade. They now leave untouched trees they might once have cut down before the digging began, and they usually start work very early in the morning and stop during the hottest hours of the afternoon. They recommend the use of hats and sunproof clothing to everyone working on the dig.

A special risk factor in sun exposure is the photosensitivity induced in some people by taking certain drugs, especially antibiotics. Tetracycline, for instance, a common and useful drug, has this side effect, but it is far from being the only one. When drug warning sheets include photosensitivity as a potential side effect, investigators should be cautious about any sun exposure at all. Reactions can be severe, even triggering heat exhaustion or heatstroke (see below).

Sunburn can also be prevented by the application of PABA creams, available without prescription from any drug store in North America, and often available overseas. These creams come with ratings from 1 to about 20, which roughly speaking can be interpreted as the multiplier of the time that one can spend in the sun before burning. In other words, covered with a PABA formula of 20, a person who could ordinarily spend only 10 minutes in the sun without damage to the skin can spend several hours (roughly 200 minutes). Of course, the amount of exposure one can tolerate differs according to time of day and individual sensitivities to the sun, to the lotion, and to other factors.

Parents who take children to the field need to be particularly careful about sunburn exposure, since children's skin is typically more sensitive than that of adults. PABA shields may be continually required for children, even when adults in the group have become acclimated. A blistering sunburn in childhood is believed to increase the risk of skin cancer lifelong.

Fieldworkers who have damaged their skin by excessive exposure to sunlight can protect themselves from the serious risks of skin cancer by informing their primary care physician of this risk factor, and by having a dermatologist check their skin for growths at regular intervals, and have any suspicious spots removed early. While the risks increase with age, anyone who has been exposed to long-term sun, or who has had even one severe sunburn, should continue monitoring skin for cancer throughout life.

In the short run, anyone who is exposed to the sun and feels that their skin is in the process of getting sunburnt should get out of the sun and drink plenty of fluids. Some advisers (Silverman 1986:4) say to take substantial doses of aspirin for the next 24 hours to interfere with the burn process and to reduce pain and fever. Cool or cold showers are also comforting and will reduce the inflammatory process somewhat after a burn. Healing may take as long as a week.

More serious forms of illness associated with exposure to the sun and to heat are heat exhaustion, an illness caused by a temporary rise in body temperature, and heatstroke, a potentially disabling or even life-threatening rise in body temperature that injures the body. Table 5.2 shows that these serious conditions are frequently experienced by the fieldworkers (some 11%) and even more commonly experienced by someone in their research group (29%).

The first signs that heat exhaustion is developing are mental confusion, irritability, nausea, diarrhea, muscle cramps, headache, and temperature elevation (of the body core) to about 105° F (40° + C). The surface of the skin may be wet or dry, hot, or even cold to the touch. The treatment needed is to get the person out of the sun and out of the extreme heat causing the condition, give fluids freely, and reduce core temperature.

Table 5.2. Heatstroke and Heat Exhaustion

	N. America	Europe	L. America	India	Africa	Pacific	Total
Total	61	17	63	17	23	23	204
Had condition, self	7	1	7	1	3	3	22
	11%	*6%*	*11%*	*6%*	*13%*	*13%*	*11%*
Others in group had it	14	5	9	1	5	3	37
	34%	*35%*	*25%*	*12%*	*35%*	*26%*	*29%*

If reduction of temperature is not achieved, the patient will proceed into heat-stroke, which is another stage of the same condition. Heatstroke is characterized by extreme confusion or unconsciousness, low blood pressure, shock, vomiting, or even internal bleeding, and a core body temperature with spikes to 115° F (46° C). Brain and nervous system damage is severe from such temperatures and the only hope of avoiding disability and death is to reduce core temperature quickly.

Heatstroke (also called sunstroke) is reported for self or other members of the research group by 31% of the respondents who say they had any risk of it, and only 13 of the 204 said that they were never exposed to this risk. Overheating can happen to anyone, but archaeologists report a considerably higher rate of its occurrence among members of the research group—perhaps because the work of archaeology sometimes requires sustained activity in the sun over long periods of time.

Archaeology student Rafael Ramos, 29, a graduate student at Tulane University, died in New Orleans in July 1983 of complications of heatstroke suffered two months earlier. Mr. Ramos was participating in a settlement pattern research project at the Mayan site of Sayil in Yucatán, Mexico. He developed symptoms of heatstroke on his first day of work in the field. First aid was provided, and he was evacuated to the local hospital, then to the hospital in the capital, and finally to Tulane Medical Center as complications developed.

Prevention of heat exhaustion is rather like prevention of sunburn, in that protective clothing and PABA sunscreens will help in the early stages. The best preventive is to recognize the early symptoms and adjust to them by getting out of the sun, reducing activity, and drinking extra fluids until acclimatization is achieved. Individual adjustments to heat stress must be recognized and respected, and special risk factors such as age, illness, and drug side effects must be taken into consideration. Persons working in hot climates should learn the signs and treatment of heat exhaustion to protect their own health and that of coworkers, especially newcomers to the field.

Sometimes the environment itself is so extreme that it is difficult to prevent heat prostration and dehydration. Listen to biologist Mark Owens's account of their first dry season in a part of the Kalahari desert that is the habitat of the animals that he had come to study, but ordinarily uninhabited by humans (Owens and Owens 1984:57):

> We were as unprepared for the hot-dry season as we had been for winter in July. Almost overnight, midday temperatures climbed above 110 degrees—then up to 116, in the shade of the fallen tree where we had posed our thermometer. The ground outside of camp was too hot for our thermometer, but it must have been over 140 degrees.
>
> We withered, like the new tender grass, in the strong easterly winds that swept hot and dry across the valley. . . . Our eyes felt scratchy; they seemed to shift into our skulls, away from the heat.

We rationed ourselves to seven gallons of water each per week, for bathing, cooking and drinking. . . . Our skin chapped and flaked, our fingers and toes split and bled. Day after day it was the same: the same T-shirt, ragged cut-offs, and holey tennis shoes, the same grey calcareous dust over everything, the same heat that sapped our strength away.

Dehydration

Loss of fluids is common in mild form among fieldworkers, producing headaches and dark urine. Prolonged mild dehydration can contribute to kidney disease. Thirst is such a strong motivation that severe acute dehydration is unlikely to occur unless the person is lost in a dry environment, as can occur on field sites where water is scarce. Research on water requirements indicates that there are few differences between racial groups or individuals in the amount of fluids needed for survival. A certain amount of fluid per pound of body weight per unit of heat is essential to survival, and rationing drinking water, as discussed by Owens (above), is irrelevant.

In 1983, a student working at Koobie Fora, in Kenya, left camp alone and became lost. Search parties found him after more than five days of wandering a few miles from camp (R. Leakey 1983:165–167). In the hospital, he died of the effects of dehydration. Subsequently the Koobi Fora field site organizers (Richard Leakey, Glynn Isaac, Jack Harris, and others) adopted rules including a requirement of team research, the carrying of water, leaving information about the direction in which one is going, and they devised a standard predictable procedure to be followed by searchers in case someone is lost.

Being lost can contribute to many kinds of accidents and risks of exposure. A person living alone in an unknown environment may easily become lost. Chagnon (1974:50), in discussing the difficulties of traveling in the Yanomamö areas of Venezuela, presents his hand-drawn maps incorporating both knowledge and misinformation, and explains the interests of those informants who deliberately gave him misinformation that could have caused him to become lost. In other situations, it may not be the informants who cause the difficulty, but merely the fieldworkers' lack of knowledge. With the availability of satellite photos, there is no area on earth that can't be mapped to some extent in advance of a visit, but such maps may be unreliable in detail. Chagnon reports (1974:49) that he learned over time to put more credence in what the Yanomamö said about geography, and less in the United States Air Force navigation charts or the maps of the National Geographic Society.

High Altitude Hazards

Altitude sickness is very much a product of the environment, although, like most physical processes, reactions to altitude include considerable individual variation. Below 1,800 meters (about 5,000 feet above sea level, approximately the altitude of Denver), altitude sickness does not occur. Above about 4,250 meters (14,000 feet, about the altitude of Pike's Peak), most people experience shortness of breath and light-headedness. At very high altitudes (Mount Everest is at 29,000 feet [8,848 meters]) virtually everyone has severe difficulties coping with even simple exertion. The problems are caused, initially, as a result of the lowered concentration of oxygen in the atmosphere. The body can compensate for a lower level of oxygen in the long run, but at first such oxygen deprivation may be a very real threat to well-being or even to life. Table 5.3 shows the proportions of all researchers who have experienced altitude sickness. Of course the proportions are much higher for those who have worked at high altitude.

Altitude sickness comes in several varieties. According to Auerbach (1986:205–210) acute mountain sickness (AMS) is the most common, least serious form. Its symptoms consist of headache, fatigue, loss of appetite, drowsiness, weakness, and apathy. Sometimes lips and fingernails turn blue (cyanosis). Children are likely to experience nausea and vomiting. Symptoms are likely to increase for the first two or three days at higher altitude, and are complicated by sleep disturbances. Advice for the condition is to avoid going to higher altitudes until the symptoms have disappeared, which should happen after three or four days. Because judgment can be affected by AMS, victims should not go hiking, exploring, or skiing alone during this period. If the person feels very ill, symptoms can be relieved by moving to a lower altitude. Minor problems caused by high altitude include swelling of the hands, face, and feet during the first few weeks, sore throat caused by mouth breathing during exertion at high altitude, and unusual bouts of flatulence caused by pressure changes. The first week or so at high altitude may be uncomfortable for many fieldworkers, even those who are making a good adjustment.

A serious complication is high-altitude pulmonary edema (HAPE), a condition of fluid in the lungs that complicates the physical problems caused by shortage of oxygen in the air. The condition is easily diagnosed by gurgling noises coming from the chest, struggles for breath, and full-body cyanosis (blue color). Collapse and coma are likely to follow within hours of the development of HAPE. The patient must be moved to lower altitude immediately.

Another form of serious complication is that of high-altitude encephalopathy (HAE), which produces alteration of mental state, confusion, difficulty walking and speaking, headache, and personality change. This condition may accompany the pulmonary edema discussed above, and is apparently caused by fluid retention in the brain. Medical care is needed, and the patient needs to be transported to lower altitude without delay.

Three reports of deaths have emerged from obituaries, but none are primarily anthropologists. Victor Valverdi, 38, head of research in nutrition at INCAP, who had recently moved to FAO, died of complications of altitude sickness in Bolivia in the 1980s. British climber Julie Tullis died of exhaustion after reaching the summit of the world's second-highest mountain, K2 in the Himalayas, in August 1986. Ms. Tullis, 47, died three days after reaching the 28,250 foot summit. In July 1986, American photographer David Shippe, 29, died in China on an expedition to the upper reaches of the Yangtze River. He came down with altitude

Table 5.3. Altitude Sickness

	N. America	Europe	L. America	India	Africa	Pacific	Total
Total	61	17	63	17	23	23	204
Had condition, self	3	0	15	1	1	0	20
	5%		24%	6%	4%	0%	10%
Others in group had it	2	0	5	0	0	1	8
	8%		32%	6%	4%	4%	14%

sickness at a base camp at 14,000 feet. Rather than go any higher, Shippe decided to join a group taking a kayak trip down river, but developed complications of altitude sickness and died on the trip.

Among our sample of fieldworkers, most of those who reported altitude sickness worked in Latin America, most frequently in Peru or Ecuador. Only one of those who worked in Nepal and Tibet reported altitude sickness, perhaps because of individual differences in susceptibility or perhaps due to the care that was taken in becoming acclimatized to high altitude slowly. One respondent who worked in the Andes felt that high altitude sickness threatened the life of a member of her research group by the extremes of high blood pressure she experienced, and reported "someone pushed her on a plane and evacuated her to lower altitude." Several researchers reported altitude sickness as the most serious threat they faced in the field. In an unrelated case, a departmental chairman, asked about health and safety in fieldwork among members of his department, reported that the wife of a project member had experienced delirium and loss of consciousness from high altitude sickness before being moved to a lower altitude. She apparently did not try to go back to a high altitude.

Lightning

Being hit by lightning is sometimes used as an example of an extremely unlikely event—and so it is, even in a group of fieldworking anthropologists. About 100 Americans die each year as a result of being hit by lightning. The individual probabilities are no doubt somewhat higher for anthropologists than for the average American because of their exposure to the elements. Only two individuals in the sample reported actually being hit by lightning during fieldwork, and two more reported that it had happened to a member of their research group. Nevertheless, the consequences of being hit by lightning can be very serious, and survival seems to be largely a matter of luck.

Irven DeVore reports that while working in the Kalahari with the !Kung in 1963, he had stepped outside the family's tent in the rain when he was struck by lightning. He saw the flash, and woke up about 30 feet across the camp, face down in a mud puddle. He had no signs of burns on his body, and struggled back to the tent, where his family huddled away from the wind and the rain, unaware that lightning had struck the camp. While he and his family can laugh about it now, they also go to some trouble to carry a roll of copper wire and a bamboo pole with them on field trips in order to construct a lightning rod.

Not so fortunate, Dennis Edward Puleston, 38, Associate Professor at University of Minnesota, Minneapolis, was killed in June 1978 when struck by lightning at the pyramid of Chichén Itzá. He was en route to Belize to do additional fieldwork at the time of the accident.

Fire Hazards

One of the distinctive features of fieldwork for many is the "camping" aspect—living simply, cooking simply, gathered around the fire. Many city dwellers have had little prior experience in building fires for heat, cooking, or light and protection. As a consequence, much time is wasted building fires inefficiently, and burns as well as frustration may result (Table 5.4). Some of the risks of field-

Table 5.4. Burns from Fire

	N. America	Europe	L. America	India	Africa	Pacific	Total
Total	61	17	63	17	23	23	204
Had condition, self	5	0	3	0	1	0	9
	8%		5%		4%		4%
Others in group had it	8	1	1	0	0	3	13
	21%	6%	6%	0%	4%	13%	11%

work, like lightning, are unlikely to occur more than once, but burns may be a frequent occurrence for those learning to cook on an outside fire.

Living in an unfamiliar house with an unfamiliar heating system also presents a danger of fire. James Nason (University of Washington) tells of a house fire on the Pacific island of Truk "from a kerosene lamp or from clan spirit action, depending upon your point of view." The Leakey family tells of several camps that have burnt (M. Leakey 1984:171; R. Leakey 1983:227).

I have no knowledge of any anthropologist that died of burns (except that some vehicle accident deaths were said to have involved fires: these are reported as vehicle accidents). Two cases of serious burning of children were reported to me. In the first, the two-year-old son of Gabriel Lasker and Bernice A. Kaplan pulled a bowl of steaming soup onto his bare chest and was severely burned in the 1950s. There were no long-term disabilities associated with the accident. A similar accident occurred in Mexico, where a pot of boiling milk was accidentally spilled on the daughter of Robert Hunt (Brandeis University) when she was 16 months old. Significant scarring due to third degree burns resulted.

In some parts of the world, bush or brush fires that sweep across vast areas may be a significant reoccurring part of the natural ecological system. Local peoples are often accustomed to the risks and are able to avoid them quite easily. Anthropologists who work with animals or with inanimate objects (archaeology) in environments where they are not guided by the local people may face greater dangers from grass and forest fires.

Delia and Mark Owens (Owens and Owens 1984:35–47) tell of coping with the sweep of fire through the otherwise uninhabited area of the Kalahari desert where they did their observations of large predators. They report relatively little danger or even stress to the animals, but complete destruction of the pleasant camp site they had organized, and considerable damage to their camp gear and threat to their truck. They also tell of the frequent hazard of spontaneous fires on the undercarriage of their truck from the accumulation of grass and seeds while driving through the Kalahari bush.

Informants who work in archaeology in the southwestern United States, especially southern California, report that brush fires are the greatest hazard in their research, and tell of expeditions that have been totally wiped out. One informant in the random sample reports that the only serious risk he and his students face each year is the problem of fire, and that they always discuss an emergency evacuation plan in detail.

Hazards of Cold

Shifting from considering the extremes of heat to those of cold, we have to recognize that the human body has a relatively narrow range of temperature in which to operate in comfort and with safety. Although only a few respondents worked in constantly subfreezing weather, most respondents recognized that cold could be a threat at times.

Frostbite refers to injury caused by the freezing of living tissue, usually in the extremities, while the body protects the core temperature by isolating the frozen part. It is much more likely to occur in children and old people than in adults, and it is in large part accounted for by poorly fitting or inadequate boots and gloves. We note in the Table 5.5 that fieldworkers who concentrate on research all over the world report frostbite occasionally. A good first aid course should teach the signs and treatment of frostbite, because it is not something that one wants to encounter in the field, without access to medical advice, for the first time.

Treatment of frostbite consists simply of rewarming the skin as quickly as possible. Some of the advice given in an earlier period, like rubbing frostbitten skin with snow, is no longer recommended since it further chills and may injure the skin. Any abrasion of frostbitten skin is dangerous and may lead to later infections.

Windburn, incidentally, is more similar to sunburn rather than frostbite, and dermatologists recommend using sunscreen (PABA lotion) to prevent windburn damage to exposed skin.

Even in tropical areas, cold can be a problem at night and at certain times of the year. Only 47 of the 204 reported that they had never experienced the risk of cold stress, or hypothermia. Note in Table 5.6 that most of the problems resulting from cold are reported by specialists in Latin America and the Pacific, and are often associated with work at high latitudes or high altitudes.

Mild hypothermia is defined as a core body temperature less than 98.6° F (37° C). While uncomfortable, mild hypothermia is not dangerous and can be reversed by exercise and shivering if the person has warm, dry clothing to contain the heat generated. Hypothermia becomes dangerous only if body temperature continues to drop. This is more likely if the clothing is wet (heat loss increases about 5 times) and vastly more likely if the body is submerged in water (loss increases by a factor

Table 5.5. Frostbite

	N. America	Europe	L. America	India	Africa	Pacific	Total
Total	61	17	63	17	23	23	204
Had condition, self	1	1	1	1	1	2	7
	2%	6%	2%	6%	4%	8%	3%
Others in group had it	1	0	0	0	0	0	1
	4%	6%	2%	6%	6%	8%	4%

Table 5.6. Cold Stress, Hypothermia

	N. America	Europe	L. America	India	Africa	Pacific	Total
Total	61	17	63	17	23	23	204
Had condition, self	4	1	8	0	1	2	16
	7%	6%	13%		8%	16%	8%
Others in group had it	3	1	2	0	0	0	6
	11%	12%	16%	0%	8%	16%	11%

of 25). To rewarm a patient suffering from mild hypothermia, one should take the natural protective system of the body into account. Drawing blood into legs and arms quickly by warming the limbs may threaten the core body functions, which were protected by the slowdown of circulation. Giving warm liquids to drink is an effective and generally safe technique for rewarming the body core (Silverman 1986:16).

Severe hypothermia is marked by muscular incoordination, stumbling gait, weakness, apathy, and mental confusion. The victim is not a good judge of his or her own condition, and is unlikely to save himself. Others must take steps to prevent any further chilling and rewarm the patient as quickly as possible. All the medical guides stress that giving alcohol, whether in brandy or in any other form, is entirely the wrong strategy.

If the victim goes into coma, or seems to have suffered cardiac arrest while extremely cold, rescuers should perform CPR (coronary-pulmonary resuscitation) and try to get the victim to medical care as quickly as possible, without attempting to rewarm the patient in the field. Extreme cold preserves the possibility of resuscitation for many hours, but it can only be done in a hospital with sophisticated equipment, as there are likely to be a wide range of complications, especially of the heart and circulation.

Boating and Water Accidents

Many deaths attributed to drowning might be attributed to hypothermia if we knew the details of the mechanism of death. Accidents with water are not frequent, compared to other hazards, but tend to be serious in their consequences.

Two people in the sample report that they personally nearly drowned in the field, and another reports that someone in the research group nearly drowned. Two others report being hit by a wave and swept out to sea while in the field.

In 1961, Michael Rockefeller, age 24, a graduate of Harvard and an art collector, was working in New Guinea on a filmmaking expedition, when he drowned. Rockefeller was in a 40-foot catamaran with two Asmat companions and his friend, Rene Wassing, when the boat began drifting out to sea from the bay they were crossing. The two Asmat men swam ashore while land was still in sight. After some 24 hours, Rockefeller despaired of rescue and attempted to swim to shore. His body was not found. Wassing was rescued some eight hours later (Forbes 1988).

Also in 1961, Sonia Cole (1975) reports that exceptional floods at Olduvai gorge required the Leakey expedition to tie ropes to trees in order to cross the river. Nevertheless, even using this rope bridge, one of their employees was swept away in the flood and rescued only with great difficulty. Richard Leakey (1983:111) reports falling off a houseboat in Lake Victoria and nearly drowning while a child. Local workers rescued him while the parents were napping below decks.

S. James Clay Young, 30, Assistant Professor at East Carolina University, who did fieldwork in Mexico, died in May 1981, in Jacksonville, Florida, one week after a swimming accident at St. Augustine, Florida. This death was apparently not related to fieldwork.

Stephen Bedwell, who was the Director of the Archaeology Field School at the University of Wisconsin, Oshkosh, was drowned in a boating accident in 1971.

He was making a test run in a boat to be used by the field school for transporting students to and from the excavation.

In anthropology boats are sometimes needed to get to field sites such as islands or isolated coastal villages or as a means of travel in the field, especially in Amazonia, New Guinea, and other areas where rivers replace roads as means of travel. Of the 528 expeditions described in some detail by respondents (up to three each) 41 (8%) involved the use of motorboats as a means of transportation, and 37 more (7%) involved use of canoes. Boat accidents are reported on four expeditions among the 204 fieldwork informants, one each among those working primarily in North America and Europe, and two among those working in Africa.

The best predictor of accidents is merely the amount of time and risk experienced in boats. James Nason, for instance, who has worked extensively on and around the island of Truk in the Pacific, had the experience of a canoe sinking while he was doing cartology, and around 1968–69, the experience of suffering rib cage cuts and bruises from being thrown into the steel deck railing of a ship during a typhoon.

Although boating accidents can occur anywhere, they are perhaps more likely given unknown shores, currents, and bodies of water, and inexperience with the particular type of boat available. The seriousness of the accident is likely to be a function of lack of back-up facilities such as the Coast Guard or the Harbor Police.

Motion sickness is a common hazard—the sort about which people say "You won't die of it, but you might wish you did." It is probably most common on boats, where it is known as seasickness, but can occur in trucks, planes, and helicopters as well. Motion sickness becomes serious in its consequences when the victim is needed to pilot or crew the boat and cannot perform the tasks. Frequently people find that motion sickness decreases over time, but others never get over it, and it is so incapacitating a condition that some people have to plan their fieldwork to avoid exposure to seasickness, for example, by being flown in and out of the field.

H. Russell Bernard, University of Florida, tells of being violently ill at sea for three days while working in Greece in 1965, as a result of seasickness and diarrhea, brought on by bad water. William Divale, York College of CUNY, tells of taking a group of 23 students at the field school in the Canary Islands on a boat trip, when they hit very rough seas. He recalls that 18 of the 23 became violently ill, and that he was the worst of all, totally unable to take the responsibilities of leadership while the voyage lasted.

Seasickness can also complicate other crises. A student from the University of New Mexico was being evacuated by boat due to a serious malaria attack, when he was stricken with seasickness, which in turn induced acute dehydration, which confounded treatment of the malaria.

Malnutrition and Dietary Deficiencies

Malnutrition is not really an environmental hazard in the same sense as the others listed in this chapter, but is produced by failure to consume adequate food. This can be related to the availability of food in the fieldwork environment, and also sometimes to the difficulty of transporting food supplies from outside sources to the research site (Table 5.7).

Many social anthropologists, in particular, believe that for research purposes they should eat only the food of the local people, and they should acquire that

Table 5.7. Malnutrition

	N. America	Europe	L. America	India	Africa	Pacific	Total
Total	61	17	63	17	23	23	204
Had condition, self	1	1	2	1	1	3	9
	2%	6%	4%	6%	4%	13%	4%
Others in group had it	1	0	1	1	3	0	6
	4%	6%	5%	12%	17%	13%	7%

food in the same way that local people do. A consequence of that belief may be malnutrition.

Dietary deficiencies among fieldworkers may result from not having the personal networks, the skills and knowledge of food acquisition, or simply from not having the appetite for local foods that local peoples do. Again, the researcher may develop acute malnutrition from following the same dietary regime as the local people, just as the local people develop that condition.

Mark and Delia Owens (Owens and Owens 1984:50) initially started their animal observations in the Kalahari on a shoestring. They arrived with only enough money to buy gear to get their research started, and it ran out before they were able to organize a new grant. Mark reports:

> Our decision to stay in Deception (Valley) until our supplies ran out did not come easily. For many weeks, even before the fire, we had been living mostly on mealie-meal, oatmeal, and pablum mixed with powdered milk. I had lost nearly thirty-five pounds and Delia had lost fifteen. We were persistently weak and lethargic, and I was sure Delia was anemic.
> In late July, I had been awakened . . . by Delia, doubled over with severe stomach pains. Though this had been happening for several weeks, she had managed to keep it from me. I was sure that her sickness was due not only to our lack of a proper diet, but also to the stress of not having the funds either to continue our research or to go home. I lay awake that night trying to think of some way I could get something more substantial for her to eat.

Despite their ability to stun and collar lions and hyenas, Mark reports nothing but abortive efforts to kill steenbok or guinea hens for food, so that they nearly starved to death in one of the richest wild animal areas in the world before their hoped-for grant finally arrived. Then, even with funds to buy food, these two solitary researchers seemed to have a hard time getting enough to eat due to the press of working nights on their observations. Delia reports:

> Our food supply was limited by what was available in Maun, what we could afford to buy, and what would survive the long haul to camp in the heat. Sometimes even staples like flour, mealie-meal, sugar, lard, and salt could not be found in the local stores. . . . When we didn't have meat, we ate various stews made of dried beans, corn, sorghum and mealie-meal. Their insipid taste could be improved a bit with onions, but it was often a matter of swallowing the food as quickly as possible and following it with a can of sweet fruit cocktail, if one was left in the tea-crate larder. [Owens and Owens 1984:85]

Malnutrition is not likely to become a serious problem in most research settings because the field trips seldom last long enough. One can certainly lose weight and good nutritional status within a few months, but you will not totally deplete your reserves in less than six months if you are a healthy and originally well-nourished adult. Anyone staying in the field for more than six months needs to consider how to avoid malnutrition, or runs serious health risks. Problems of malnutrition are much more serious for children, for pregnant women, and for anyone who is sick or fighting infection.

Weight Loss

Moderate weight loss is common during fieldwork, due to the availability of only unfamiliar foods and sometimes due to a higher rate of exercise than normal. Occasionally, severe weight loss will follow upon severe restriction of food or, more often, upon illness. Overall 16% of the sample of fieldworkers reported weight loss as a notable problem (Table 5.8).

It is striking that weight loss is more common among Latin Americanists than others. Volunteers who reported weight loss as a severe problem always cited it as secondary to sickness, and their stories are told under those headings. Most North Americans are glad to experience some weight loss if not complicated by malnutrition, and may actually end up healthier and stronger because of it.

Margaret Mead (1972:226) notes that one's ability to maintain weight and health depends upon the conditions found in the field. Speaking of her joint field-work with Gregory Bateson, she wrote:

> Fieldwork in New Guinea was grueling, especially on the Sepik where we had met, the mosquitoes and the heat providing a constant irritation of bites, cuts, itches and small vexatious infections that might turn into tropical ulcers. There was no skilled help, no way of getting anything done that one did not initiate and take responsibility for oneself. And no matter how long one managed to stay in the field, managed to piece together meals of local foods and scarce canned food and managed to outlast the heat and the fatigue, and, on the Sepik, the discomforts of high water, the torrents of the rainy season, and recurrent attacks of malaria, there never was any guarantee that one would in the end see the ceremony that might provide the key to an understanding of the culture.
>
> To all these vicissitudes, Bali presented an extraordinary contrast. In New Guinea I routinely lost between twenty-five and forty pounds on each field trip. In Bali I never lost any weight at all.

Aram Yengoyan (1977:246) reports that when he goes to the field, he takes only catsup, a necessity of life especially when working with the Mandaya of the Philippines. With catsup, he once managed to work for 26 months, eating almost only tubers. He speaks with appreciation of an Australian field site where there was a local store and a supply of fresh beef to enhance his diet while working with the Pitjandjara.

Consumption of Toxic Foods

Although poisoning by toxic foods is not exactly an environmental hazard, it fits better here than elsewhere. Most poisonous foods taste bitter, which reduces the likelihood of accidentally eating them. The dangerous ones are those that look

Table 5.8. Weight Loss in the Field

	N. America	Europe	L. America	India	Africa	Pacific	Total
Total	61	17	63	17	23	23	204
Had condition, self	3	1	7	2	5	4	22
	5%	6%	11%	12%	22%	17%	11%
Others in group had it	1	1	8	0	0	0	10
	7%	12%	24%	12%	22%	17%	16%

like and taste like favorite foods, such as some of the mushrooms. No one in this study reported poisoning from mushrooms. The only frequent kind of toxic food poisoning reported was from manioc, mentioned by several respondents. Christine Hugh-Jones (Cassell 1987:62), who took her 8-year-old daughter, Leo, and her 5-year-old son, Tom, to spend most of a year in the jungle in Colombia under extremely dangerous conditions, reports:

> We were lucky: Tom's worst accident was to cut his foot badly with a machete; Leo's was to drink poisonous unboiled manioc juice, which she thought was banana soup. The Indians assured us she would be sick and dizzy for a day and night, and she did have to be carried for much of the journey we made the next day, but she got better that night.

A volunteer tells of arriving one evening at the house of a potential linguistic informant, a North American Indian, who was sitting on his porch, squeezing berry juice. Before he would talk to her, she was required to drink the berry juice. It turned out that he was making a medicinal concoction, and the usual dose was a spoonful or two. She drank about a pint and was very sick for a week. But from the locals' point of view it had been a test; she gained his confidence and he eventually gave her much good data.

As this last example illustrates, while the hazards of the environment are straightforward, the hazards of animals, humans and others, can be much more complicated. We will look at these complications in more detail in the next two chapters.

CHAPTER 6   THE HAZARDS OF ANIMALS

If we relied on stories about "archaeologist" Indiana Jones (or Tarzan, for that matter) to guide our awareness of dangers in the field, we would focus primarily on snakes, wild animals about to leap out of any tree, and evil people. While we smile at the naiveté of such stories, the fact remains that there are some risks from snakes, animals, and hostile people. We will look at the evidence of dangers from animals (including snakes, insects, and others) in this chapter, and the dangers from people in the next.

Creatures of the Water

Having seen the hazards of boats and water in the last chapter, let us pick up the story of "critters" with those of water creatures—leeches, jellyfish and other stinging sea animals, poison fish that sting or bite, and sea snakes.

Leeches are remarkably ugly and persistent water worms that attach themselves to skin and feed on blood. In some parts of the world, they are unavoidable when wading in the water or even when walking through wet vegetation. If the "leeches scene" in *The African Queen* made you weak in the knees, you had better inquire about their prevalence in your projected field site before you go. On the other hand, we see in Table 6.1 that none of the European specialists had any experience with them, and only the Pacific area and the Indian subcontinent have notably high rates.

Leeches inject an anticoagulant when they attach to their host, and constant exposure could in principle lead to anemia or even more serious reactions. No one reported serious consequences to their health or their ability to work from leeches.

The highest rates of accidents with jellyfish, sponges, sea urchins, stingrays, and other stinging sea creatures comes from South Asia, where Indianists report fairly frequent problems with them (Table 6.2). South and North America are other areas where they present a problem on the beach. No one who worked in the Pacific reported experience with them, but I believe that they can be a problem in Australia and on Pacific islands.

Table 6.1. Leeches

	N. America	Europe	L. America	India	Africa	Pacific	Total
Total	61	17	63	17	23	23	204
Had condition, self	4	0	4	3	1	9	21
	7%		6%	18%	4%	39%	10%
Others in group had it	1	0	1	1	0	0	3
% Any Experience	*8%*	*0%*	*8%*	*24%*	*4%*	*39%*	*12%*

Table 6.2. Jellyfish and Other Stinging Sea Creatures

	N. America	Europe	L. America	India	Africa	Pacific	Total
Total	61	17	63	17	23	23	204
Had condition, self	0	0	0	2	0	2	4
Others in group had it	3	0	3	1	0	0	7
% Any Experience	*5%*	*0%*	*5%*	*18%*	*0%*	*9%*	*5%*

Prevention requires learning about the habits of the local species and finding ways to avoid contact with them. Prevention may require wearing shoes or sandals when wading in the water, for example. Treatment consists in removing spines or stingers carefully, trying not to break them off below the skin. Many contain skin irritants, so careful washing and sometimes soaping or soaking is needed. The best course is to get medical advice about the locally dangerous species from a doctor near the field site before an accident happens.

Emilio Moran (Indiana University) reported having stepped on a stingray in the Xingui river in Brazil while wading. He had the barbs removed surgically, but three abscesses formed in the affected area before healing was completed about four months later.

Napoleon Chagnon reports that a danger of water travel in the Amazon jungle where the Yanomamö live is that canoes and small boats turn over or sink with some frequency. The water is generally shallow enough to stand while you bail, but water creatures are a danger.

> About midday, as we were bailing out after one of our mishaps I stepped on a log beneath which lived an electric eel. I didn't know what hit me, but I felt a sharp pain in my leg and was knocked flat from the jolt. I saw the eel swim into deeper water as I got to my feet. [Chagnon 1974:39]

About a third of the sample report that they were never exposed to the presence of poison fish or sea snakes during their fieldwork, and only a few of those who were exposed report any contact. Sea snakes are found only in the Pacific and Indian Oceans, where they are among the most abundant reptiles in the world. They bite, and their venom is extremely toxic. The few who may be exposed to the risk of their bites should explore the dangers carefully before meeting them.

Hazards of Land Creatures

Snakebite

Snakebite is probably the most misperceived problem in anthropological fieldwork, as it is emblematic of the dangers of an unknown environment. Many anthropologists carry a snakebite kit as a talisman against dangers that they hope will never occur and, in fact, the frequency of snakebite is sufficiently low that most never discover that the snakebite kit is not actually very useful in an emergency. According to Table 6.3, North American workers have the highest rates of contact with snakebite, followed by Latin Americanists, with some risk in South Asia and Africa, none reported by those who specialize in Europe and the Pacific.

To say that snakebite is rare is not to say that snakes are rare in the places where anthropologists work. From my own experience of 22 months in the Kalahari, I

Table 6.3. Snakebite

	N. America	Europe	L. America	India	Africa	Pacific	Total
Total	61	17	63	17	23	23	204
Had condition, self	1	0	0	0	1	0	2
% Bitten	*2%*	*0%*	*0%*	*0%*	*4%*	*0%*	*1%*
Others in group had it	3	0	3	1	0	0	7
% Total Experience	*7%*	*0%*	*5%*	*6%*	*4%*	*0%*	*4%*

recall once seeing a snake going into my tent, which was searched until the snake was found curled in my sleeping bag. On another occasion, I slept next to the canvas wall of a tent, and found that a fat spitting cobra had slept on the outside of that wall, apparently drawing some heat from my body on a chilly night. I remember looking up from a work table to see an enormously long *boomslang* drop out of a tree onto the sloping roof of a tent, then slide down and off into the bush before it could be caught. On one memorable afternoon, we held a picnic on what the Bushmen later called "the doorway of a mamba's house." The people were deeply impressed by our courage and resourcefulness in challenging the mamba in this way. And during an energetic spell of tent cleaning one day, I reached into a wooden box in which books were stored, and found a snake sleeping behind them. But none of those snakes bit me, and merely seeing snakes cannot be considered a serious hazard of fieldwork.

The rate of snakebite is low because most snakes do their best to avoid humans, and none has evolved to hunt and kill humans. The prey of snakes, even extremely large snakes, are much smaller. Typically the mouths of snakes are such that they have a hard time getting hold of any part of a human other than a finger or a toe. Most bites occur when a human accidentally trips over a snake, or reaches out and grabs it. (Injuries are high for those who actually collect and handle snakes, but that is another set of dangers.) Venomous snakes inject paralyzing substances into their prey, and some venoms are extremely toxic to humans. The venom of the *boomslang* of southern Africa is said to be always fatal, and the black and green mambas found in the same area can kill within seconds. A Botswana crocodile hunter, Bobby Wilmott, was bitten by a black mamba and died almost immediately in 1968. But most snakes are not poisonous to humans, and the toxicity of a bite can vary widely even within the same species, depending on the placement of the bite, the time of the last injection of venom by the snake, and so on. Many or most bites can be survived.

The best strategy for dealing with snakes is avoidance. Many can be avoided by knowledge of the snake's habits and by looking carefully into places where they are likely to be. Other bites can be avoided by wearing boots and long pants when walking through gravel or grass that prevents a clear view of where one's foot is about to be put down. Similarly, the hands and arms may need protection when visibility is not totally clear. Long sleeves and leather gloves will protect from snakes as well as other hazards (such as scorpion stings, poison ivy, and cuts) when one is collecting stone tools, bones, food, or firewood.

If one is bitten, then knowledge of the local snakes and their habits becomes essential, and it is far too late at that point to start consulting the reference books on snakes. In advance of exposure, one needs to learn about the kinds of snakes present locally, their appearance, their habits, their characteristics, their bites, and the treatment called for. Some books suggest that the first priority after a bite is to kill the snake, for identification purposes, but that only makes sense if the patient can be transported to a sophisticated treatment center quickly, where the knowledge of the snake can be used to tailor treatment. Attempting to kill the snake introduces a risk of further bites and delays attention to the patient.

Richard Leakey (1983:325) tells of treating a snakebite victim at Koobi Fora by psychological reassurance, among other methods. He tried to keep the victim from seeing the snake, so that he would believe the assurances that it was only a small one and wouldn't cause trouble if the bitten one would only keep calm. Unfortunately, someone killed it and showed it to the victim.

East Africa has many snakes: Richard Leakey tells of being bitten several times, man and boy. A colleague of Mary Leakey, Bobby Sticketon, a geologist, was bitten by a puff adder while Mary Leakey was in the field with her three-year-old son. She left the child in the care of the patient while she ran several miles to the truck for the snakebite kit (M. Leakey 1984:117). And that child, Jonathan Leakey, has always loved snakes. Over the years he has been bitten by a carpet viper, a green mamba and a black mamba, and has been treated with antivenin so many times that he is now allergic to it. But as an adult he keeps a snake farm for commercial production of antivenin.

Many authorities now believe that applying a tourniquet in a case of snakebite is not useful, but is painful and introduces the risk of gangrene, which may be more harmful than the original snakebite. Similarly, giving "snakebite medicine" (whiskey) is not useful, can injure the patient's ability to recover from the bite, and may interfere with everyone's best judgment about what to do. Many doctors advise that cutting and sucking venom out of a snakebite is usually a bad idea, unlikely to help and likely to contribute to making a badly infected wound much larger than it needed to be.

Napoleon Chagnon (1974:38) tells of an exhausting trip from a remote Yanomamö village back to his research headquarters. In the course of telling of his strategy of escape from difficult and demanding people, he reveals his attitude toward the snakebite kit he routinely carries for emergencies:

> I was feeling pretty low. It really did not matter very much if they did steal everything, did it? I humored them by pretending I was still concerned about my worldly possessions. I took only those items that were absolutely essential for survival, and those that had some scientific value, keeping my field notes and leaving behind things like antivenin for snake bites.

Delia Owens (Owens and Owens 1984:92) tells of her not entirely successful strategy for avoiding snakebite by encouraging the presence of all kinds of birds in their camp in the Kalahari.

> Early one morning, still groggy from sleep, I threw back the cover from the dilapidated tea crate. When I reached inside, looking for a tin of oatmeal, my breath caught. The long grey body of a banded cobra was coiled on the cans, inches away from my hand. Boomslangs, puff adders, black mambas, and other poisonous snakes frequently appeared in camp. That we had not been bitten was due mostly to our own private warning system. Since there were sometimes as many as 200 birds in camp, the racket they made always tipped us off that a snake was on the prowl. Sometimes they would keep it up for hours . . . and we would begin to prefer the quiet snakes to the noisy birds.

Carmel Schrire of Rutgers University (personal communication, 1985) tells of learning how what one person considers an emergency may be a routine and uninteresting event to others. While excavating in Australia, she was visited by two men, who stopped at her camp for a cool beer and a chat. It was only after they had been relaxing for a while that they mentioned that they were on the way to the hospital to get treatment for a snakebite that one of them had suffered the day before.

Scorpion Stings

Scorpion stings, although they are mentioned much less in the mythology of the dangers of fieldwork, have apparently caused more pain and suffering to field-workers than snakebite (Table 6.4).

Those who have been stung agree that a scorpion sting is exquisitely painful. A neurotoxin is injected from the stinger on the tail, and the degree of toxicity seems to vary widely by the species of scorpion, the placement of the sting, and the characteristics of the victim. Small children are especially likely to be stung and also to suffer severe reactions. It seems to be life-threatening primarily to children and perhaps to old people. Some of the most dangerous species are found in the southwestern United States, Mexico, and Central America. The incidence of stings is high among those who work primarily in Africa (26%). Nevertheless, scorpion bites were rarely listed as one of the worst things that had happened to respondents, and were not often mentioned in interviews of volunteers, perhaps because there are few lasting consequences once the intense pain has passed.

Prevention of scorpion stings is basically common sense. It helps to know the habits of the creature and to protect hands and feet with gloves and boots, especially when picking up food, firewood or other objects off the ground when visibility is not perfectly clear. In this regard, scorpion stings and snakebites are reported about twice as often by archaeologists (combined they are reported about 20%) as by social-cultural anthropologists (about 10%).

Bee, Wasp, and Insect Stings

Bee and wasp stings, too, are exquisitely painful for the moment. But while scorpion stings are experienced singly and infrequently, bees and wasps may attack in a swarm and sting relentlessly. In some sites they are a constant threat; in others, the bees may be stingless, and the risk nonexistent.

The amount of neurotoxin injected by a bee or wasp is typically small but with many stings it can become life-threatening. Some people, previously sensitized by stings, develop an allergic reaction to the neurotoxin which, in the extreme form of anaphylactic shock, can be quickly fatal unless appropriate first aid can be provided. Anyone who has ever had an allergic reaction to a bee or wasp sting

Table 6.4. Scorpion Stings

	N. America	Europe	L. America	India	Africa	Pacific	Total
Total	61	17	63	17	23	23	204
Had condition, self	1	0	3	1	3	0	8
	2%		*5%*	*6%*	*13%*		*4%*
Others in group had it	6	1	8	1	3	2	21
	11%	*6%*	*17%*	*12%*	*26%*	*9%*	*14%*

Table 6.5. Bee and Wasp Stings

	N. America	Europe	L. America	India	Africa	Pacific	Total
Total	61	17	63	17	23	23	204
Bees							
Had condition, self	14	3	15	2	6	1	41
	23%	*18%*	*24%*	*12%*	*26%*	*4%*	*20%*
Others in group had it	17	2	9	1	5	3	37
	51%	*29%*	*38%*	*18%*	*48%*	*17%*	*38%*
Wasps							
Had condition, self	16	1	13	1	3	3	37
	26%	*6%*	*21%*	*6%*	*13%*	*13%*	*18%*
Others in group had it	13	4	4	1	2	1	25
	47%	*29%*	*27%*	*12%*	*22%*	*17%*	*30%*

in the past should carry injectable epinephrine in the field, and others in the research group should be warned of this possibility and shown how to use the epinephrine in advance of trouble. Fortunately, severe allergic reactions usually develop only after a number of warning events, characterized by symptoms such as hives, severe swelling and itching around the sting. Between field trips, allergic individuals should see an allergist for desensitization shots.

Louis Leakey was attacked by a swarm of bees on the Kenya coast in 1971, an incident that started his final decline in health. Stung by hundreds of bees, he fell and injured his already bad hip. A concussion from the fall left him with memory loss, and it was later discovered that he had had a stroke, probably at the time of the bee attack. He was hospitalized for a month and never recovered entirely (Cole 1975:368).

The problem of bee stings has increased in Latin America and is likely to increase in North America as the so-called "killer bees," originally from Africa, replace the European honey bees.

Biting and stinging ants and flies are common discomforts of fieldwork (Table 6.6). You will note that the ratio of people who reported these problems themselves to those who reported it only for other members of the research group is high, reflecting the frequency of bites and the wide distribution of the insects, such that it is unlikely that any member of the group would be entirely spared.

Mary Leakey tells (1984:80) of army ants stinging her baby in the cradle. Thousands of *siafu*, army ants, got into the director's house at the Nairobi Museum where the Leakeys were living, and surrounded the crib of baby Jonathan, getting under the mosquito netting and surrounding the baby before stinging. All of them bit at once, and only the screams of the baby and the quick response of the parents saved him from a horrible death. After that, the legs of his crib and cot stood in shallow pans of water and paraffin to prevent *siafu* from crawling up.

Biting and stinging insects are best discouraged by wearing protective clothing, creating protected spaces in tents or under mosquito nets, and using insect repellents. This preventive advice applies as well to the insects of the next category, those that transmit disease with their bites or stings.

All of the insects in the next category sometimes transmit diseases along with the irritations of their bites and stings. We will look at the incidence of the diseases

Table 6.6. Stinging Ants and Black Flies

	N. America	Europe	L. America	India	Africa	Pacific	Total
Total	61	17	63	17	23	23	204
Black Ants							
Had condition, self	7	2	8	2	4	3	26
	11%	*12%*	*13%*	*12%*	*17%*	*13%*	*13%*
Others in group had it	3	0	3	0	1	0	7
	16%	*12%*	*17%*	*12%*	*22%*	*13%*	*16%*
Army Ants							
Had condition, self	2	1	7	2	5	1	18
	3%	*6%*	*11%*	*12%*	*22%*	*4%*	*9%*
Others in group had it	1	0	3	0	0	0	4
	5%	*6%*	*16%*	*12%*	*22%*	*4%*	*11%*
Black Flies							
Had condition, self	17	2	16	5	4	4	48
	28%	*12%*	*25%*	*29%*	*17%*	*17%*	*24%*
Others in group had it	0	1	1	0	1	0	3
	28%	*18%*	*27%*	*29%*	*22%*	*17%*	*25%*

later, just noting here that these creatures are frequently a nuisance, that some exposure to them is more common than avoiding them, and that the rates for particular insects vary sharply by areas of the world. One might say that willingness to tolerate insects is a defining characteristic of anthropologists.

Prevention of exposure to bites and stings from insects can involve three aspects. The first is providing shelter, especially at night, in the form of a house or tent that can be closed from entry by screens. A second line of defense is the old-fashioned mosquito net, once a feature of life in Africa and India for Europeans, now more rarely used. The great advantage of the mosquito net is that it is non-toxic (compared to chemical defenses) and that it affords a rest and retreat from the constant irritation of insect pests. Acceptance of the widespread notion that the mosquito net is "not used any more" or is obsolete seems to me to be a mistake, especially if there are children on an expedition, or anyone who has trouble sleeping when insects buzz.

A second line of defense from insect pests are the chemical insecticides that are spread around the living area to kill insects, and the insect repellents that are applied to the skin. Rather than live in close proximity to disease-transmitting insects it is sensible to use insecticides, but some of them are very toxic to humans as well as insects, and one must be cautious, especially that they are not permitted to get into the drinking water. Mary Leakey (1984:57) tells of collecting rainwater in Kenya from a tent fly that she did not realize was impregnated with insecticide. They all became extremely ill as a result of drinking it. Skin-applied insect repellents are useful for short-term exposure but probably should be avoided whenever possible.

The third and safest line of defense is clothing—long sleeves and pants with elastic to prevent insects getting to the skin, along with gloves and boots if necessary. In the presence of tsetse flies, bees, or wasps, one might also wish to wear a wide-brimmed hat with netting tucked into the shirt.

Table 6.7. Disease-transmitting Insects

	N. America	Europe	L. America	India	Africa	Pacific	Total
Total	61	17	63	17	23	23	204
Mosquitos							
Had condition, self	45	9	46	13	19	14	146
	74%	*53%*	*73%*	*76%*	*83%*	*61%*	*72%*
Others in group had it	4	2	2	0	1	1	10
	80%	*65%*	*76%*	*76%*	*87%*	*65%*	*76%*
Fleas							
Had condition, self	11	2	24	4	9	8	58
	18%	*12%*	*38%*	*24%*	*39%*	*35%*	*28%*
Others in group had it	8	5	5	1	3	2	24
	31%	*41%*	*46%*	*29%*	*52%*	*43%*	*40%*
Ticks							
Had condition, self	28	2	20	2	7	6	65
	46%	*12%*	*32%*	*12%*	*30%*	*26%*	*32%*
Others in group had it	7	1	1	1	2	1	13
	57%	*18%*	*33%*	*18%*	*39%*	*30%*	*38%*
Chiggers							
Had condition, self	17	3	26	3	5	3	57
	28%	*18%*	*41%*	*18%*	*22%*	*13%*	*28%*
Others in group had it	4	1	1	0	3	0	9
	34%	*24%*	*43%*	*18%*	*35%*	*13%*	*32%*
Lice							
Had condition, self	3	1	9	5	5	8	31
	5%	*6%*	*14%*	*29%*	*22%*	*35%*	*15%*
Others in group had it	3	2	5	1	0	1	12
	10%	*18%*	*22%*	*35%*	*22%*	*39%*	*21%*
Sandfleas							
Had condition, self	5	2	12	2	6	7	34
	8%	*12%*	*19%*	*12%*	*26%*	*30%*	*17%*
Others in group had it	1	2	1	2	1	1	8
	10%	*24%*	*21%*	*24%*	*30%*	*35%*	*21%*
Tsetse Flies							
Had condition, self (No one else in group	0	0	0	2	3	0	5
had it)				*12%*	*13%*		*2%*

Protective clothing may make one look conspicuous, and may be uncomfortable under some circumstances, but it has the advantage of helping one guard against a range of hazards—sun, wind, and extremes of temperature, as well as insect bites, minor cuts, and bruises. It may be that the often-observed concentration of problems within the first week or two in the field results from adding protection after it is found to be needed rather than starting out overprotected and discarding unnecessary safeguards.

Bites and Attacks from Mammals

One hundred and fifty of those in the random sample did not work around animals and felt that they were not exposed to the risk of bites or injuries from animals. Fifty-four of the 204 considered that they were exposed to animal bites or injuries, and of those 65% (35) report that they were bitten, scratched or otherwise hurt at some time (Table 6.8).

Only four persons report having an immediate problem with rabies in the field: one was bitten by a dog suspected of having rabies; one was licked by a certainly rabid dog; one was bitten by a vampire bat; and one was scratched and perhaps bitten by a rabid racoon. All had to have a course of rabies treatment in the field, which is an unpleasant but life-saving procedure.

Dian Fossey was exposed to rabies in the field and started the treatment very late out of an unwillingness to leave her research and go to the hospital, but survived (Mowat 1987:136).

Bites from animals are sufficiently common in all parts of the world that being inoculated against rabies before going to the field is almost certainly a good idea. It is still necessary to get another series of injections if bitten by a probably rabid animal, but previous injections give a margin of safety.

The species mentioned by the 35 fieldworkers as sources of bites and injuries are dogs (24), cats (2), rats (3), a fox, vampire bat, llama, sheep, patus monkey, rhesus monkey, skunk, and racoon. Threats from large animals were mentioned by four people in the sample, including elephant (2), bear, crocodile, lion, leopard (2), hyena (2), and rhinoceros. One of the 35 listed red ants (apparently a memorable attack), one listed bedbugs, and another listed a carnivorous fish.

Primatologists have special problems with animal bites and injuries because their work often requires close contact and many hours of exposure. Angus Booth died from the bite of a monkey in Ghana in 1958. A professor reports, "several students of mine were seriously bitten by rhesus monkeys in the course of their fieldwork." He doesn't attribute the accidents to the normal hazards of fieldwork, but to the failure of the students to pay proper attention to the behavior of the animals. James Loy, at the University of Rhode Island, Kingston, suffered serious bites that required stitches from a rhesus monkey bite on Cayo Santiago island.

Richard Leakey (1983:185) tells of hundreds of crocodiles that have been known to chase the boats and hover around shore at his East African sites. At the end of the day students and fieldworkers relaxed by swimming and by catching fish while crocodiles lurked nearby. After a student died (of other causes), rules of safety were drawn up and the hazard of crocodiles in the water was explicitly mentioned as a risk that could be taken or avoided by the decision of the fieldworker.

Garth Owen-Smith and Margaret Jacobsen, who was then an honors student, Capetown University, were attacked by a lion at night when they were camping out in sleeping bags on a tarpaulin in southern Africa. Owen-Smith was bitten

Table 6.8. Bites and Attacks from Mammals

	N. America	Europe	L. America	India	Africa	Pacific	Total
Total	61	17	63	17	23	23	204
Animal Bites or Injuries	9	4	13	3	2	4	35
	15%	24%	21%	15%	9%	17%	17%
Rabies Scare or Treatment	0	1	1	0	2	0	4
Self (1) or others	0%	6%	2%	0%	9%	0%	2%

(through his sleeping bag) on the leg. The two of them shouted and made noise, and Jacobsen got a gun and shot over the lion's head to frighten him off. She writes of this event in her honors thesis (1985), and says she wouldn't camp out again without her faithful dog to warn of the approach of animals in the night.

Adrianne Rankin, laboratory director and field assistant on a University of Wisconsin 1973 field school, suffered a dislocated right shoulder handling one of the two mules rented for the field season. The mule reared up and yanked Rankin up by her arm. Surgery was needed after the field season but it was unsuccessful in totally repairing the damage, and she now has only partial use of her arm.

Gianni Roghi, an Italian journalist and anthropologist, was accompanying L. L. Cavalli-Sforza's research group during the early years of the Pygmy research. He died in 1967, a few days after the end of the research season, from being trampled by an elephant while on safari in the Central African Republic. He was taken to a hospital in Bangui and operated on, but died, probably of an embolism (Cavalli-Sforza 1986:8).

Biologist Joanna Copley, 23, of St. Andrews University in Scotland, was killed in South Africa in 1988 when a rhinoceros attacked her while she was observing a pack of baboons with a colleague as part of a research project. According to game park officials, the rhino was believed to have been searching for its calf when it charged. Also in the summer of 1988 a field assistant on an archaeological project in Africa was trampled by a rhino and injured, but not fatally.

Dogs are simultaneously a form of protection from dangers, animal and human, and a source of danger in themselves, especially for those who walk the roads alone in Third World countries. The student attacked by a lion by night vowed in consequence never to go to the field without her dog again. Mary Leakey got her first dog in response to attack, and has never worked without them again. Yet clearly dogs protect their owners but threaten others, and are the animals that most frequently cause trouble among anthropologists (24 of the 35 cases). Dog bite prevention has been studied by the U.S. Post Office, among other high risk organizations, and it can be shown that protective boots and leggings can prevent most injuries. Carrying a stick or a spray can of an irritating material is sometimes advised. In parts of the world where dogs guard yards and fields, anthropologists may need to obtain advice from locals or from canine behavior experts to protect themselves.

On the other hand, problems that stem from attacks by the human species are more frequent and not so easily preventable. Human hazards are so common that we will consider them in a special chapter, subdivided into criminal or informal attacks (robbery, assault, and harassment) and formal problems (such as arrest and other problems with the government).

CHAPTER 7   HUMAN HAZARDS OF FIELDWORK

If we were thinking of the hazards of humans as disease and accident vectors, many of the hazards experienced in the field could be put in this section. Venereal disease, for instance, is a "contact disease" of humans, but we will classify it as an infectious disease and confine our attention here to the hazards of human hostility and conflict.

More than other hazards, interpersonal assault and threat are touchy subjects for anthropologists, calling into question the relationship that the fieldworker is supposed to establish with colleagues and with the subjects of his or her study, as a matter of professional competence. Nevertheless, these failures do happen, and whether the anthropologist is in some sense to blame or is blameless, many anthropologists suffer interpersonal attacks during the course of their fieldwork.

Some anthropologists, when reporting these kinds of problems during fieldwork, are quick to point out that the same kinds of problems of criminal attack might occur in the home society—and, indeed, some are sure that the field is much safer than home in these respects, even if there is still some danger.

We start by looking at the frequency of the kinds of events that we consider "criminal": theft, fighting, assault, rape, and murder. Table 7.1 gives the overall table of numbers reporting one or more interpersonal problems, to self and to other members of the research group. Note that the percentages given are cumulative, so that the percent under "others" includes those that reported the hazard for self. And the categories are nested, so that if an event occurred to oneself and to others in the group it is coded as happening to self. Political problems, stemming from governmental or political movements such as arrest and military threat are not included in Table 7.1 and will be considered later in this chapter.

We note that the majority of those who work in Africa report one or more kind of interpersonal hazard, and that those who work in North America have the best record of avoiding these problems.

We also note that most of those who report any such problem report it as having occurred to themselves rather than to others of the group. Generally speaking,

Table 7.1. Criminal Interpersonal Hazards, Combined Rate

	N. America	Europe	L. America	India	Africa	Pacific	Total
Total	61	17	63	17	23	23	204
Had condition, self	19	6	25	8	12	9	79
	31%	35%	40%	47%	52%	39%	39%
Others in group had it	1	0	4	0	1	0	6
	33%	35%	46%	47%	56%	39%	42%

common events show this pattern of being reported primarily for self, while rare events are more often reported for others than for self. Criminal hazards seem to be highly variable by area. Where they are common, they are reported primarily for self, and in other areas they are not reported for either self or others in the group. A similar pattern would be expected if some respondents reported while others denied interpersonal hazards.

About one third of those who work in Latin America, Africa, and the Pacific report having been robbed during fieldwork (Table 7.2). In South Asia, the rate is about one quarter. In North America, despite the American reputation for law-lessness and incivility, only about 13% report having been robbed in the field. Overall, about one in four report one or more robberies during fieldwork, and some have been robbed many times. Countries with particularly bad reputations for robbery are Kenya, Peru, Colombia, and New Guinea. Maintaining the distinction between criminal and political acts is often difficult in these parts of the world. Many of the robberies reported occurred in national capitals or other big cities on the way to fieldwork but were not directly a part of the fieldwork experience.

During traveling to and from the field, one is at risk of robbery because one is burdened with carrying luggage while being disoriented, tired, and unsettled. Pickpockets may lift a wallet, and luggage, cameras, and backpacks are frequently stolen in transit, in airports, while getting a taxi, checking in to a hotel, and so on. Shoulder bags are especially common targets in some parts of the world, where the experience of having one's bag grabbed by someone on a passing motorbike is frequently reported. The difficulty of replacing a stolen passport or travelers' checks is both common and disheartening.

Hotel rooms are another frequent site of theft for travelers, by hotel employees or by outside thieves who might be ex-employees, ex-residents in the hotel, or just ordinary thieves. Some travelers bring along a wedge-shaped doorstop for use in hotel rooms, which will not eliminate the danger of theft but at least will prevent break-ins while one is in the room. Some people leave passports, tickets, and travelers' checks in the hotel safe while visiting a dangerous area. (Good advice on managing the risks of theft is given in Hatt 1985.)

Circumstances of robbery are likely to vary by areas of the world. In some places, anyone walking around who does not look like a local is at high risk, whereas in other areas it is the knowledge of the tempting money and goods that might be taken that seems to pose the greatest risk.

A matter of great concern under such circumstances is the keeping of guns. Some researchers want to have a gun in order to prevent or retaliate against robbery, but the knowledge that there is a gun in camp may enormously increase the

Table 7.2. Robbery (including theft)

	N. America	Europe	L. America	India	Africa	Pacific	Total
Total	61	17	63	17	23	23	204
Had condition, self	5	2	13	4	4	7	35
	8%	*12%*	*21%*	*24%*	*17%*	*41%*	*17%*
Others in group had it	3	0	7	0	3	0	13
	13%	*12%*	*32%*	*24%*	*30%*	*41%*	*24%*

probability of being robbed, as a gun is a very valued possession in many areas. Knowledge that one keeps a gun may also lead robbers to come armed with guns, increasing the danger to everyone.

One may also be robbed by informants or employees. Many anthropologists have reported that they have lost valuable possessions in the field, but few are willing to describe the incidents "on the record." It is easier to talk about thugs in the capital or bandits who sweep down into the village, but hard to talk about breakdowns of reciprocity at the field site, especially for social-cultural anthropologists. For all robberies combined, 20% of archaeologists report robbery, while 27% of social-cultural anthropologists report the same thing.

Many examples can be cited. Napoleon Chagnon (1974) tells of a number of instances where temporary employees or village bullies stole trade goods, food, or research equipment from him, some of which were later recovered. When Louis and Mary Leakey were newly married, they were working at Hyrax Hill in Kenya. Local bandits broke in and stole everything from their tents. In response they got a dog, and have kept dogs with them in the field ever after (M. Leakey 1984:71). Dian Fossey was robbed of a case containing her money, checkbook, passport, and car papers (Cole 1975:345).

In Nairobi, Kristen Hawkes and Jim O'Connell (University of Utah) had their entire truckload of supplies for an expedition to the Hadza stolen. Not only camping gear, but notes, cameras, and research supplies were taken, leaving only a case of bully beef. This delayed the research considerably and almost threatened to end it, since the materials were essential and they could not easily replace them. Again in Nairobi, Hawkes and O'Connell were robbed by four men on foot, while they were walking from the hotel to dinner. Her jewelry and money were taken, and his watch, wallet, and pocket knife. A passerby in a car saw the robbery going on and stopped and rescued them, but the robbers were not caught. This crime was reported to the local police and embassy.

Mark Owens (Owens and Owens 1984:107), who worked with his wife in the Kalahari, reports:

> Later, when we unloaded in camp, we found that our three months' supply of flour and sugar had been stolen from the truck, along with some other grocery items. We were furious. On our limited budget, there was no going to Maun until our next regularly scheduled trip, so for three months we were without bread, an important part of our diet. Since most of the door and window locks on the old Land Rover were broken, there seemed to be no defense against being robbed, other than for one of us to watch our goods every minute while in the village.

Owens also reports (1984:107) that he protected his goods in the truck after that disastrous theft by killing a couple of large and feared mamba snakes and draping their bodies over the fresh supplies in the back of the Land Rover. He says that even after the locals realized that the snakes were dead, no one touched the goods, probably because the bizarre sight of them suggested witchcraft to locals.

Physical Violence

The three categories—assault, fighting, and beating—are similar in that they all refer to interpersonal struggles in which physical injuries were inflicted, but they seem to differ in the locus of the responsibility being assigned. Note that fighting and beating are more frequently reported for others in the research group, while assault is much more commonly reported for self. It may be that "assault" is a word we use to describe circumstances where the victim is held to be innocent of blame, whereas "fighting" implies more aggression, and being beaten implies defeat. In interviews, it has emerged that the "others" referred to in these responses are typically male graduate students and junior colleagues.

There are many known instances of assault to anthropologists, and they are found in all parts of the world. In Papua New Guinea, Robert Welsch, then a student at the University of Washington and now at the Field Museum in Chicago, was assaulted and stabbed in a robbery attempt while staying in a university residence for researchers in Port Moresby. There had been an outbreak of robberies around the university in 1980. Welsch was sleeping in his room one hot night, when seven of these "rascals" broke into the housing unit. Three entered his room, armed respectively with a baseball bat, an ax, and a long kitchen knife. Welsch resisted and was stabbed between the ribs in the struggle. They fled without taking anything of his, although others in the residence were robbed that night. He was taken to the hospital by colleagues, underwent surgery, and recuperated in the hospital 12 days, and then in the home of Mac Marshall. Welsch partially blames himself for the attack, for sleeping with his door open on a hot night. Afterward, the university installed a simple whistle in each room as a low-tech alternative to burglary alarms.

Lorraine Sexton reports that one time she was driving with Mac Marshall and his wife and child near her field site in Papua New Guinea when they were approached by ax-wielding "highway men" attempting to rob them. Marshall adds to her account that when he realized the threat "I sped up and aimed right for the guy with the ax. When he finally realized that I would hit him, he flung the ax to one side and ran, looking very scared."

Charlotte Ikels, Case Western Reserve, writes that when she was interviewing in Hong Kong she was robbed at knifepoint in the stairwell of a building.

Napoleon Chagnon (1974:4) tells of many instances among the Yanomamö of threats of violence and occasional hits or planned attacks, especially when the

Table 7.3. Assault and Physical Violence

	N. America	Europe	L. America	India	Africa	Pacific	Total
Total	61	17	63	17	23	23	204
Assault							
Had condition, self	5	2	4	1	4	4	20
	8%	*12%*	*6%*	*6%*	*17%*	*17%*	*10%*
Others in group had it	0	1	6	0	0	0	7
	8%	*18%*	*16%*	*6%*	*17%*	*17%*	*13%*
Fighting							
Had condition, self	1	3	0	1	1	1	7
	2%	*18%*	*0%*	*6%*	*4%*	*4%*	*3%*
Others in group had it	4	1	6	0	3	0	14
	8%	*24%*	*10%*	*6%*	*17%*	*4%*	*10%*
Beating							
Had condition, self	0	1	0	1	1	0	3
	0%	*6%*	*0%*	*6%*	*4%*	*0%*	*1%*
Others in group had it	3	0	3	0	0	1	7
	5%	*6%*	*5%*	*6%*	*4%*	*4%*	*5%*

locals had been taking hallucinogenic drugs. On one occasion, Chagnon tells of one of the village men, under the influence of drugs, coming toward him with an arrow aimed directly at his chest. Chagnon believed that the purpose of the behavior was to make the anthropologist turn and run, exposing his rear as a target, and he decided that he would stare the aggressor down, despite the dangers of provocation. As it happened, this dangerous gamble was rewarded with success.

A recent encounter with violence occurred in Philadelphia, in April 1988, when an employee attacked four archaeologists with a knife. According to the *New York Times* of April 12, 1988, Glynn W. Sheehan, the director of a salvage archaeology project on the Schuylkill River, and his wife, Anne Jensen, were attacked when they attempted to come to the rescue of two women being raped by the employee, Arthur Faulkner, who was arrested in New York City the next day. Sheehan and Jensen were stabbed, seriously injured, and were apparently left for dead. Sheehan crawled for help to the nearest house and got an ambulance and the police.

Rape and Attempted Rape

Before Sheehan and Jensen arrived, the employee, Faulkner, had cornered Clarice J. Dorner, of Elk Grove, Illinois, in the barn that was used for the headquarters of the archaeological excavation on the banks of the Schuylkill River outside Philadelphia. He was in the process of raping her when another archaeologist, Annaliese H. Killoran, of Lynn, Massachusetts, arrived and tried to stop the attack. According to the account in the *Times*, he raped and killed both women.

Rapes occur among many occupational groups, and in many parts of the world. The special risk factors in this case seem to have been the relatively isolated location of the site and the need for manual labor rather than any features of the archaeology itself. Generally speaking, rape seems to be a special danger to women who are unknown to the local power structure, which protects most women most of the time. Women anthropologists may be outside protective networks, even if only temporarily, and may be unaware of the signals of challenge and deference with which local women protect themselves.

Rape, including attempted rape, is a difficult topic to study, since many women do not want to discuss the topic. Table 7.4 shows that rape was reported by 2% of all fieldworkers, 7% of the women in the study. Some of them are motivated by the fear that women who have been raped lose status and respect and are seen as pawns in the male game of aggression and competition. Other women are more concerned about issues of employment and research opportunities that could be denied to them on the excuse (or perhaps the true motive) of wanting to protect

Table 7.4. Rape and Attempted Rape

	N. America	Europe	L. America	India	Africa	Pacific	Total
Total	61	17	63	17	23	23	204
Had condition, self	0	0	2	0	1	2	4
	0%	*0%*	*3%*	*0%*	*4%*	*9%*	*2%*
Others in group had it	1	1	5	0	1	0	8
	2%	*6%*	*11%*	*0%*	*8%*	*9%*	*6%*

94   *Chapter 7*

women from the risk of rape in the field. All in all, it is a touchy subject, and one that I am quite sure is underreported in this sample.

In all, four anthropologists in the sample reported that they personally had been raped in the field, but two of these are women reporting an attack on themselves and two are men reporting an attack on their wives. Eight researchers, in addition, reported that someone in their study group other than self or spouse was raped (or experienced an attempted rape) during fieldwork in which the respondent had participated. Overall, about 6% reported a problem with rape in their fieldwork.

While the data are uncertain, it seems to be the case that the threat of rape is highly localized: in some areas, at some periods of time, there is little or no risk, while in other areas it is hard to avoid. North Africa, localized parts of East Africa, New Guinea, and parts of Latin America (Peru stands out in the accounts) have been cited as particularly dangerous, while Europe seems to be relatively safe. Nader (in Golde 1986:111) states that threats to women in the Middle East have been highly exaggerated, and cites customs of protection of certain categories of women (''sisters of men'') that should make foreign women safe. Other informants, however, disagreed that fieldwork was safe for women working alone in Muslim areas. Generally speaking, knowing the area and knowing people in the area seem to be factors in safety, whereas being alone, tired, and disoriented seem to be factors in danger.

Murder, Suicide, and Other Mysterious Deaths

Murder attempts against themselves were reported by five anthropologists in the sample (two Latin Americanists, two Asianists, and one North Americanist), and another four reported a murder attempt against a member of the research group (two in Latin America, two in Europe). One researcher reported a suicide attempt by a member of the research group in India. Another in the sample was arrested and tried for the murder of a member of his research group.

A famous old case of an anthropologist killed by the people he went to study is that of the death of William Jones, who was at the Field Museum in Chicago until he was killed by the Ilongot of Northern Luzon in the Philippines around 1908. There have been other cases—in Latin America, New Guinea, and Africa—and there have been cases where anthropologists simply disappear and no one ever knew what happened to them.

Another well-known murder case in the history of anthropology is the death of Henrietta Schmerler, a graduate student at Columbia who died during fieldwork at the Fort Apache Reservation in Arizona in 1931. Schmerler, a student of Ruth Benedict, was described by Morris Opler, who was a member of the research group, in the following way:

> According to Goodwin, Miss Schmerler, who greatly admired Margaret Mead, was determined to duplicate her South Seas work in the Apache context and especially to gather material about Apache sex life. This is a subject about which Apache elders do not speak easily to virtual strangers, and they refused to cooperate. The youth who slew her interpreted her emphasis on sex in her research as a sign of looseness and invited her to ride behind him on his horse, something that young people of opposite sex among the Apache do not do unless they are courting. Miss Schmerler, unaware of this, accepted. When he made advances and was rebuffed, the young man was angered at what he perceived as enticement and then rejection; the struggle, assault and death followed. [Opler 1987:3]

The Schmerler case is almost a litmus test of whether anthropologists assume that they have to take the blame for everything that goes wrong in the field, or whether others are seen as independent agents who might be held responsible. The possibility that women might not be permitted to do fieldwork because of their susceptibility to rape and murder came close to the surface in this situation. Franz Boas wrote to Ruth Benedict when he heard the news:

> I cannot tell you how shocked and also worried I am by the fate of Henrietta. I am trying to imagine what may have happened and cannot conceive of anything that should have induced nowadays an Indian to murder a visitor. [In another letter after receiving a detailed report on the events:] It is dreadful. How shall we now dare to send a young girl out after this? And still. Is it not necessary and right? [Mead 1959:408–410]

It is still true that women hesitate to speak out about rape or threats of sexual assault for fear that their freedom of action will be restricted.

No doubt the most famous case in recent years of an anthropologist killed in the course of her work is the death of Dian Fossey, hacked to death with a *panga* knife in her research hut in Rwanda, during the night of December 27, 1985. Fossey had been working with the mountain gorillas of that area for some 15 years, and had been in frequent conflict with local residents and local officials who resented her high-handed ways. No one knows who broke into her cabin and killed her, as was shown in the recent film of Fossey's life *(Gorillas in the Mist)*, but Mowat's book (1987) entertains several hypotheses. Local authorities charged one of the graduate students and one of her long-time local employees. These two people were convicted of the murder, *in absentia*, and the case is considered closed by the Rwandan government, although primatologists familiar with the case are convinced that neither was guilty.

Not all murder attempts are successful. Napoleon Chagnon (1974:178–180) tells of being in a hostile village among the Yanomamö with a severe allergic reaction. Throughout the night, as he tossed and turned in itching and discomfort, he shone his flashlight around the village to orient himself whenever he woke up. Later he learned that the village leader and his two brothers, carrying axes, had crept up close to his hammock intending to crush his skull while he slept, but just then he had shined the light on them, and they had stopped in fear of his knowledge and his powerful gun. Hearing this story, Chagnon decided to avoid work with this group for the foreseeable future.

In some cases of mysterious death in the field, how the death occurred is not known, and perhaps never will be known.

A German anthropologist, Harold Herzog, from the Max Planck Institute near Munich, was found shot with his own gun in the jungle of Venezuela where he was doing fieldwork with the Yanomamö. Despite the reputation of the Yanomamö as the "fierce people" there is reason to believe that his death was due to accident or suicide rather than murder, although his entry to his daily diary gave no hint of despair that day. The Yanomamö reported the death to local authorities and said that they had just found the body near the gun (Polly Weissner, personal communication, 1986).

In the early 1980s, Melanie Fuller, a graduate student in the biology department at the University of Chicago, and a student of Stuart Altmann, was in East Africa attempting to get started on dissertation research when she ran into difficulties. She broke off her agreement with her supervisor and spoke of establishing another topic with another supervisor. Then she was not heard of for some weeks. Her parents got in touch with local authorities in Kenya and investigators found her body in the bush, and identified it by dental records. The cause of her death is unknown; her money and documents had not been taken.

Political Hazards

It is often difficult to distinguish during fieldwork between the kinds of threats that stem from criminal impulses on the part of others, and those that arise from political motives and circumstances. What feels like irrational rejection by a segment of the village may follow ancient cleavages of the local power structure, and the arrival of hostile army officers with questions and demands to inspect papers may arise from racial hatred, a desire for bribes, the presence of an organized guerilla movement aiming to overthrow the government, or the suspicion that the researcher has broken a law of the land.

We tend to assume that our colleagues are innocent of offenses, but we can probably all think of instances where a colleague broke local laws.

Don Johanson tells (Johanson and Edey 1981:158–159) of needing a human knee joint for comparison with a fossil when they found important new *Australopithicine* bones in Ethiopia. In the excitement of an important find, he compelled a reluctant graduate student to help him take a bone from a modern Afar burial mound, although he had been warned that any approach to the modern burials would be considered an outrage to local feelings. Some researchers feel that consequences of that act have had negative implications for all foreign research in Ethiopia.

Whether or not the individual was guilty of law breaking, about 5% of our sample of fieldworkers report having been arrested in the field, and about 9% experienced an arrest in their group (Table 7.5). Some of the charges were minor, but one was the arrest of the group leader on murder charges, and two were arrests on drug smuggling charges in South America.

Military Attack

Like arrest, involvement with the military in other countries can be a frightening event. The hazard was described as "military attack," but apparently respondents included harassment and questioning by the military, not just armed attack. Table 7.6 shows the experiences reported with the military.

In areas of guerilla warfare, anthropologists may be suspected by the military of helping or supplying the rebels. The rebels may see anthropologists as allies of the government or as competitors for resources or people. In Peru, guerillas have been known to retaliate against villagers who sold food to an expedition. We re-

Table 7.5. Arrests in the Field

	N. America	Europe	L. America	India	Africa	Pacific	Total
Total	61	17	63	17	23	23	204
Had condition, self	1	0	6	1	2	2	11
	2%	0%	10%	6%	8%	8%	5%
Others in group had it	3	0	3	1	0	1	8
	7%	0%	14%	12%	8%	13%	9%

Table 7.6. Military Attack

	N. America	Europe	L. America	India	Africa	Pacific	Total
Total	61	17	63	17	23	23	204
Had condition, self	1	1	2	0	0	0	4
	2%	6%	3%	0%	0%	0%	2%
Others in group had it	0	0	2	1	1	1	5
	2%	6%	6%	6%	4%	4%	4%

Table 7.7. Suspicion of Spying

	N. America	Europe	L. America	India	Africa	Pacific	Total
Total	61	17	63	17	23	23	204
Had condition, self	4	2	8	2	4	7	27
	6%	12%	13%	12%	17%	30%	13%
Others in group had it	1	1	2	0	0	0	4
	8%	17%	16%	12%	17%	30%	15%

call that 31% of our informants reported having been unable to work somewhere when they wished to because of political instability (see Table 3.3).

Another difficulty that anthropologists sometimes have in the field is being suspected of spying. Bruce Schroeder of the University of Toronto tells of being arrested by the Syrian Border Patrol while surveying in the Anti-Lebanon Mountains for sites in Lebanon in 1972, apparently due to suspicion of his motives for working so close to the border. His group was taken across the border to several civil and military authorities in small villages until they reached Damascus. They were released at the Lebanese border within a day, but they then faced the difficult task of explaining to the Lebanese border authorities why they had no Lebanese exit or Syrian entry stamps in their passports. Schroeder concedes that they probably did look like spies, "wearing khaki, and encumbered with maps, binoculars and cameras." There were spies in the country, and he stresses that the Syrian authorities did not harass or mistreat them. But they spent a day "riding around Syria with armed troops, machine guns and bazookas at our backs." They eventually decided that it was not possible to work at that site until the political situation was resolved.

An indicator of the degree of trust and good will of the local population is probably found in the frequency with which investigators are accused of spying, a charge that is difficult to defend against when one is there in search of information, and the uses to which it will be put cannot easily be explained to the locals. Overall, 15% of fieldworkers report that someone in the research group was suspected of spying (though only a few of these were arrested) (Table 7.7).

We note that suspicion of spying is most frequent among those who work primarily in the Pacific and Asia (30%). The rate for those who work in Africa is moderate (17%), and is about 12% for those who work in Europe, Latin America, and India. Among those who work in North America, the suspicion of spying is not frequent, although it has been known (Kurt Wolff 1964:240). It is striking that suspicion of spying is much more frequently reported by social-cultural anthropologists (about 25%) than among archaeologists and physical anthropologists (about 10%). And sometimes the suspicion is correct: after the crisis, Louis Leakey openly admitted that he had been working for the Kenyan government, as Mary Leakey put it, "broadcasting propaganda to the loyalists and gathering intelligence about Mau Mau groups and their leaders" (M. Leakey 1984:111). His fluency in Kikuyu and his knowledge of the people and the history of all participants in the conflict made him invaluable to the government. His love of Kenya made him willing to do whatever he could to preserve a state with room for Europeans as well as Africans.

Another kind of hazard even more frequently reported by fieldworkers is living through a period of political turmoil in the country where the work is being done. These episodes are not necessarily focused on the researchers, but it may be stressful and dangerous at times when one's presence and intentions may suddenly come into question. Examples are periods of revolution, war, or rioting. Naturally, the rate of such problems depends very much upon the countries in which one is working. June Nash (1979), for example, tells of living through a strike in a Bolivian mining community, where she was forced to, and chose to, take sides with the strikers against the government, at considerable personal and professional risk.

We note that about 30% of those who have worked primarily in India and in Africa report experiencing political turmoil during their fieldwork, as do 24% of those who have worked in Latin America (Table 7.8). North America, and Asia and the Pacific were places of political turmoil to about 13% of the workers, and Europe had the lowest reported rates, at only 6%. There is no striking difference in the rates for social-cultural versus archaeological fieldworkers. We notice that the hazard usually occurs to all or none in the research group, although there are a few cases where it was said to have happened to others in the group but not to self.

Often the events involve several categories of problems at the same time. For instance, Ronald Cohen (University of Florida) tells of having a vehicle accident in Nigeria, during the period of Ibo massacres in northern Nigeria in 1966. People were being killed, and he was in the process of getting his family into the country. Just then, he had the bad luck to hit a cow with his truck. What might have been a minor mishap in peaceful times was extremely stressful during a period of national crisis. Cohen's African advisers helped him to resolve the problems quickly with the owner of the animal, and he and his family were able to go to the peace of their field site destination.

Factional Conflict

A milder form of the same phenomenon is the experience of living through acute conflict within the unit being studied, for example, a struggle between fac-

Table 7.8. Living through Political Turmoil

	N. America	Europe	L. America	India	Africa	Pacific	Total
Total	61	17	63	17	23	23	204
Had condition, self	8	1	15	5	7	3	39
	13%	*6%*	*24%*	*29%*	*30%*	*13%*	*19%*
Others in group had it	2	0	2	0	0	2	6
	16%	*6%*	*27%*	*29%*	*30%*	*22%*	*22%*

tions in the village or organization under study, which might include violence. Overall, about 11% report having had this kind of experience as a part of field-work (Table 7.9).

Hostage-taking

A rare but severe form of interpersonal threat, almost always politically moti-vated (although the desire for ransom may be a motivation), is taking hostages. Five of the 204 respondents (2%) were involved in hostage-taking incidents in the field—two in Latin America, and one each in Indian subcontinent, Africa, and Asia and the Pacific (Table 7.10).

Perhaps the most famous incident of this kind was the abduction of three Stan-ford University students and a Dutch citizen by paramilitary kidnappers from the Congo. They were taken in 1975 from the Gombe Stream Reserve, where chim-panzees were being studied in the field by Jane Goodall and her associates. A ransom was paid by Stanford University before the students were released. One of those students, Barbara Boardman Smuts, went on to get a Ph.D. in neuro- and biobehavioral sciences and became a professional anthropologist.

More recently, a woman archaeologist and her four-year-old child were kid-napped by guerillas in Peru and later abandoned in the desert. They managed to get back to safety.

Assassination

Mowat speculates whether the death of Dian Fossey should be attributed to poachers or whether it was a product of a faction in the resentful power structure of Rwanda. The case reminds us that anthropologists may be killed in the field for motives that are political rather than personal.

Another example is the death of Ruth First Slavo, a South African-born an-thropologist who was a professor at Maputo University in Mozambique, where

Table 7.9. Factional Conflict

	N. America	Europe	L. America	India	Africa	Pacific	Total
Total	61	17	63	17	23	23	204
Had condition, self	6	2	5	1	3	3	20
	10%	12%	8%	6%	13%	13%	10%
Others in group had it	2	0	2	0	0	0	4
	13%	12%	11%	6%	13%	13%	12%

Table 7.10. Hostage-taking Incidents

	N. America	Europe	L. America	India	Africa	Pacific	Total
Total	61	17	63	17	23	23	204
Had condition, self	0	0	1	1	0	0	2
Others in group had it	0	0	1	0	1	1	3
	0%	0%	3%	6%	4%	4%	2%

she was killed in her office in 1982 by a mail bomb. It is suspected that the bomb was sent by the South African secret service to end her effective political protests against apartheid. First died on the job, even if she was not at the moment doing research "out in the field." Bridgit O'Laughlin, who works in the same research institute in Maputo, was injured in the same explosion.

Despite the difficulty of distinguishing political from criminal or merely interpersonal causes of dangers from other people, the hazards of political problems can readily be seen to be real and frequent. Overall, 42% of those who worked in the Indian subcontinent reported experiencing one or another of these kinds of problems, as did 37% of those who worked in Latin America, 35% of those who worked in Africa, and 26% of those who worked in Asia or the Pacific. Rates for those who worked in North America (22%) and especially in Europe (12%) were notably lower.

We have seen that interpersonal problems make a substantial contribution to the difficulties of fieldwork. They are not the major cause of death—our next topic, accidents, is that. And very likely the rates of interpersonal violence and difficulty are no higher for fieldworkers than they are for other members of the society under study, and maybe not any higher than in one's own society at home.

Human nature includes variation everywhere, and a person who has no difficulty at home may have a difficult time in the field setting. Conversely, a person with a reputation for difficult interpersonal relations at home sometimes does well in the field. And the best balanced and most socially skilled person may not find it possible to live and work in some circumstances without interpersonal conflict. A field site that is easy to work at one time may be very difficult a decade later. It is part of the nature of anthropology that anthropologists tend to take credit for fieldwork that goes smoothly, and to feel guilty or unprofessional when serious difficulties arise, especially in human relations. While these feelings are understandable, it is likely that many of the elements in the interpersonal equation are not under the control of the anthropologist.

We return to some of these issues in Chapter 12, where problems of sustaining mental health are considered. It is important that these problems should not be denied, especially to young people starting to think about becoming anthropologists.

CHAPTER 8   INJURY ACCIDENTS: VEHICLES AND OTHER CAUSES

Accidents and traumatic injuries, in addition to the kinds we have already considered, are common in fieldwork. Problems arise from transportation to the field and in the field, from burns, falls, cuts, and explosions. These causes account for most of the serious injuries and deaths that fieldworkers experience, and are at once the most dramatic and probably the most easily preventable causes of field danger. We will start with vehicle accidents, and move on to the other kinds of accidents reported.

Car Accidents

In most occupations in North America, the single largest cause of occupational deaths is car accidents. In anthropology, as in other occupations, these rates are high, but in anthropology there are additional risks as well.

We see in Table 8.1 that car accidents in the field are frequent and widespread. Among those who work in Africa, 35% report occurrence to someone in the research group, as do 17% of those who work in Latin America. Where the rates are low, we wonder the extent to which this reflects the absence of roads that permit the use of cars in fieldwork, or the safety of the available roads.

Car accidents are frequent all around the world. Indeed, the rates of injury and property damage per mile driven is much higher in some areas than it is in North America, where there is a relatively good system of engineered roads, strict licensing requirements, and more or less regular car upkeep. In other parts of the world, although a smaller proportion of the population may have access to cars, and the cars may be driven fewer miles, the accident rates may be much higher. Poor roads, vehicles in poor shape, and lack of safety training and equipment produce many accidents. Lack of seat belts, lack of efficient means to call for help, and lack of a readily available system of emergency rescue and trauma treatment means that the injuries from a given accident are likely to have far worse results in rural and underdeveloped areas than in North America.

Table 8.1. Car Accidents

	N. America	Europe	L. America	India	Africa	Pacific	Total
Total	61	17	63	17	23	23	204
Had condition, self	1	0	2	2	4	0	9
	2%	0%	3%	12%	17%	0%	4%
Others in group had it	6	1	9	0	4	1	21
	11%	6%	17%	12%	35%	4%	15%

Some deaths due to car accidents among anthropologists include:

Ellen R. Brennan died in March 1983 from an auto accident in the United States.

Royna Craig, 33, died in August 1978 in a multi-car accident at Truckee, California, while driving from her field site in California to the University of Nevada.

Harvey Crew, in his 40s, died in the Sierras during fieldwork of spring 1986.

Hal Charles Foss, 28, graduate student at SUNY-Buffalo, died in a car accident near Albion, New York, where he was starting fieldwork.

Roald Fryxell, 40, died May 1974 in an auto accident.

Mark Allen Grady, 32, Southern Methodist University, died in June 1978 on the way to an archaeological field project in New Mexico.

Cesar Grana, about 60, died in a car accident in 1986 in Spain, where he was doing fieldwork on Spanish art.

Jennifer Beth Greenfield, 25, graduate student at the University of Wisconsin, Milwaukee, died in Dublin, Ireland, from injuries in a car accident, 1981.

Mary C. Hale, 35, died (with Royna Craig) in a multiple car accident near Truckee, California, August 1978.

Jon B. Higgins, 45, Director of Wesleyan University Institute of Ethnomusicology, died December 1984 in a car accident in Middletown, Connecticut.

Patricia Jones-Jackson, 39, of Howard University, died in an auto accident on Johns Island, South Carolina (Sea Islands), where she was doing fieldwork, June 1986.

L. Jill Louchs, 29, Assistant Professor, Appalachian State University, died in an auto accident November 1982 in North Carolina.

B. Mark Lynch, Assistant Professor, University of Santa Clara, died in December 1983.

Donald Mixon died in 1967 in a car crash while doing fieldwork near his home in Napa County, California. He was teaching at Napa Junior College while working on a Ph.D.

T. Stell Newman, 46, Superintendent of "The War in the Pacific National Historical Park" in Guam, died in a car accident on Guam, December 1982.

Paul Pascon, 46, a French anthropologist living in Morocco, died in a car accident in Mauritania, April 1985.

Scott Patterson (M.A., Sonoma State), a contract ethnographer working in Lake County California, was killed when a newly licensed driver hit him broadside in his parked car.

Jane Katherine Sallade (Brawn), doctoral candidate at the University of Michigan, died in Ann Arbor, July 1979.

This list of deaths, even though it is incomplete, has several notable features: (1) It is long. Auto accidents are a common cause of deaths among anthropologists. (2) Many of the cases are difficult to separate into fieldwork related and non-fieldwork-related. Obituaries do not generally provide kinds of information that would be useful (i.e., whether fieldwork was under way, were other cars involved in the same accident, were the various parties wearing seat belts, or whether alcohol contributed to the accident). (3) Many of the deaths are to graduate students and other very young anthropologists. A lot of promising careers are ended in this way and most deaths of young anthropologists result from vehicle accidents.

In addition to the cases derived from obituaries, 20 additional cases of car accidents have been reported by volunteer informants. Eight of the 20 were said to involve students. Three of these (involving a total of seven people) occurred to students attending field schools. In one of these cases, driving off pavement was said to have been a factor. A departmental chairman noted ironically that three of the four students involved in a serious accident were veterans of fieldwork in Panama and Africa, but were badly injured in North America. Another accident, which seriously injured a student, was attributed to a seat belt that failed to hold. An undergraduate student at Lawrence University in Wisconsin died January 1973 in a car accident on the day she arrived in Costa Rica to start work on an archaeology project. Two students from Arizona State University died in a car accident in 1969 at their archaeological field school.

Eight additional car accidents to faculty were described as having serious consequences, including broken bones, severe cuts and bruises, and (in three cases) an early termination of the field season. Two of the accidents produced long-term consequences, one a serious and long-term back injury, which in combination with altitude sickness and poor diet made continued fieldwork in the Altoplano of Peru impossible. The wife of an anthropologist had a miscarriage as a result of a car crash in Europe in the 1950s, and was never able to have another child. Four additional car accidents reported involved hitting an animal on the road or hitting another car, a complicated situation that can destroy fieldwork rapport in addition to the hazards of the accident itself. A faculty member working in Pakistan had a death to a local employee in the field due to a car accident.

There has been a lot of research on the reduction of accidents that can be applied. Drivers' training (especially for off-road and gravel surface conditions), driving sober, and driving a vehicle in good mechanical condition will each contribute to a reduction of the accident rate. But the rates of injury and death from accidents can be reduced, independently of the rate of accidents. Large and well-controlled studies by traffic safety councils across North America and Europe show that the keys to reducing death and injury from car accidents are (1) consistent use of seat belts for all passengers, and (2) prompt and effective emergency medical treatment after accidents. Although it takes extra effort, anthropologists could arrange to have seat belts installed for all passengers in their vehicles (even if that is not standard for the country). We could take substantial and effective first aid courses so that uninjured persons can help the injured. And we can find out in advance of accidents what emergency services are available and how to obtain them as quickly as possible.

Truck Accidents

It is striking that the car accidents happen in relatively developed areas and in urban areas, while the truck accidents occur in the more remote countries and districts of those countries. While car accidents are more frequent, as Table 8.2 shows, the truck accidents tend to be more serious and expensive.

Naturally, one is not at risk of truck accidents unless a truck is used in fieldwork at least some of the time, a condition reported by 122 of the 204 fieldworkers. Of those who ever used a truck, 14% of our respondents reported one or more accidents to self or others on the expedition—a rate of accidents very similar to that of cars. Many more fieldworkers use cars, so that overall about twice as many car as truck accidents are reported.

It is therefore striking that while accounts of 20 car accidents have been volunteered by departmental chairmen and others, 25 truck accidents were similarly

Table 8.2. Truck Accidents

	N. America	Europe	L. America	India	Africa	Pacific	Total
Total	61	17	63	17	23	23	204
Had condition, self	0	0	1	2	2	0	5
	0%	*0%*	*2%*	*12%*	*8%*	*0%*	*2%*
Others in group had it	4	1	5	1	1	0	12
	7%	*6%*	*16%*	*18%*	*13%*	*0%*	*8%*

reported. Although fewer trucks are used, more of these accidents were fatal than among the car accidents.

A graduate student, David Derry, died in August 1976, when the truck he was driving went off a rough road north of Fairbanks, Alaska, during fieldwork. Two local employees of a prominent professor who prefers not to have his name used were killed when their truck turned over during an accident. Another faculty member rolled his van over on an icy road in the mountains in Arizona, wearing no seat belt. He suffered a serious head injury, is permanently disabled, and has taken early retirement. Truck accidents are more often fatal or very seriously injurious in part because trucks, with their higher center of gravity, are far more likely to roll over in a crash than cars are.

Another factor in the higher rate of injuries in truck accidents is the lesser frequency of seat belts in trucks, and the much greater rate of people riding in open backs and sitting on the load. Generally speaking, the only potentially safe seats in a truck are in the cab, and even there seat belts are a rarity in many parts of the world. This principle is illustrated by a rare happy story among the reports of disasters: there was an accident to departmental researchers in Nevada in 1980 in which the truck was totaled, but there were no serious injuries because seat belts were in use.

Ronald Cohen, University of Florida, tells of experiencing whiplash injuries in Nigeria, when a Hausa trader in a Land Rover hit Cohen's truck from behind. Cohen was immobilized on his back for ten days. He got up too soon, and has experienced years of back problems.

Trucks tend to be operated where roads are bad and other people and creatures do not reliably follow "the rules of the road." Several of the truck accidents involved hitting cattle on the road (especially at night), and one accident involved hitting a deer. One, involving a female student working alone in the back country of the United States, occurred when she came around a blind corner and slammed into a county truck parked in the middle of the road. Both drivers were injured sufficiently to need emergency hospitalization. Another truck, this one in Africa, hit a tractor stopped on the road without lights. The injuries were inflicted when the driver and passenger went through the windshield. All such accidents are far more destructive if the passengers have no seat belts.

The typical truck accident occurs when a truck is being driven on gravel or sand. The truck comes to a curve, sometimes even a very moderate curve, and the driver finds the truck skidding and finally overturning. Such an accident could have been prevented by driving at a slower speed, but it is difficult to judge how fast a truck can go around a curve without tipping. Even experienced drivers have been known to have this kind of accident, and inexperienced drivers have an enormously higher probability of overturning on any curve. For this reason it is extremely important that drivers—who may have driven cars for many years—need to consider themselves new drivers when it comes to trucks. And indeed, not all trucks (or all roads) have the same driving characteristics, so that any new vehicle or new field site should be the occasion for relearning how to drive safely. Courses in the safe operation of the truck, formal or informal, are sometimes offered by dealers, by the government, or by adult education or job training facilities, in North America or around the world, and could be life-saving for an anthropologist going where trucks will be used.

Louis Leakey experienced such an accident in the 1920s, when his "lorry skidded and overturned" (Cole 1975:91) while he was driving alone on the road from Gambel's cave to Nairobi. While recovering from his injuries, he was stricken with malaria, and between the two problems he was out of work for a month.

Frances Wenrich Underwood, 64, Associate Professor emeritus from San Jose State, died in 1982 after a truck accident. She had taken early retirement and went to live in Dominica, her field site in the Caribbean.

A serious accident occurred on an expedition led by investigators Kristen Hawkes and Kim Hill, working in Paraguay, when their truck was sideswiped and pushed off the road by a careening bus. The truck was totally demolished as it overturned, and rolled down the highway, and Kevin Jones's right hand was crushed. Hill and Jones had to hitchhike to the nearest hospital, as there was no emergency transport available. After ineffective emergency surgery locally he was evacuated to the United States for treatment by specialists in reconstruction of the hand. Loss of Jones, loss of the truck, and minor injuries to other members of the team delayed the research for several weeks. For Jones, the consequences were much greater.

> It prevented my conducting any field research (fieldwork I had planned for over two years) and effectively eliminated planned ethnoarchaeological studies from the research. As a result of the accident, I spent six weeks in the hospital and months in physical therapy. My right thumb was amputated, and I lost a great deal of function of my entire right hand. I underwent eleven surgeries, including two skin grafts.

Another frequent kind of accident with trucks starts with a blow-out of a tire and also involves overturning. Given the frequency of overturned trucks with blow-outs, and given the state of roads in most Third World countries, roads that make severe demands upon tires, it really doesn't make any sense to drive upon old and patched tires.

Finally, a cause of deaths in truck accidents that is not paralleled in car accidents is caused by the dangerous conditions of riding in the open back or on top of a load in trucks. There is no natural limitation on the number of passengers that can be carried on a truck (as cars have), and anthropologists frequently adopt local customs and carry as many passengers, natives, and researchers as can fit in the space. One reason this is dangerous is that the truck can be overloaded or the center of gravity may shift to an unstable high point. A second source of danger is that it is not possible or practical, under most circumstances, to provide seat belts and rollbars to prevent passengers from being thrown from the truck in an accident, so that the heavy metal body of the truck can absorb most of the impact. A third source of danger is that trucks are often loaded with heavy and sharp items—tools, tool boxes, tents, heavy cans or drums of water or gasoline, tanks of propane, and so on. The heavy items will hit passengers in the back of trucks in case of an accident, and crush or injure them. Modifying trucks with compartments or fixtures for securing drums and boxes could help prevent injuries in milder accidents. The deaths associated with riding in the back or on the top of trucks tend not to be to the anthropologists but to native employees and local hitchhikers, whose names are less likely to be known in a study like this.

Melissa Knauer, 31, a new Ph.D. from the University of Toronto, on her way to her first overseas fieldwork with the !Kung, died in June 1985 in Botswana in a single vehicle accident. She died of skull injuries from falling from an observation seat on the top of a truck when the truck overturned from a blow-out. The other occupant of the observation seat, 14-year-old Alex Lee, also died. The six people inside the truck, all without seat belts, were injured.

Courses in safe driving may be combined with courses in maintenance and emergency repair of trucks. Trucks are typically needed in areas where support from a garage and mechanics may not be available, at least not readily available. One needs the manual for the vehicle, a supply of spare parts, and sufficient knowledge to install them. Repairs to trucks can sometimes be dangerous too, especially for those who have not been trained in this work. Neil Smith (Emory University) was changing a tire on his truck in the field when the jack slipped and his hand was trapped in the tire so that he was pinned down to the truck. He was fortunate that someone came along and helped him get free, as he could easily have died a painful death of dehydration in an isolated spot. There are many parts of the world where one cannot expect help to arrive promptly, so that emergency water, blankets, and first aid should be carried, and better yet, a form of emergency communication such as a two-way radio should be carried to summon help.

Those who arrive on the scene of the accident will not always help. An example comes from researchers working at Koobi Fora in the early 1980s. They were in two Land Rovers loaded with enough tinned food and petrol to last for two months when a tire blew out. Jeanne Sept (Indiana University) broke her pelvis and clavicle, colleague Zefe Kaufulu broke his pelvis and lumbar vertebra, and one of the two field assistants was badly cut. They were unconscious on the road for several hours. While unconscious, they were robbed by people who happened to pass by. Others at the scene flagged down a lorry headed back toward town and had them transported to the nearest clinic where they eventually regained consciousness and could start making decisions. On balance Sept feels that passersby helped more than they hurt. She writes:

> the lessons I learned from this episode were not the ones you mentioned (theft at the scene of the accident—fairly trivial). I learned: never to cut corners when maintaining field vehicles; don't overload them with people or supplies; don't allow students to do field work without adequate accident/health insurance and financial/airticket provisions in case of emergencies.

Motorcycles, Motor Scooters, and Bicycles

There are many parts of the world where motorcycles, motor bikes or scooters are a practical way of getting around in the field. In many of these places the local people use these vehicles too, and it may contribute to establishing rapport to avoid the use of cars or trucks. But mile for mile, accident for accident, small vehicles are more dangerous than cars and trucks.

The danger, of course, is that in case of an accident the rider is unprotected from the impact by the metal of the vehicle, so that at any speed the damage to the body coming into contact with the road, or the vehicle, or other objects is substantial. Wearing a helmet helps to reduce the consequences of such accidents, but cannot reduce them as seat belts can in a car or truck.

Table 8.3 suggests that one should beware particularly of motorcycles in India, motor scooters in Africa, and bicycles in Europe, but basically we need to recognize that these vehicles are dangerous anywhere.

These kinds of accidents are not, of course, confined to fieldwork, and anthropologists can be injured like anyone else, right at home. Alice Singer, a graduate student at Brandeis in the 1970s, was hit by a truck and fatally injured while bi-

Table 8.3. Injury Accidents from Motorcycles, Motor Scooters, and Bicycles

	N. America	Europe	L. America	India	Africa	Pacific	Total
Total	61	17	63	17	23	23	204
Motorcycle (*N* = 121)							
Had condition, self	0	0	0	3	1	1	5
				18%	*4%*	*4%*	*2%*
Others in group had it	0	0	1	0	2	0	3
	0%	*0%*	*2%*	*18%*	*4%*	*4%*	*4%*
Motor Bike or Scooter (*N* = 125)							
Had condition, self	1	0	0	1	1	1	4
	2%			*6%*	*4%*	*4%*	*2%*
Others in group had it	0	1	3	0	2	1	7
	2%	*6%*	*5%*	*6%*	*13%*	*9%*	*5%*
Bicycle (*N* = 120)							
Others in group had it	1	3	0	0	1	0	5
	2%	*18%*	*0%*	*0%*	*4%*	*0%*	*3%*

cycling in Cambridge. Professor Zilberman, a faculty member at Brandeis, was killed by a car while bicycling in Newton, Massachusetts, a few years later.

Thomas Zwickler, a graduate student at the University of Pennsylvania, died in a bicycle accident in India, in 1985. He was struck by a bus and killed while riding a bike on a rural road at night.

Bus or Public Transport Accidents

Some anthropologists who work in areas where public transportation exists, especially cities, prefer not to maintain a private car (or cannot afford to do so). Public transport may be crowded and dusty but it is an opportunity to get where one wants to go while sharing the experience of the locals. Only one accident was reported from riding on public transport. Charles Leslie of Delaware University was exiting from a trolley-bus in Calcutta in 1960 when his foot was seriously injured. His foot might have been amputated in the Calcutta hospital to which he was taken, but colleagues intervened. Instead he was transferred to another and perhaps better hospital in Calcutta, and then sent back to the States for a long series of operations. Many years later, he still suffers from the injury. Nevertheless, he continues his fieldwork as well as other professional activities.

Pedestrian Accidents

Walking along the roads and trails would seem to be the safest means of transport in the field, but there are risks there, too. Here these risks have been classified by the type of agent of threat rather than the pedestrian status of the victim. Pedestrians hit by cars or trucks are mentioned under car or truck accidents, those bitten by dogs or other wild animals while walking are considered under the heading of animal hazards, and those who have been attacked by assailants are discussed in the section on human hazards. A few others are included in the section on falls, which concludes this chapter.

Helicopter Accidents

Many anthropologists use air transport to get to the field, but relatively few use it as a regular technique for fieldwork. Helicopters seem to be used primarily for survey work in archaeology.

Several cases of deaths in helicopter accidents have been reported, or have been extracted from obituaries in the professional journals. Ruth Croxton, who was a former student at the University of Alaska, Fairbanks, worked as an agency archaeologist after getting her B.A. She was killed in a helicopter crash in 1982 while on survey in "bush" Alaska. R. Powers, Professor of Anthropology, University of Alaska, Fairbanks, was in a helicopter crash in 1976 on Stewart Peninsula. Fortunately they crashed into a lake so that none of the crew were seriously injured. Mark Wimberly, a subcontractor to the Office of Contract Archaeology, University of New Mexico, suffered serious injuries in a helicopter crash while on a BIA contract on the Mescalero Reservation in southern New Mexico in fall 1980. He died after six months in the hospital.

Airplane Accidents

Relatively few anthropologists use airplanes to get around in the bush, and relatively few are pilots. Where available, planes (and helicopters as well as other means of transportation) may save lives by providing a means of evacuation of the ill and injured to hospital, but they also bring dangers. Planes are undeniably dangerous as a means of transportation.

Elgen Annis, a graduate student at Brandeis University, buzzed the campus in his small plane at low altitude in the 1970s, and caught a wing on a tree, crashing and killing himself and a passenger. He came close to hitting the anthropology building, where many students and faculty were working at the time.

Ron Douglass, Bruce Jenkins, and Ed Gardner were employed by Larry Seemans and Associates on a cultural resources contract. They all died in 1981 in a plane crash as the plane developed mechanical trouble while taking off from Happy Camp, California. The pilot also died in the crash.

Richard Leakey tells of learning to fly in order to increase the efficiency of the East African prehistory research. In *One Life* (1983) he tells of first trying camels, then later, airplanes, to avoid the problems of using trucks under difficult off-road conditions. He acquired his pilot's license first in 1963, but gave up piloting after what he calls "a stupid incident at Olduvai the previous year in which I very nearly killed several good friends":

> I was trying to land against the early morning sun which was so bright that I was quite unable to see the markers on the little grass airstrip that I had built myself some weeks before. I made three attempts but each time I aborted the landing at the last moment when I realized that I was not straight on the runway. I became very anxious: my pride was at stake. Instead of going away or attempting the landing from the other direction, I foolishly determined, on the fourth attempt, to put the plane down regardless. This I did but hit the rocks marking the edge of the runway and in a few moments we had shed two wheels, the tail of the plane and half of one wing. [Leakey 1983:140–141]

Leakey goes on to discuss getting his license back in the 1970s in order to supply the Omo expedition, and reports that he can fly safely again. He adds:

> Our landing strip near the camp is unpopular with pilots because it is very short; a total runway length of 428 yards and often there is a strong cross wind that can reach 25 knots at a 75° angle! I

have now landed and taken off from this field well over a thousand times without incident but it always calls for special concentration and effort.

Many friends have asked why we do not extend the length of the strip and the answer is very simple. If we did all sorts of uninvited people would fly in to Koobi Fora and it would become a real nuisance. By having an airfield that is tricky to use visitors are forced to use the larger strip which is about six miles away from our camp. To visit us they require ground transport and so their visit has to be arranged in advance with our consent. In this way, we have a very effective visitor filter. [Leakey 1983:141]

A group from Brigham Young University had a plane crash while doing field-work in Guatemala, where the only access to the site was by small plane. The passengers were able to get out before the plane burned, and no one was seriously injured.

Bill Durham, of Stanford, who works in a remote area of Panama, tells of feeling safe getting to the country and safe once in the field, separated by a terrifying few hours of dependence upon one of the dare-devil bush pilots to move him and his family and colleagues into the field, with their supplies. See, too, the accounts by David Maybury-Lewis (Maybury-Lewis 1988) of getting into and out of field sites by depending upon either the military or bush pilots for hire. As a guest of the military one cannot very well complain about risk-taking, and the bush pilots seem to work on a "take it or leave it" basis. Investigators who have worked in the Arctic also express concern about the degree of dependence upon bush pilots.

Anthropologists also undergo some risks in dealing with commercial airlines, getting to the field and around the world in pursuit of their business. Alan Park-hurst Merriam, 56, was killed in an airline crash en route to Warsaw University for a brief visiting appointment. He did fieldwork in Africa and in the United States. Michael Nimtz, a graduate student at Pennsylvania, a Near Eastern ar-chaeologist, was killed in 1974 while returning from his dissertation fieldwork when the roof of the airport in Tehran collapsed. Cesar Fonseca, 50, Professor at the National University of Peru in Lima [working with Enrique Mayer (Uni-versity of Illinois) and Steven Bush (University of California at Davis)], was leav-ing Canete, Peru, on a small commercial airplane to return to Lima. Fonseca climbed the steps to board just as another plane buzzed the field, creating a wind that knocked him off the ladder. He fell about 12 feet, and died of head injuries, in March 1986.

Nonvehicular Injury Accidents

Accidents with Weapons

Only one of our 204 fieldworkers reported an accident with a gun—a person who worked in the Pacific (in this case, New Guinea). The injury was fortunately not serious, but of course with guns, injuries are likely to be fatal.

One of the departmental chairmen who responded to my inquiries wrote back a long and interesting letter about the use of guns in the field. He believes that they can contribute to safety in situations of interpersonal threat. By having the reputation of a person who has and uses guns, some kinds of incidents may be avoided. He feels that the urban background of many anthropologists leads to an unrealistic fear and loathing of guns.

Napoleon Chagnon writes (1974:16) of spinning a tall tale to the Yanomamö about his prowess with guns for shooting imaginary river monsters. As evidence of his claim, he "showed them several cartridges with rifled slugs protruding from the plastic jackets. Back in 1965 it was possible to make such an argument, since none of the Yanomamö had yet been given shotguns. Now it is impossible: I know of at least forty Yanomamö in various villages along the Orinoco, including the Bisaasi-teri, who have shotguns."

Knives

Injuries from knives are more common than those from guns. Our 204 informants tell of 19 incidents of knife injuries to themselves and to members of their expeditions (Table 8.4).

Somewhat contrary to my expectations, I note that there are no such accidents among those who work primarily in Africa, but many among those who work in Europe, and to a lesser extent those who work in North and Latin America. Perhaps this is due to the mix of weapons that are in use in different parts of the world. Injuries from a category called "local weapons"—including bows and arrows, clubs, and digging sticks—were reported by an additional seven investigators.

Perhaps the most chilling of these accidents was reported by Kim Hill (University of Michigan) who was working on foot with colleague Magdalena Hurtado among the Ache hunter-gatherers of Paraguay in 1982. Hill tells how he went hunting with an Ache man who repeatedly shot arrows at a monkey some 20 meters above them in a tree. The hunter released an arrow and a gust of wind caught it, bringing it directly back down towards the pair. Unfortunately, Hill looked down to write in his notebook at the moment the arrow began to fall. It hit Hill in the back and penetrated about four inches. Because Ache arrows are barbed, the arrow had to be twisted around several times to be removed by the hunter. As Hill bled profusely the pair walked an hour back to the Ache band where Hurtado applied antibiotic powder and a makeshift bandage. Because they were so deep in the forest, and without any means of outside communication, Hill and Hurtado were forced to walk with the band for another week before they arrived at the nearest mission outpost.

Traps represent another danger to investigators and their parties, particularly as city people are often not familiar with the mechanisms of traps or the places where they are likely to be found. Only two injury accidents were reported from traps, one from a Europeanist and one from a specialist in Asia and the Pacific.

Special Hazards of Archaeology

There do not appear to be any distinctive differences in rates of accidents from weapons between the archaeologists and physical anthropologists, on the one

Table 8.4. Injury Accidents from Knives

	N. America	Europe	L. America	India	Africa	Pacific	Total
Total	61	17	63	17	23	23	204
Had condition, self	1	1	3	0	0	1	6
	2%	*6%*	*5%*	*0%*	*0%*	*4%*	*3%*
Others in group had it	4	4	2	2	0	1	13
	8%	*29%*	*8%*	*12%*	*0%*	*9%*	*9%*

hand, and social-cultural and linguistic anthropologists, on the other. There are, however, two kinds of accidents that occur primarily or uniquely to archaeologists. One of these is injuries from the use of digging equipment. A few years ago a backhoe, being used to move earth in an excavation, tipped over and fell upon an archaeological worker, injuring him badly. Other injuries reported consisted of cuts from shovels and pickaxes while digging in the field, wielded by oneself or another worker at close quarters in the trench. An eye was put out by a chaining pin that was thrown instead of handed to the next worker. Rules for safe conduct during digging must be learned, and field schools are frequently used in archaeology for transmitting this training—the one exception to the rule that anthropologists do not explicitly train their students and workers for health and safety.

A second kind of special danger in archaeology is the cave-in, a kind of accident that is in principle predictable and preventable. Two such incidents were reported among the 112 archaeologists (and physical anthropologists) in our sample, neither fatal or even very injurious. Other examples were cited by volunteers: Barbara Thiel (Northern Kentucky University) reports that in the Philippines in 1976 her foot was hurt when stone from the wall of a cave fell on her. There was a trench collapse on an excavation associated with Brigham Young University, and an employee was caught in it.

Falls

Another relatively common injury accident for archaeologists is falling off cliffs, into holes, and from the tops of structures. But falls, it turns out, are relatively common hazards for social-cultural anthropologists as well.

Only 130 of the 204 respondent fieldworkers claimed exposure to the risks of falls, and almost 30% of these reported experience with falls during their fieldwork (Table 8.5). Results of these falls include broken bones, cuts, bruises, and concussions. None of the people in the sample were killed, but falls cause a substantial portion of the accidental deaths in the field.

Similarly, falls are among the cases that come most readily to the minds of chairmen reporting on the history of health and safety in the fieldwork done by members of their departments. Excerpts from letters include: "a student suffered a fall at a field school in New Mexico in 1982 and was hospitalized for concussion"; "a student suffered a broken arm from a fall at the excavation site in Israel in 1986"; "in 1973 (I) fell from a cliff while doing archaeological research at Chaco Canyon, New Mexico"; "a faculty member's young son took a serious fall during field work in Mexico"; "an individual fell into a deep pit at our field project in Arizona and broke his pelvis"; "a graduate student fell and injured her ankle"; "a student on the excavation of a historical graveyard fell and injured her

Table 8.5. Injury Accidents from Falls

	N. America	Europe	L. America	India	Africa	Pacific	Total
Total	61	17	63	17	23	23	204
Had condition, self	2	2	2	1	1	3	11
	3%	*12%*	*3%*	*6%*	*4%*	*13%*	*5%*
Others in group had it	10	1	9	3	1	1	25
	20%	*18%*	*17%*	*24%*	*9%*	*17%*	*18%*

knee, needing surgery and a year of physiotherapy.'' Clearly falls are a frequent hazard, especially on archaeological excavations.

But falls are not confined to archaeological projects. Margaret Mead (1977) reported injuries from falls on several occasions during fieldwork, and at least once had to be carried to her site on a hammock because of the danger to her weak ankle.

Georgeda Buchbinder, now at the School of Public Health at the University of Hawaii, then a graduate student at Columbia, fell at a rest house in New Guinea while on the way to the latrine at night. She broke her ankle in the fall. The Patrol Officer and the local men made a stretcher and carried her for 22 hours through the rain over ''incredibly rugged terrain'' where she was given a splint and flown out to a hospital in the morning. There the leg was put into a cast but nerve damage was done and the fracture never healed properly. She traveled first to Australia and then to the United States for orthopedic surgery. The injury cost Buchbinder a year of lost field time and many months of treatment, and she was uninsured for the costs.

One of the most mourned deaths in anthropology during the past decade occurred on a social-cultural project in the Philippines, working with the Ilongot. Michelle Zimbalist Rosaldo, 37, Associate Professor at Stanford University, died in a fall from a mountain path in the Philippines, October 11, 1981. She was walking with informants, when she lost her footing and fell down the cliff. She was in the field with her husband, Renato Rosaldo, and their two children for a year's study when the accident occurred.

Klaus-Friedrich Koch, 42, Associate Professor at Northwestern University, died in Cairo in 1979 from a fall from an apartment building balcony while doing research in Egypt.

An example of difficulty in classification of accidents arises in the case of a student at the field school of the University of Wisconsin, Oshkosh, in 1973. He suffered a crushed cervical vertebra after diving head first into shallow water along the bank of the Mississippi river in LaCrosse, Wisconsin. The swimming was recreation rather than fieldwork. He is said to have made a full recovery eventually, but he did not finish the field school course or continue to work in archaeology.

Miscellaneous Accidents

One cannot prepare for every kind of potential hazard that fieldworkers face in the field. Some of them are models of unpredictability. In one case, for instance, a social-cultural investigator in the Near East went to the door of a house where he hoped to talk with an informant, and was electrocuted when he touched the door. Apparently the homeowner had been attempting to change the wiring of the house that day and had not realized that lines were crossed and that the metal door was charged. The investigator was badly burned but recovered.

Another accident involving electrocution was more predictable, and probably would not happen to a trained researcher today. In the 1930s, a crew member, wanting to take photos of an archaeological site, climbed a power line tower in the central valley of California. He touched a power line and died of electric shock.

A woman collecting corn pollen with a group of Navajo scratched the cornea of her eye and needed treatment. She recalls that she had very little previous ex-

Table 8.6. Injuries from Accidents

	N. America	Europe	L. America	India	Africa	Pacific	Total
Total	61	17	63	17	23	23	204
Cuts (in skin)							
Had condition, self	33	6	29	4	12	12	96
	54%	35%	46%	24%	52%	52%	47%
Others in group had it	8	3	4	1	3	1	20
	67%	53%	52%	29%	65%	57%	57%
Cuts and Bleeding (injury accident)							
Had condition, self	10	4	8	3	3	7	35
	16%	23%	13%	18%	13%	41%	17%
Others in group had it	13	3	7	1	4	0	28
	38%	41%	24%	24%	30%	41%	31%
Broken Bones (Other)							
Had condition, self	2	0	1	2	5	1	11
	3%	0%	2%	12%	22%	4%	5%
Others in group had it	7	2	9	2	3	0	23
	15%	12%	16%	24%	35%	4%	17%
Broken Limbs (injury accident)							
Had condition, self	1	2	1	3	4	1	12
	2%	12%	2%	18%	17%	4%	6%
Others in group had it	7	1	9	2	1	0	23
	13%	18%	16%	29%	22%	4%	17%
Sprains							
Had condition, self	12	0	9	3	5	3	32
	20%	0%	14%	18%	22%	13%	16%
Others in group had it	17	4	7	2	4	0	34
	48%	24%	25%	29%	39%	13%	32%
Dislocations							
Had condition, self	0	0	2	3	0	2	7
			3%	18%		9%	3%
Others in group had it	2	0	4	0	0	0	6
	3%	0%	10%	18%	0%	9%	6%
Spinal Injury							
Had condition, self	2	0	0	0	1	0	3
	3%				4%		1%
Others in group had it	2	0	1	0	0	0	3
	6%	0%	2%	0%	4%	0%	3%
Fractured Skull							
Had condition, self	2	0	3	0	0	0	5
	3%		5%				2%
Others in group had it	0	0	0	0	0	0	0
	3%	0%	5%	0%	0%	0%	2%
Electric Shock							
Had condition, self	1	0	2	0	0	1	4
	2%	0%	3%	0%	0%	4%	2%
None of the Above							
Self only	11	6	22	9	5	7	60
	18%	35%	35%	53%	22%	30%	29%

perience with corn fields or the nature of corn plants at that time. Her experience reminds us that it would be difficult to design a training program that would anticipate all of the dangers that fieldworkers will encounter.

Injuries Received from Accidents (Cumulative)

Overall, 70% of the 204 informants report one or another kind of injury from one or many accidents in the field over the years. About 10% of the archaeologists say they have never been injured, and about 20% of the social-cultural investigators report no injuries. Another 10% left the question blank. Others report injuries, as seen in Table 8.6. Note that individuals can be included in more than one category, so that the rows cannot be summed to find the percentage of those injured.

Note that there is a close replication of two categories in Table 8.6, included for the purpose of checking the internal consistency of the responses. Fieldworkers were asked to check whether ''cuts'' ever occurred to self or other members of the expedition under the heading of skin problems, and also asked about ''cuts and bleeding'' under the category of injury accidents. Also they were asked about broken bones under the heading of ''other illnesses'' and ''broken limbs'' under the category of injury accidents. This comparison reminds us that while we are undoubtedly learning a great deal about the kinds of risks that people encounter during fieldwork, these questions are not standardized and there are no readily available comparative data.

Table 8.6 shows us that the consequences of accidents—cuts, broken bones, bad backs, dislocated joints, etc.—are commonly experienced by anthropologists. This table will repay reflection on the question of the need for first aid training and emergency procedures in the field. Although there are only a few cases in each of these categories, the accumulated effect of accidents is so great that some 70% of the anthropologists surveyed have had to cope with at least one such injury during the course of their research. We see here that most expeditions experience emergencies, and so most anthropologists need to learn to deal with serious injuries.

CHAPTER 9 PARASITIC DISEASES

Most urban North Americans are not exposed to parasitic disease in their daily lives, and most of us know little about recognition or prevention of such diseases. Indeed, many doctors in North America have never seen most forms of parasitic disease except in textbooks during medical school, and have no experience of identifying or treating the kinds of illnesses that anthropologists may encounter and bring home. So parasitic diseases, while not the most frequent or dangerous, are among the most striking and impressive of the occupational hazards of anthropology. If the people who live in the area where the anthropologist will be working get parasites, the anthropologist is at some risk of getting them also, and parasites are still very common among some of the populations that anthropologists study.

Parasites are life forms larger than bacteria, which spend some or all of their life cycle within the bodies of other creatures, including humans and animals. Prevention and control of them depend on knowing about the parasites in the immediate environment, their life cycles and customary hosts, their methods of invasion of the host, and the treatment that will kill them internally or interrupt their reproductive cycle. Malaria is the most prevalent and dangerous of the parasites for anthropologists. In this presentation of the dangers, we will start with malaria and other insect-borne parasitic diseases, and go on to those transmitted through water, food, and soil.

Parasites Transmitted by Insects

Malaria

Malaria parasites are protozoa, of one of four species. They are long-term inhabitants of the human body, carrying out reproductive cycles that produce illness and periods of quiescence in which the illness recedes. The illness is marked by high fever, chills, aches and pains, headache, and often a cough. Longer-term symptoms include anemia, jaundice, kidney failure, coma, and sometimes death. When illness is described as "fever," it is usually (but not always) malaria that is the cause.

All species of malaria are ordinarily transmitted from one person to another by the bite of an infected female *Anopheles* mosquito. Rarely it is transmitted by blood transfusion or from mother to fetus. Malaria is an intensely local disease, of high risk in some districts of some countries and virtually impossible to contract in other areas. The U.S. Centers for Disease Control (CDC) keep track of where malaria is found, and where specific strains of the chloroquine-resistant malaria will be found. They are the experts who should be consulted before planning a detailed control program for malaria, if one is needed.

Malaria can be prevented by interfering with the cycle of transmission of the protozoa from one person to another through mosquito bites. Methods include draining swamps and waterholes where mosquitos breed, putting up screens and mosquito nets, dressing in protective clothing to prevent being bitten, and treating the body with repellents and prophylaxis to become an unfriendly host to the parasite. Taking quinine (and drinking "bitters" or quinine water) is an old-fashioned form of malaria prevention. The more modern version is to take chloroquine phosphate or an alternative prophylactic medication while exposed, usually once a week, starting from a few weeks before exposure to the parasite begins and continuing for several weeks after exposure ends.

Most people find that they can tolerate chloroquine on a weekly basis with no complications, but a minority report side effects of ringing ears, increased blood pressure, and even sight or hearing loss.

Despite some drug complications, chloroquine has been an invaluable product in the prevention of malaria, but unfortunately, resistant strains of malaria have evolved. And chloroquine has always required a rigid adherence to schedule to prevent malaria. Not only does one have to remember to take it on the same day each week, but it has to be absorbed at the proper dosage, so that people with diarrheas and dysenteries may fail to keep their dosage up even if they remember to take the pill during sickness. Thus, while public health officials insist that no one should get malaria who takes their medication conscientiously (unless the local strain is chloroquine-resistant), in fact many anthropologists who are exposed to the disease do get it sooner or later, as Table 9.1 shows.

Malaria is by far the most common of the parasitic diseases among anthropologists, not only as measured by the reports from our random sample but as witnessed by the 52 individual reports of malaria from departmental chairmen and volunteered accounts of problems. There are so many reports of malaria to named people that we won't report any of them here. Malaria is a global health problem, and anthropologists will encounter it when they work outside North America (where there is virtually none) and Europe (where there has not been much since World War II). Among South Asian experts, 100% of the sample report having been exposed and 41% have experienced malaria; among Africanists, 87% report exposure and 35% experience; and among those who concentrate on Asia and the Pacific, 78% report exposure and 31% experience. Obviously malaria is a hazard that must be carefully considered by many fieldworkers.

The course of malaria is an alternation of attacks and recoveries, occurring on a cycle of a few days to a few weeks. It usually begins with chills and often severe headache for an hour or two. This is followed by fever for several hours, which may produce delirium. Finally the high fever breaks with an outburst of sweating

Table 9.1. Malaria, 24% of Those Exposed (and 64% Have Been Exposed)

	N. America	Europe	L. America	India	Africa	Pacific	Total
Total	61	17	63	17	23	23	204
Had condition, self	2	1	2	3	5	5	18
	3%	6%	3%	18%	22%	22%	9%
Others in group had it	2	1	2	4	3	2	14
	6%	12%	6%	41%	35%	30%	16%

that reduces the temperature, and after a few hours the person may feel weak but recovered. Untreated, this sequence may be repeated within 24 hours to within a few days. After one has endured the disease for some time, the cycles may lengthen to once each few weeks or even months. The disease is sufficiently severe that it seriously interferes with work and is extremely unpleasant. As Katharine Milton (University of California at Berkeley) put it, "It is one of the symptoms of the disease that you think you are going to die."

Delia Owens (Owens and Owens 1984:167) tells of contracting malaria in the Kalahari desert in the rainy season, despite their isolation from other humans.

> A vise crushed both sides of my head, and a sharp wedge pressed down from above, splitting my brain. The pain of resting my head on the pillow was unbearable. I tried to sit up but a wave of nausea swept over me. . . . Without moving my head I nudged Mark . . . "some pills . . . I must have malaria." . . . The hut was dank, dark. I was buried under heavy blankets of scratchy wool, but I was still stone-cold, my skin clammy. Mark lay next to me, trying to keep me from shivering, but I could feel no warmth. The blood in my head pounded against my skull, and a brilliant light from one tiny window stabbed at my eyes. Then my body began to burn. With all my strength I shoved Mark away and threw back the covers. The sheets were damp and a putrid odor smothered me. For a long time my mind floated in darkness.

In some parts of the world, fieldworkers may prefer to avoid the locally available medical facilities. Delia Owens (1984:167), for instance, says

> There was no reason (for Mark) to take me to the mission clinic in Maun, which had nothing better for malaria than chloroquine and where there was a good chance of picking up tuberculosis or something worse. In the rainy season Maun was rife with malaria. According to the hunters, "You either take the pills, sweat out the fever, and get better, or you die."

Generally speaking, the same medications are used for prevention and treatment. If the suppressive dose has failed to prevent one from contracting the disease, a larger dose is used to kill the parasites within the body. Some anthropologists choose not to take continual lower doses for suppression of malaria, hoping to avoid the disease by preventing mosquito bites, because they fear the side effects of the drugs. If the disease is contracted, however, it is important to take a curative dose, because malaria is not self-limiting (as most diseases are), but will settle into a chronic state in the body, and also because one's infected body becomes a source of disease when mosquitos bite it and pass the disease on to others. Naturally, this is particularly important if one has acquired malaria somewhere else and is working in an area where the population has mosquitos but not malaria. The curative dose will help prevent transmission to others but may not totally wipe out the disease on first treatment, so after an attack one might want to reconsider the question of taking a suppressive dose.

Exactly which medications to use depends upon the strains of malaria found locally; it is a complicated question that requires the best possible local medical knowledge. A warning from many anthropologists, but most particularly from Robert Carneiro (American Museum of Natural History) is that North American physicians may know virtually nothing about malaria, especially one's particular strain of malaria, and may take a very long time to diagnose the disease and to provide the proper treatment. Some of the medications available are dangerous and others are ineffective. A number of informants warn particularly about the dangers of taking the medicine Fansidar, and wish that they had not taken it routinely. And while some anthropologists have become experts on the characteristics of malaria and its treatment, and others, like Peter Brown of Emory University, are professional experts on it as a topic in medical anthropology, many anthropologists have only a vague understanding of the issues.

The sample was asked to report what treatment program they used to control malaria, if any. Their answers reveal that many have only a vague recollection of what was done ("I took the pills my doctor gave me"). Carneiro insists that most anthropologists are in a position to become much better informed on the treatment of malaria than their doctors are likely to be. His view is seconded by Henry Wright (University of Michigan) who strongly recommends developing special knowledge of the treatment used successfully in the area of research, and carrying the most useful drug with you when you leave that area in case you need it later when it will not otherwise be available. All experts recommend continuing suppressive therapy for some weeks or months after one leaves the field, so that parasites in any mosquito bites received during the last days of fieldwork are not permitted to multiply freely in the bloodstream.

If one should become ill with malaria in the six months or so after leaving the field, keep in mind that it is not a diagnosis that is likely to occur to a North American physician unless it is pointed out, and even if the possibility is considered, inexperienced laboratory workers frequently miss diagnosis of it in blood tests. Several fieldworkers tell of their frustration in realizing that they were coming down with malaria in North America after leaving the field, and being unable to convince their physicians to start a course of treatment early, while the multiplication of the parasite could still be limited to a mild case. In one instance, symptoms started at the beginning of a long summer weekend, but the diagnosis was not made and treatment started until well into the second attack of malaria.

There are two severe complications. The first is cerebral malaria, whereby the parasites get into the brain and can do a great deal of damage. The treatment needed is injection of chloroquine (or the medication of choice) which should be performed by and the consequences monitored by a physician. A nutritionist at Columbia University nearly died of cerebral malaria a few years ago, despite sophisticated treatment received after she was evacuated to the United States.

The second complication—"blackwater fever"—was once common but is rarely seen or reported now. This urinary-bladder illness usually results from months or years of recurrent malaria. Louis Leakey's boss on his first African archaeological expedition, Cutler, died of it in Tanzania in the 1920s when Leakey was back in Cambridge finishing his studies (Cole 1975:36). Bernard Deacon, a brilliant 24-year-old from Cambridge, died on Vanuatu of blackwater fever in the 1920s after only 18 months in the field (see also Chapter 12).

Stuart Altmann, Department of Biology, University of Chicago, writes (1986, personal communication) a warning on the implications of the medication chosen to fight malaria. For a small proportion of people, quinine derivative medicines are *ototoxic,* that is, they poison one's hearing by high frequency hearing loss and "tinnitus," a continuous buzzing or ringing of the ears. Altmann says "two of us monkey-watchers have hearing damage that probably is due to antimalarials." He reviews the dangers of each of several strategies, and points out that available information on treatment of malaria is still changing rapidly, and that people who work in malarial areas should keep themselves informed of the latest information.

Among the 50 or so reports of malaria to departmental members reported by chairs, three refer to graduate students whose illness led them to drop out of anthropology rather than continue fieldwork and get a degree. We cannot know, of course, how much of the decision was caused by malaria and how much by second thoughts that anyone might have confronting the reality of fieldwork. In two of these cases, it was noted that malaria was complicated by the simultaneous or close occurrence of another disease, in one case hepatitis and in another chronic dehydration from dysentery. The juxtaposition of malaria and hepatitis seems to be common, and produces a debilitating illness.

African Sleeping Sickness (Trypanosomiasis)

To continue with consideration of the parasitic diseases transmitted by the action of insect bites, we take up trypanosomiasis. This is a public health danger of considerable magnitude in the part of the world where it is prevalent—tropical Africa, roughly between 15° n and 20° s. While one might be infected with malaria by a mosquito bite and not be aware of the danger until the fever starts, the bite of the tsetse fly will rarely go unnoticed. The insect is large, slow, and it takes a great ripping bite out of the skin, rarely failing to cause bleeding and pain. Indeed, the bites tend to infect even if the trypanosomiasis does not result. Hence one is highly motivated to avoid the bites, and few will fail to notice whether they were exposed.

Symptoms of trypanosomiasis, according to the *CDC Manual* (1987:79), may not show up for months or years after exposure. It is a serious, potentially fatal disease and will require expert treatment. No one among the 204 fieldworkers, including the 17 Africanists in the sample, reported having anyone on their expeditions experience the disease (although contact with the tsetse fly was often reported).

American Trypanosomiasis (Chagas' Disease)

Two of our 204 fieldworkers report experience on their expeditions with Chagas' Disease, the American continent version of trypanosomiasis, found from Central America to Argentina. The parasite is transmitted in America by contact with the feces of an infected reduviid bug, which lives in the cracks of walls and roofs of houses, and bites by night. This disease is also a risk of blood transfusions in Central and South America. The CDC recommends complete avoidance of overnight stays in dwellings which might possibly be infected by reduviid bugs, but of course this is very difficult advice for some anthropologists to take. The risk can be reduced by spraying one's own dwelling with insecticide, and by sleeping under mosquito nets.

Leishmaniasis

Leishmaniasis, also called "sandfly fever," is transmitted by the bite of phlebotomine sandflies. It can cause a disfiguring, nonhealing ulcer at the site of the bite, and the visceral form will cause fever, enlargement of the liver and spleen, and anemia. According to the CDC, it is a risk to health in all continents which have tropical areas.

Six of the 204 fieldworkers reported problems with leishmaniasis on their expeditions. Three of these report contracting it themselves—one each among the experts in North America, South America, and Africa. Among those who reported that others in their research group contracted the disease, all three were South American regionalists.

Filariasis (Microfilariasis), Also Called Onchocerciasis and River Blindness

Filarial disease is caused by a parasite worm transmitted by blackflies that breed in river water near the equator, in both Africa and Latin America. An estimated 18 million people worldwide suffer from the disease onchocerciasis, reducing their resistance and interfering with circulation. In extreme cases, the disease is caused "elephantiasis" for the grotesque enlargement of body parts that some-times results from the multiplication of the parasites. The offspring of the adult worms are called microfilariae and they cause the eye problems that so often pro-duce blindness.

Four of the 204 fieldworkers report that there were problems with filariasis on their expeditions, one of the Latin Americanists, two of the South Asian special-ists, and one Africanist. One of the sample reports contracting river blindness (onchocerciasis) in the field in West Africa. He reports he is "still trying" to obtain satisfactory medical treatment.

The researchers of the Pygmies, including Irv DeVore, Bob Bailey, Nadine Peacock, and their colleagues, have researched and summarized knowledge about filariasis. One of their project members contracted onchocerciasis and was treated by the drug Ivermectin (Merck Sharp), developed to treat parasites in domestic animals. This drug is currently being widely distributed in West Africa as the best hope of bringing this common disease under control. Other members of the Pygmy Project contracted LoaLoa (loaiasis) and were treated with Hetrazan. These treatments should be administered under hospital conditions, however, because the dead bodies of the parasites can cause a severe reaction after treatment, which may be worse than the disease itself. Irv DeVore (personal communication) has been severely ill several times as a result of infestation and its treatment.

Desmond Clark and Glynn Isaac contracted filariasis when they visited the Pygmy research station briefly in 1984. Barbara Isaac was similarly sick, but the diagnosis was never established. Brooke Thomas (University of Massachusetts, Amherst) got filariasis in lowland Peru in 1983. Geza Teleki at George Washing-ton University has been very ill, hospitalized many times here and in Great Brit-ain, for a form of filariasis that has resisted treatment.

Water-borne Parasites

Schistosomiasis (Bilharzia)

Transmitted not by insects but by water infested with snails, the schistosomiasis parasite is a free-swimming larval fluke that burrows through skin or enters through the mouth, anus, or urethra to infect the body. During its life cycle, it sheds eggs into the urine and feces of the victim, and these eggs, deposited near water, infect snails which hatch the eggs into larva and release the parasite into water where it reinfects humans. Worldwide, it is estimated to infect 200 million people, and causes some 800,000 deaths per year. None of these deaths, as far as I have been able to learn, has been to anthropologists.

Schistosomiasis is a chronic disease, rarely cured without treatment. Wading and swimming in fresh water in most rural areas of developing countries involves a substantial risk of schistosomiasis. The best indicator of its risk is whether the local people have it.

Three of the 204 fieldworkers report that researchers have contracted it on their expeditions. Frequently the first symptom is blood in the urine. Diagnosis can be made during the early weeks of the disease by microscopic examination of stool and urine, where eggs of the fluke will be found in large numbers. Additional symptoms in the early stage are fever, lack of appetite, weight loss, abdominal pain, weakness, headaches, joint and muscle pain, diarrhea, nausea, and cough. Chronic infections can be extremely debilitating, including serious disease of lungs, liver, intestines, and bladder. Fortunately, curative medication is available, although chemoprophylactic treatment has not been successful, as in the case of malaria. Neglected bilharzia can produce very badly damaged kidneys, causing general swelling of the body and ultimately, death.

According to Louis Leakey, "nobody bothered much about bilharzia," which is endemic in the water where they did their work on the islands in Lake Victoria. The whole family got bilharzia in 1954, and Louis, Jonathan, and Richard were hospitalized. Mary was treated at home and had bad reactions to the treatment, which consisted of doses of antimony tartrate (M. Leakey 1984:114). Louis Leakey got it three times, and the painful treatment left him weak and thin for a year afterward (Cole 1975:219). He also tells of bathing in bilharzia-infested water during visits of distinguished American visitors. "I've had it so often it doesn't matter any more," he told the horrified Americans.

Most of those who work in Central Africa seem to run the risk of bilharzia. Nicholas David (University of Calgary) had intestinal bilharzia in Cameroon (1986). Robert Netting (University of Arizona) has had mild cases in Nigeria, but has become more cautious about taking risks with it over the years. He said one day, "I guess many of us start out willing to risk it, but the first time you see blood in your urine you might starting thinking again."

The risk can be reduced by avoiding wading and swimming in infested water, or temporarily, one can spread insect repellent on the exposed parts of the body. Longer term protection might consist of covering exposed skin with clothing or waterproof waders or boots. Some investigators say that smearing Vaseline on the exposed parts of the body prevents infection but another informant comments that it is time consuming and a source of merriment to others to see the Vaseline being applied, so that it is really a serious interference with the ability to work. In the long run, the solution to the problem of schistosomiasis will be a vaccine to produce immunity, and medical research on that subject is moving forward steadily (Capron et al. 1987:1065–1072).

Aside from bilharzia, contracted from wading, bathing, or swimming, other parasites are transmitted by water through drinking or by eating infected food.

Amebiasis

Amebiasis is an infection of protozoan life forms, carried usually in water, sometimes in food (Table 9.2). It is a diarrheal disease, and cysts of the protozoa are passed in human stools and are extremely infectious to others. It may be transmitted by food, or drink, from the cook or from the hands of the patient.

Table 9.2. Amebiasis

	N. America	Europe	L. America	India	Africa	Pacific	Total
Total	61	17	63	17	23	23	204
Had condition, self	1	1	11	5	4	3	25
	2%	6%	17%	29%	17%	13%	12%
Others in group had it	1	0	9	1	3	1	15
	4%	6%	32%	35%	30%	17%	20%

Table 9.3. Amebic Dysentery

	N. America	Europe	L. America	India	Africa	Pacific	Total
Total	61	17	63	17	23	23	204
Had condition, self	3	1	10	4	5	3	26
	5%	6%	16%	23%	22%	13%	13%
Others in group had it	2	1	6	3	5	1	18
	8%	12%	25%	41%	43%	17%	22%

Thomas Gibson, University of Rochester, was hospitalized for amebiasis in 1979 in the Philippines. Alfred Harris, also of the University of Rochester, had hepatic amebiasis and was finally diagnosed and treated in the Hospital for Tropical Diseases in London.

Amebic Dysentery

Amebic parasites are carried in food and water, ultimately from the feces of infected people who cannot help but shed the parasites and risk infecting others. They produce a diarrheal disease, which is called dysentery when accompanied by blood in the stool (Table 9.3). Severe amebic dysentery produces abscesses in the liver which can be life-threatening. Amebic dysentery can be distinguished from bacterial dysentery (see Shigella, or bacillary dysentery, Chapter 10) by the absence of fever in the amebic form. Amebic dysentery can be treated, but is better prevented by protecting your sources of food and drink from infection.

Some 36 cases of notable illness were reported by volunteers, making it one of the most frequent complaints. People tend not to go into details about the form this illness took, probably because it is an unattractive and even humiliating illness. The most complete case histories are provided about the illness of children who contract amebic dysentery in the field; their loss of weight and dehydration can be dramatic and frightening. Several parents tell of having to leave their fieldwork to take a child to a hospital or to a place where treatment by a physician was possible, and one parent tells of moving the field site from a remote island to a mainland village after his child nearly died from dysentery and the parents could · not reach help quickly.

Giardiasis

Another form of parasitic diarrhea is giardiasis, caused by a common small parasite, giardia, that is carried in fecal contamination of food or water (Table

9.4). It can be diagnosed by its symptoms and treated specifically. Knowing whether giardia is locally prevalent will help with diagnosis, but again prevention, by maintaining hygienic standards in the camp kitchen and water supply, is the best treatment. Because the giardia parasite is considerably larger than bacteria and viruses, filtering water can provide an effective shield against giardia, but other microbes will remain as a problem. In the northwest United States, some of the apparently pure mountain streams now contain giardia, and protection can be obtained by filtering water. Boiling continues to be a superior method of water purification for most situations.

Many people who have giardiasis call it "travelers' diarrhea," or "Gyppy belly," "Montezuma's revenge," and other names. Those who have had it properly diagnosed include Jim Green (University of Washington) who had it several times in Pakistan in the early 1980s, and Charles Keyes and his wife (University of Washington) who got it in Thailand in the 1960s, 1970s, and 1980s. Robert Levy (University of California at San Diego), who is an M.D. as well as a Ph.D., got giardiasis in Nepal, where the infection did permanent damage by scarring the lining of his intestinal tract. He has persistent difficulties with digestion.

Ascariasis (Roundworms)

The large worms called ascarids are transmitted as eggs through fecal contamination of food or drink to another body, where they hatch and grow. The young worms travel to the lungs, from which they are coughed up and swallowed, and thereby reach the intestines, where they attach themselves and grow to their full size (up to 30 cm.). Ascariasis is an example of the kind of hazard and experience that North Americans do not ordinarily meet in their everyday lives, and which can be truly horrifying to those unprepared for them. In addition, more serious consequences of ascariasis can include pneumonia, asthma, choking, and convulsions (especially in children).

Table 9.5 shows that overall, about 10% of researchers have had to deal with ascariasis in the field at some time, and that those who work in Asia and the Pacific and in the Indian subcontinent are particularly likely to encounter it.

Among volunteer informants, Alan Beals reports being infected in India in the 1950s. Geoffrey A. Clark (Arizona State University) got ascariasis in Turkey in the late 1960s and early 1970s. Clark's weight dropped from a normal 145 pounds to 117 pounds and remained there for more than two years while the infection persisted. The treatment (at Billings Hospital, University of Chicago) was primarily doses of arsenic, which produced unpleasant side effects of headaches and nausea.

Table 9.4. Giardiasis

	N. America	Europe	L. America	India	Africa	Pacific	Total
Total	61	17	63	17	23	23	204
Had condition, self	1	1	5	2	1	2	12
	2%	*6%*	*8%*	*12%*	*4%*	*8%*	*6%*
Others in group had it	2	0	5	1	2	0	10
	5%	*6%*	*16%*	*18%*	*13%*	*8%*	*11%*

Table 9.5. Ascariasis

	N. America	Europe	L. America	India	Africa	Pacific	Total
Total	61	17	63	17	23	23	204
Had condition, self	1	0	4	3	3	6	17
	2%	0%	6%	18%	13%	26%	8%
Others in group had it	0	0	2	1	0	1	4
	2%	0%	10%	24%	13%	30%	10%

Table 9.6. Tapeworm

	N. America	Europe	L. America	India	Africa	Pacific	Total
Total	61	17	63	17	23	23	204
Had condition, self	0	0	2	1	1	1	5
			3%	6%	4%	4%	2%
Others in group had it	0	0	2	0	0	1	3
	0%	0%	6%	6%	4%	8%	4%

Meat-borne Parasites

Tapeworm Infestation and Trichinosis

These two unpleasant conditions come from parasites transmitted to humans by the meat of cattle, pigs, and, less often, other animals, domesticated or wild.

The tapeworm grows to be several meters long in the intestines, and diagnosis may occur when large pieces are found in feces or extruding from the body (Table 9.6). The life cycle starts when animals (especially pigs) eat human and other feces containing eggs of tapeworms. The eggs hatch in the pig's body and form cysts throughout the flesh. When a person ingests live cysts from eating infected meat that has not been sufficiently cooked, the cysts develop into tapeworms in the human intestine, and the tapeworms may grow to large proportions, while continuing to shed eggs and continue the cycle. When humans eat tapeworm eggs as opposed to cysts (by fecal-oral contamination), the cysts can form throughout the human body, including, in some cases, in the brain.

Steven Piker (Swarthmore) developed tapeworms in Thailand in the 1960s. Michael S. Hopkins (American University, Cairo) got them in the early 1960s in Mali.

Trichinosis is perhaps a less grotesque condition than tapeworm, but a more serious threat to life (Table 9.7). The parasite is obtained by eating pork containing parasitic cysts that have not been killed by thorough cooking. The cysts hatch into worms in the human body and burrow through the intestines into the muscles. They produce serious illness, including fever with chills, muscular pain and internal hemorrhage. They are difficult to eradicate, and medical care is needed. The reaction may be fatal, especially in poorly nourished patients, although no anthropologists are known to have died of them. Both of these conditions can be prevented by strict avoidance of meat that has not been thoroughly cooked.

Table 9.7. Trichinosis

	N. America	Europe	L. America	India	Africa	Pacific	Total
Total	61	17	63	17	23	23	204
Had condition, self	0	0	1	0	1	0	2
			1%		*4%*		*1%*
Others in group had it	0	1	1	0	0	0	2
	0%	*6%*	*3%*	*0%*	*4%*	*0%*	*2%*

Table 9.8. Hookworm

	N. America	Europe	L. America	India	Africa	Pacific	Total
Total	61	17	63	17	23	23	204
Had condition, self	0	0	2	0	2	6	6
			3%		*9%*	*26%*	*3%*
Others in group had it	0	0	4	1	0	0	5
	0%	*0%*	*10%*	*6%*	*9%*	*26%*	*5%*

Soil-borne Parasites

Hookworm

Hookworms are small, red worms that can live in large numbers in the intestines without necessarily revealing their presence (Table 9.8). Symptoms are anemia, weakness, and failure to grow (in children). They are contracted by walking on soil infected with the minute worms, which burrow through bare feet. They circulate through the bloodstream, eventually settling in the lungs, from which they are coughed up into the throat and swallowed. The adult hookworms attach themselves to the intestines where they can live, producing eggs, for long periods. A heavy infestation of worms can produce severe anemia. The eggs in the feces hatch in damp soil and migrate to the surface, to be taken into the feet (or paws) of a new host. We note that all regionalists except those of North America and Europe report some experience with hookworm, with the rates for Latin America and Asia and the Pacific being especially high.

Air-borne Parasitic Diseases

Histoplasmosis

Histoplasmosis is a disease of the immune system caused by inhaling fungus. Its symptoms are fever, anemia, and emaciation. No one in the sample reported histoplasmosis, but it has been known to occur to archaeologists and physical anthropologists.

Valley Fever (Coccidioidomycosis)

Valley fever is not confined to archaeologists. Farmers and others who work closely with the soil in the Central Valley of California and a few other locations where the spores are found get it too, and indeed, some of them get very sick and even die. But valley fever is remarkable in that it corresponds in eerie ways to the fantasy of ''the Pharaoh's curse''—the cause of death that lurks in old materials and kills anyone who disturbs their peace. Dozens of students and professionals who have dug in the western United States, and especially in California, have contracted this disease, and at least one student died of it during the 1970s.

Valley fever is a disease of fungus, which is inhaled into the lungs and establishes its colonies there. It is very hard to dislodge, and the body's reaction to its presence causes the sickness.

Table 9.9 shows that valley fever has been experienced by something like 15% of the North American researchers. Those classified as European and Latin American almost surely had their experience with valley fever while working in North America. It is interesting to see one condition that does not affect anyone in India, Africa, or the Pacfic.

Most of the cases of valley fever have been contracted in the central valley of California, but other areas have it (or a very similar organism). According to Jane Kelley, of Calgary, a number of the crew members working at "Head Smashed-In" site, a University of Calgary project in southern Alberta, in 1965–66, came down with a fungal illness identical or similar to valley fever. Excavations have continued at that site over the subsequent 20 years without further outbreaks, as the crew now wears masks while in contact with the fine, dry soil of the site. Elizabeth Grobsmith (University of Nebraska) got valley fever during the excavation of a mission site near Tucson, Arizona, some years ago.

Because valley fever is so localized in the soil of specific sites, it ought to be avoidable. Indeed, at least one university was sued by parents for exposing students who could not have known about the threat of the disease in a location where it was predictable. Joe Chartoff (Michigan State University) writes that his experience with valley fever was part of his education as a fieldwork manager. Although he has not dug in a known valley fever area since 1967, he reminds us that good health practices are important for the control of all hazards.

> When I got valley fever as a student in 1962, the crew I was on was living in the worst possible conditions—no tents or other housing, slept on the ground in sleeping bags, no bathing facilities (we were in the field about 3 weeks). Our diet ran to peanut butter, pasta and beer. All but one crew member was stricken [with valley fever]. Since then I have been able to avoid similar problems by keeping my crews clean, well-fed, adequately sheltered and by not driving them to exhaustion.

A difficulty about valley fever is that it is unlikely to be diagnosed outside the specific area where it was contracted. Dirk van der Elst, the Chair at California State University at Fresno, writes that

Table 9.9. Valley Fever

	N. America	Europe	L. America	India	Africa	Pacific	Total
Total	61	17	63	17	23	23	204
Had condition, self	4	1	2	0	0	0	7
	7%	*6%*	*3%*	*0%*	*0%*	*0%*	*3%*
Others in group had it	5	1	4	0	0	0	10
	15%	*12%*	*10%*	*0%*	*0%*	*0%*	*8%*

In 1975, I came down with a fever ranging up to 105° when I was working in Surinam. After two weeks, my wife brought me back to the States. In 1983 I was found to once have had a hefty case of valley fever and it is assumed that this was my jungle fever of 1975. If so, no wonder it wasn't recognized in Surinam.

Parasites can place a heavy burden on the physical functioning of anthropologists, primarily through malaria, but also through a range of diseases. Prevention is always preferable to cure, and any steps that can be taken to prevent exposure to parasites, such as wearing protective clothing and shoes, boiling water, supervising the cook, and digging latrines, are well worthwhile. When a parasitic disease is contracted, the fieldworker must use care and energy in obtaining prompt and adequate medical treatment; and even with the best treatment, some parasitic diseases leave lifelong consequences. Finding out the risks of parasites before going to the field, making a conscious decision to take those risks, and knowing the available treatments are necessary and rational steps toward taking responsibility for health and safety in the field.

CHAPTER 10   INFECTIOUS DISEASES

Infectious diseases are those in which the active agent is a bacteria or a virus. Like parasitic diseases, they may be transmitted from one person to another by insects, the air, water, food, or soil and other surfaces. Instead of acting as a host, however, as it does with most of the parasitic diseases, the human body has evolved elaborate defenses against infectious diseases in the form of antibodies produced by the immune system in response to the presence of the microorganism. In this sense, most of the infectious diseases are "self-limiting," in that the body's response, if successful, brings them to an end.

Leaving the outcome to the body's natural defenses, however, has two great disadvantages: the patient may be miserably sick as the disease runs its course; and the patient may die or be permanently disabled by the results of the sickness. Therefore, medical science assists the body in the struggle with the infectious diseases with two approaches.

Dramatic advances have been made in the preventive area through immunization—delivery of small amounts of the microorganisms (vaccine or toxoid) to trigger the immune process without causing the disease itself. This approach began with the development of a vaccine against smallpox (in the 18th century) and has advanced in the 20th century to a series of shots routinely given to the general population, starting in childhood. These vaccines are effective against most of the highly contagious diseases—measles, mumps, rubella, chicken pox, diphtheria, tetanus, influenza, and poliomyelitis—and are so effective that these diseases have almost disappeared in many parts of the world.

Another series of shots is available for travelers to protect against cholera, yellow fever, tetanus, hepatitis B, rabies, meningitis, pneumonia, and the immune globulins, which protect against hepatitis A and a range of other possible infections. The Centers for Disease Control, U.S. Public Health Service, continually update advice to physicians about immunizations recommended for travelers to each country in the world. A physician can advise in detail about possible side effects of the inoculations, such as allergies and counterindications in pregnancy. The hepatitis B vaccine, for instance, is expensive, but is highly recommended for those in high-risk categories for exposure, which include many anthropologists, especially those who practice bush medicine, treating the local populations for injuries and infections.

Inoculation schedules can be complicated, so it is a good idea to keep a single document on which all immunizations are recorded. The World Health Organization form for documenting the required yellow fever and cholera immunizations has space for recording all shots.

Prevention also involves avoiding the circumstances or conditions by which the disease is transmitted. For this reason, the information on infectious diseases in this chapter is organized by the primary method of transmission, to focus our attention on avoidance, which is prevention's first line of defense.

The second approach of medical science is to treat the disease after it has been contracted. Antibiotic drugs, available for administration in pills, liquids, or injections, have been extremely successful in stopping the reproduction of bacteria in the body or even killing them directly (there has been much less success in control of viruses). When people study "bush medicine," it is usually the drug treatment of infectious diseases that they focus on, since these drugs are the "miracle cures" of Western medicine.

Until the medical advances that followed acceptance of the germ theory of disease in the 20th century, infectious diseases were the primary killers of mankind everywhere, and in many of the parts of the world they still are the major causes of death and disability. Many infectious diseases are so rare in North America today that the risk of contracting them is very slight, while they may be prevalent in parts of the world where fieldwork is done. Hence it is particularly important to keep up immunizations for the entire period during which foreign fieldwork is being done, and to be aware of the means of prevention and treatment of the diseases that are found in the field area.

Air-borne Infections

Colds, Bronchitis, Tonsillitis, Sore Throat, Strep Throat

Infections of the respiratory tract were commonly experienced by our sample during fieldwork, and contributed to the complications of getting the work done. Some of these sicknesses were reported to be severe, and some of them required medical care, but none of them produced long-term consequences, an end to fieldwork, or death.

The rate of respiratory infections is fairly high in or out of the field: the average person gets a cold at least every few years and some people get several a year. If the rates are somewhat higher in the field, it may be that fieldworkers are exposed to wider extremes of temperature than they would be at home, or to more irritants, such as the smoke of cooking fires, in the field than at home, and they may be in close contact with a larger population experiencing these infections.

The respiratory virus diseases tend to be highly contagious and highly local. The visiting anthropologist, unprotected by antibodies created in previous exposures, can expect to contract the local strains. Similarly, the local people will be vulnerable to the respiratory infections that the anthropologist inadvertently brings to the field. At my own research site in the Kalahari desert, when a truck from another area would arrive, a wave of colds could be seen moving through the population like a circle of ripples moving out from a stone tossed in the water.

None of the volunteer informants reported colds, which are so common as to be invisible. Two volunteers reported hospitalization or serious illnesses that resulted as complications of "strep" throat or tonsillitis, one to self and the other to a child. In addition to the infections listed in Table 10.1, diphtheria was reported by three individuals out of the 204 respondents, and six reported problems with whooping cough. These diseases are rarely seen in the United States and Canada, but may still be common in other parts of the world, and their occurrence in the sample should remind us of the need to keep inoculations up to date.

Table 10.1. Colds and Respiratory Infections

	N. America	Europe	L. America	India	Africa	Pacific	Total
Total	61	17	63	17	23	23	204
Colds							
Had condition, self	29	10	32	11	15	16	113
	47%	*59%*	*51%*	*65%*	*65%*	*70%*	*55%*
Others in group had it	16	3	8	0	2	1	30
	74%	*76%*	*63%*	*65%*	*74%*	*74%*	*70%*
Sore Throat							
Had condition, self	10	4	13	5	9	9	50
	16%	*24%*	*21%*	*29%*	*39%*	*39%*	*25%*
Others in group had it	12	5	10	4	4	2	37
	36%	*53%*	*37%*	*53%*	*56%*	*48%*	*43%*
Bronchitis							
Had condition, self	2	3	10	3	5	3	26
	3%	*18%*	*16%*	*18%*	*22%*	*13%*	*13%*
Others in group had it	6	3	3	2	3	2	19
	13%	*36%*	*21%*	*29%*	*35%*	*22%*	*22%*
Tonsillitis							
Had condition, self	0	0	3	1	0	0	4
	0%	*0%*	*5%*	*6%*	*0%*	*0%*	*2%*
Others in group had it	2	1	4	0	2	1	10
	3%	*6%*	*11%*	*6%*	*9%*	*4%*	*5%*

Table 10.2. Tuberculosis

	N. America	Europe	L. America	India	Africa	Pacific	Total
Total	61	17	63	17	23	23	204
Had condition, self	0	1	1	0	1	0	3
	0%	*6%*	*2%*	*0%*	*4%*	*0%*	*2%*
Others in group had it	1	0	3	1	0	0	5
	2%	*6%*	*6%*	*6%*	*4%*	*0%*	*4%*

Tuberculosis (TB)

The tuberculosis (TB) bacillus is as common as the cold virus in some parts of the world, and researchers and their families who have never been exposed to TB may suddenly be surrounded by coughing people who carry it (Table 10.2). Generally speaking, this is not a terrible risk for well-nourished adults. Even if the infection is contracted, it can generally be cured by drug treatment without long-term consequences for health. But occasionally a child may have a more severe reaction to the infection, and one volunteer informant reported having to curtail fieldwork in order to provide the conditions for a cure for her child. Pulmonary TB, acquired by droplet inhalation from infected patients, can usually be successfully treated with a doctor's guidance without leaving the field. Bovine TB, which is acquired by drinking milk from infected cows, may cause dangerous lesions in bones or organs and may require careful management under a physician's care.

An important part of a pretrip health examination is a tine TB test, to determine whether one is negative in antibodies to the bacillus before one goes. That way, a positive test after the trip will tell you that you have been exposed recently. After a positive TB skin test your doctor may want to X-ray your lungs as a baseline for treatment after exposure. There is an immunization, B.C.G., against tuberculosis, and your doctor can advise whether it would be a good idea for you and other members of your research group to have it before you go.

Pneumonia

Pneumonia, in its various forms, is a potentially serious disease that is not much of a threat to well-nourished people with access to antibiotics. However, when a person is worn down, overtired, poorly nourished, under stress and so forth, the illness may develop into a serious pulmonary infection in which fluid accumulates in the lungs and the patient suffers lack of oxygen. Among the !Kung and many people in the world, the primary cause of death of the local people is pneumonia. It is rarely the initial cause, but is often a complication that develops after a fall, a hunting accident, dysentery, or malaria.

When fieldworkers contract pneumonia in the field they should consider, along with the immediate treatment of the disease, whether they have been taking adequate care of their health by getting good food, enough rest, and so on. Pneumonia, like fatigue and sores that won't heal, may be a signal that the body needs better care. A vaccine is now available that protects against the 23 types of *Streptococcus pneumoniae* that account for 90% of bacterial pneumonia. The vaccine is recommended for workers who have suffered from other diseases that put them at high risk of pneumonia, such as malaria and hepatitis. It may also be recommended for anthropologists who provide medical care to local people.

Table 10.3 shows that about 10% of the fieldworkers have had to deal with pneumonia in the field among their research group at one time or another, indicating that those who work away from easy access to medical care need to learn to use antibiotic treatment.

Water- and Food-borne Infectious Diseases

Diarrheas and Dysentery

Infectious hazards to the intestinal tract include salmonella (often called "food poisoning"), typhoid fever (a severe variety of salmonella), and paratyphoid, *E.*

Table 10.3. Pneumonia

	N. America	Europe	L. America	India	Africa	Pacific	Total
Total	61	17	63	17	23	23	204
Had condition, self	2	2	3	1	1	1	10
	3%	12%	5%	6%	4%	4%	5%
Others in group had it	2	0	5	1	2	0	10
	7%	12%	13%	12%	13%	4%	10%

Coli infections, and the vague complaint that people describe as "travelers' diarrhea," which might be any of the above or one of the parasitic gut infections. Generally speaking, those who used the vaguer terminology did not see a doctor about their complaint.

Travelers' diarrheas, like colds, are common and might have been experienced even if the researcher had stayed home, as the microorganisms are plentiful almost everywhere. When traveling, however, people eat more food in restaurants and other places that may not be sanitary, may eat food that has been stored without refrigeration under conditions that encourage bacterial growth, and they may be particularly susceptible to infection due to jet lag, fatigue, stress, unfamiliar conditions, and so on. It is common to encounter different strains of microorganisms while traveling than one might have known at home, and to respond by illness until an immune defense is built. In any case, these problems are more the rule than the exception, and although many patients feel miserable, they are only mildly ill.

Few escape the experience of diarrheal disease entirely when they do fieldwork (Table 10.4). Effects can be minimized by eating and drinking sparingly or (better) not at all when the sources are suspect, and by providing oneself with a continual supply of safe food and water. Disinfecting or boiling water consistently

Table 10.4. Diarrheal Diseases

	N. America	Europe	L. America	India	Africa	Pacific	Total
Total	61	17	63	17	23	23	204
Travelers' Diarrhea							
Had condition, self	20	5	48	13	17	16	119
	33%	*29%*	*76%*	*76%*	*74%*	*70%*	*58%*
Others in group had it	3	5	6	2	4	1	22
	38%	*59%*	*86%*	*88%*	*91%*	*74%*	*69%*
E. Coli Infections							
Had condition, self	4	2	14	5	5	2	32
	7%	*12%*	*22%*	*29%*	*22%*	*9%*	*16%*
Others in group had it	2	2	7	2	3	1	17
	10%	*24%*	*33%*	*41%*	*35%*	*13%*	*24%*
Typhoid fever							
Had condition, self	0	0	3	1	2	0	6
	0%	*0%*	*5%*	*6%*	*9%*	*0%*	*3%*
Others in group had it	2	0	6	0	2	0	10
	3%	*0%*	*14%*	*6%*	*17%*	*0%*	*8%*
Paratyphoid							
Had condition, self	0	0	6	1	0	0	7
	0%	*0%*	*10%*	*6%*	*0%*	*0%*	*3%*
Others in group had it	2	0	3	1	1	0	7
	3%	*0%*	*14%*	*6%*	*4%*	*0%*	*7%*
Salmonella (Food Poisoning)							
Had condition, self	2	0	10	2	0	2	16
	3%	*0%*	*16%*	*12%*	*0%*	*9%*	*8%*
Others in group had it	4	1	7	1	1	1	15
	10%	*6%*	*27%*	*18%*	*4%*	*13%*	*15%*

would prevent a great deal of intense discomfort. The lucky and the careful have diarrheal disease only occasionally and for brief periods, while some who cannot or choose not to control their intake of food and water may have diarrheas more or less constantly. When diarrhea is contracted, giving fluids to prevent dehydration is the major concern. Dark urine and headaches accompanying diarrhea may be a sign that more fluids are needed. And of course it is particularly important that the fluids offered are free of microorganisms and parasites.

The immediate problem with diarrheal disease is dehydration. Longer-term complications of chronic diarrhea include weight loss, malnutrition, and scarring of the intestinal tract, which can cause lifelong problems. There is a vaccination against typhoid fever, which is 70–90% effective, but it cannot substitute for care in protecting food and water sources from contamination. The vaccine that combines protection from typhoid and paratyphoid is not recommended by the CDC (but up-to-date advice should be sought).

By volunteer accounts, nine people have been reported to have suffered from typhoid fever during fieldwork, and two reported paratyphoid. Peru, Mexico, and India are the most frequently mentioned sites at which these illnesses were contracted. Many of these cases required hospitalization, and several caused the curtailment of a fieldwork project.

Children are much more susceptible to diarrheal disease than adults, because their smaller body volume suffers dehydration more quickly. The key to treatment of diarrheal disease is rehydration, with plain (pure) water for mild cases, and with a special rehydration solution for serious cases and especially for infants and small children. A serious first aid kit should have many packets of the inexpensive powder that makes the rehydration formula for local distribution as well as for treatment of the members of the research group. With clean water and this powder, lives can be saved.

Cholera

Cholera is an extremely dangerous and unpleasant infection of the digestive tract that causes virtually continual diarrhea for days. The risks of severe dehydration are very great for the patient, especially for children. Two anthropologists in the sample, one who works primarily in North America and one in East Asia, report that they suffered from cholera in the field.

There is a cholera vaccine available, and anyone who works in a cholera area where the food and water supply cannot be protected from infection should have the inoculation. It is particularly needed for children, although the vaccine is not known to be safe and effective for children under six months of age. The treatment of an active case of cholera is rehydration therapy, which is particularly difficult to achieve because of the rapidity of the fluid loss. Cholera is extremely contagious from the diarrheal material, and those doing the nursing must be careful not to become infected.

Bacillary Dysentery (Shigellosis)

Bacillary dysentery is a serious infection of the digestive tract that produces diarrhea and dehydration. About a fifth of the sample report that they or someone in their field group had it (Table 10.5). The rate is particularly high for those who

Table 10.5. Bacillary Dysentery—Shigellosis

	N. America	Europe	L. America	India	Africa	Pacific	Total
Total	61	17	63	17	23	23	204
Had condition, self	4	2	10	8	8	3	26
	6%	*12%*	*16%*	*47%*	*35%*	*13%*	*13%*
Others in group had it	2	0	8	1	1	0	12
	10%	*12%*	*29%*	*53%*	*39%*	*13%*	*19%*

work in Latin America, Africa, and India, where the majority of anthropologists reported experience with it in the field. (Dysentery, incidentally, technically means the presence of blood in the feces, and physicians generally prefer to describe the disease by its causative agent, shigella, rather than its symptoms.)

Bacillary dysentery tends to be experienced by everyone in a research group, if anyone gets it. Eleven volunteers came forward to tell of experience with bacillary dysentery. One was a chairman, who took an informal survey of his department of twenty professionals: four of them reported bacillary dysentery. Five of the eleven volunteers mentioned that children and other family members also were sick from it when the primary fieldworker got it, and another five mentioned that they had had multiple experiences with it. One, who reported seven separate occasions in central Niger, said "I simply wasn't sufficiently careful in what I ate." Another reported, "We had dysentery, dehydration and malnourishment as a result of living like the people, drinking the water, the summer heat, and our impoverished graduate student finances."

Bacillary dysentery is a disease of poor hygiene, and can be controlled by boiling the drinking water and taking care that food is fresh and uncontaminated. There is no vaccine against bacillary dysentery, and the CDC does not recommend prophylactic use of antibiotics to prevent it. To obtain the best medical advice for controlling and responding to all these diarrheal diseases, consult the CDC annual, *Health Information for International Travel* when planning research.

Hepatitis: Type A, B, and "Non-A, Non-B"

If we judge the importance of diseases by a combination of prevalence and seriousness of consequences, hepatitis might be said to be the most (or one of the most) important diseases of fieldwork (Hesser 1987).

Hepatitis is a viral disease that involves the liver. There are several types—A, B, and a kind called "non-A, non-B." In Table 10.6 we use the term *Other* for those who don't know which kind they had or what the difference is. It is an indicator of the lack of accurate perception of the dangers of fieldwork that so many of the references to hepatitis fall into this vague category. I also add "jaundice" to this table, although jaundice is technically a symptom rather than an infectious disease, because of this same lack of clarity as to what sickness is involved.

The liver diseases together form an identifiable group, and this table includes an indicator of those who reported none of them, as well as the numbers for each type. Note that 70% of those who work in South Asia report having had some experience with liver disease, and 44% of those who work in Africa. Hepatitis stands out from the other risk factors as having a strong correlation with the type of living conditions in the field, specifically as related to situations in which an-

Table 10.6. Hepatitis and Other Infectious Diseases of the Liver

	N. America	Europe	L. America	India	Africa	Pacific	Total
Total	61	17	63	17	23	23	204
Hepatitis A							
Had condition, self	1	0	3	2	3	2	11
	2%	0%	5%	12%	13%	9%	5%
Others in group had it	1	0	8	4	3	0	16
	3%	0%	17%	35%	26%	9%	13%
Hepatitis B							
Had condition, self	0	0	1	1	1	0	3
	0%	0%	2%	6%	4%	0%	1%
Others in group had it	1	0	1	1	0	0	3
	2%	0%	3%	12%	4%	0%	3%
Hepatitis "Other" (Non-A, Non-B, and Type Not Known)							
Had condition, self	0	2	0	5	1	0	8
	0%	12%	0%	29%	4%	0%	4%
Others in group had it	2	2	5	2	0	0	11
	3%	23%	8%	41%	4%	0%	9%
Jaundice							
Had condition, self	0	1	0	1	0	1	3
	0%	6%	0%	6%	0%	4%	1%
Others in group had it	0	1	1	1	2	0	5
	0%	12%	2%	12%	8%	4%	4%
None of the above	56	12	47	5	13	19	152
Percentage of Total	92%	71%	75%	29%	56%	83%	75%

thropologists employ local cooks to prepare their food for them. It seems that those who prepare their own food and even those who eat in hotels and institutions manage better to avoid the fecal contamination of food that is the immediate cause of most liver disease.

Type A, or infectious hepatitis (also sometimes called infectious jaundice) is spread by fecally contaminated food and water. Overall, 13% of the sample report that they contracted it in the field, or someone in their research group did. Type A hepatitis is the usual cause of the yellowish skin of anthropologists, of their inability to drink liquor, and of the early nights of a substantial portion of the participants at the annual meetings of the American Anthropological Association. It is very easy to contract, it can be found in practically all parts of the world, and it makes one terribly sick.

Some of the people who report having had hepatitis A are:

Michael Agar (University of Maryland) in India in 1965.
Alan Beals (University of California, Riverside) (and his wife and two children), in India in 1965.
H. Russell Bernard (University of Florida) in Mexico in 1968.
Ronald Cohen (University of Florida) in Nigeria, in the 1970s, was in the hospital 2 months, nearly died.
Lauren A. Corwin (Cleveland State) in Calcutta in 1974, hospitalized a month, out of work fall quarter.
George Cowgill (Brandeis), northern Guatemala in 1959, ill for a month.
Irv DeVore (Harvard) in Africa in 1968.

Bernard Gallin (Michigan State), 1970, returning from a year's fieldwork in Taiwan and travel in Africa and Asia.

Charles Leslie (University of Delaware) (and wife and 4-year-old child) in Mexico, 1954.

Herb Lewis (University of Wisconsin, Madison), and wife, Marcia, contracted hepatitis in Ethiopia, 1966.

Robert A. Littlewood (Washington State) (and wife) in New Guinea in 1962.

David Lubell (University of Alberta) (and team) working in Algeria. Lubell was evacuated to a hospital in Algeria, a team member returned to Belgium. The field season was cancelled early.

Sheryl Miller (Pitzer College) had a very serious case in India while she was a student.

June Nash (City University of New York) had it bad in Mexico in 1954.

Miles E. Richardson (Louisiana State), 1972 in Costa Rica.

Susan Stonick (University of West Virginia) in Central Mexico, 1986.

R. Brooke Thomas (University of Massachusetts, Amherst), during 1968 in Highland Peru.

Deborah Winslow (University of New Hampshire), was sick 3 months in Sri Lanka in 1973.

Clearly this list is not complete: the reader and compiler become exhausted long before the number of cases. The cost of hepatitis to anthropologists has been very high over the years, and we note in the list of dates above that researchers are still getting it.

For a double knock-out, there is a tendency to come down with hepatitis A a few weeks after contracting malaria. Among those who report having had this nasty combination of ills are Laura Nader (1969:103–104) in Mexico, Hildred Geertz (Princeton) in Sumatra in 1958, and Katharine Milton (University of California, Berkeley) in Venezuela, in 1987.

Hepatitis B, also called serum hepatitis, can be contracted through sexual relations, through contact with blood, through transfusions and unsterile needles, and through insect bites (especially those of bed bugs). It has a substantial fatality rate. In some parts of the world, it is very prevalent.

Bernice Kaplan (Wayne State University) had a badly infected flea bite in the field while working in Mexico at high altitude. The local doctor who lanced the infection sterilized his instruments inadequately, and she developed a serious case of what was probably hepatitis B.

Glynn Isaac (Harvard University) died October 1985 at a U.S. Naval Hospital in Japan where he was airlifted from China, after he had become seriously ill while on a lecture tour. His wife, Barbara Isaac, writes that the final diagnosis of the cause of his death was hepatitis B. Glynn Isaac's fieldwork in Africa over a period of 30 years had exposed him to many risks, and although he was a thoughtful and sensible worker, aware of a wide range of dangers, his level of exposure over a long period of time must have been very great. The death of Glynn Isaac at 47, in the middle of an enormously productive career, has been a very great loss to the field of African prehistory.

Another prominent anthropologist, Lawrence Angel (Smithsonian Institution) contracted non-A, non-B hepatitis from a blood transfusion during an operation, and died from it in 1986. Angel's work in physical anthropology with skeletal material might have involved special hazards, but it seems that Angel's illness was not field- or laboratory-related. Many fieldworkers contract the non-A, non-B form of hepatitis, especially in India, according to our sample.

Insect-borne Diseases

Insect-transmitted infectious diseases are rather like parasitic diseases in that one must know the actions of the insect vectors in order to avoid or control them.

The diseases listed here are not as prevalent or life-threatening as some, but are unpleasant and debilitating.

Dengue Fever

Dengue fever, a viral disease transmitted by mosquitoes, is often called "breakbone fever" because of the severe muscle cramps and aches it produces in its victims. It is endemic in the South Pacific, tropical Asia, most of the Caribbean and Central America, and in some parts of South America and Africa. It is found in urban areas as well as rural, and tends to break out in the form of local epidemics. The mosquito that transmits it is unusual in that it is primarily active in the daytime rather than the evening or night; thus, prevention depends more upon protective clothing and insect repellent than on screens and mosquito nets.

There was at least one case at the 1985–86 field school in Jamaica, according to the Texas A&M chairman. Donald Sade contracted a severe dengue type II infection while working in the Caribbean. Art Hansen (University of Florida) got it in the Dominican Republic. Others report contracting it in Sri Lanka, the Philippines, and India. One person reports getting hepatitis A simultaneously with dengue fever, under conditions where he could not get medical help. He reports tersely, "I just rode it out." The random sample reports the following experience with dengue fever (Table 10.7).

Rocky Mountain Spotted Fever, Lyme Disease, and Tick Typhus

Rocky Mountain Spotted Fever is caused by the bacteria *Rickettsia rickettsii*, and is transmitted to people by the bite of a wood or animal tick. There is no reliable vaccine available to protect against it in advance. The course of the illness is fairly slow but extremely severe and life-threatening, so medical care should be obtained if one is fairly sure that it has infected someone in the research group.

Tick bites should be avoided by wearing protective clothing in endemic areas and avoiding transfer of ticks from dogs. At least once a day, researchers in such an area should inspect their bodies to look for ticks, which have the habit of attaching themselves to the skin for a long meal where they have bitten. If a tick is found, it should be carefully removed with tweezers and the wound cleaned, in the hope of avoiding the transmission of bacteria and infection.

Three to 14 days after an infected bite, the disease starts with mild symptoms of chills, loss of appetite, and sense of illness. Some 2 to 6 days later, a red rash appears, along with chills, fever, headache, photosensitivity of the eyes, and mental confusion. This stage lasts about two weeks, with an increasingly severe

Table 10.7. Dengue Fever

	N. America	Europe	L. America	India	Africa	Pacific	Total
Total	61	17	63	17	23	23	204
Had condition, self	0	0	0	4	1	2	7
				24%	4%	9%	3%
Others in group had it	2	0	1	1	0	0	4
	3%	0%	2%	29%	4%	9%	5%

rash and subdural hemorrhages. In untreated cases, the mortality rate is said to be 20–30%; treated, the rate is reduced to 3–10% (Wilkerson 1985:364).

Five cases of Rocky Mountain Spotted Fever were reported by our 204 informants, three by North Americanists and two among Asian scholars. The chairman of a major department who was particularly conscientious in reporting the hazards to health and safety experienced by members of that department tells of five cases—two in the summer of 1979 and three in the summer of 1981—all in rural western state archaeology sites. A two-year-old child accompanying his parents on a dig just outside Los Angeles got Rocky Mountain Spotted Fever a generation ago.

Lyme disease, similar to Rocky Mountain Spotted Fever in that it is transmitted by ticks, has recently been recognized as prevalent in the western United States as well as in Connecticut and the eastern United States where it was first recognized. It is a danger to archaeologists and others who work in areas where wildlife is common. The ticks may be carried by deer, dogs, or other animals, and they may be picked up from vegetation where they have fallen off infected animals, as well as from contact with the animal itself. The disease consists of arthritis-like symptoms in the early stages, followed by brain and central nervous system involvement. It can be extremely debilitating, and those who work in U.S. forest areas should explore its distribution, prevention, and treatment carefully. The California Archaeological Society has an informative booklet on the disease, as an occupational hazard of local archaeology.

People living in East Africa, South Africa, and especially Ethiopia have to watch out for the severe influenzal disease of tick typhus. The microorganism is injected into the human host by the bite of a tick, most often picked up from a dog, but also possibly encountered walking through long grass. Tick typhus can be fatal, but it was not reported by anyone in the sample.

Yellow Fever

People are likely to have more trouble from the yellow fever shots that they must undergo for travel to certain areas than from yellow fever itself. The disease still does exist in parts of Africa and South America.

There is an urban type—an epidemic viral type transmitted person-to-person by mosquito bite infection—and a jungle type, also transmitted by mosquitoes. The jungle type is maintained in nonhuman primate reservoirs, which might imply that primatologists are most likely to be infected. This is a fever rather than a diarrheal disease. Three of the 204 in the sample of fieldworkers reported that someone in their research group had experienced yellow fever, in each case a colleague. Two of these were Latin Americanists, and one a North Americanist who was working in Africa when this sickness struck his colleague.

Brucellosis (Undulent Fever, Malta Fever)

This is a milk-borne infection, not primarily diarrheal, which is transmitted from cattle and goats to humans. It can also be acquired by workers who milk affected cattle or goats or who handle hides. Only one researcher reported experience with this in the field, a Latin Americanist who had it occur to someone in his research group. It can be prevented by boiling any milk consumed and handling hides of possibly infected animals with care. A volunteer informant tells of contracting the disease from a recently dead bear in the wild. She was aware of the danger but knew that the people she worked with value bear paws highly for making jewelry, and she took the risk of a close examination of the animal. The illness was very debilitating and long-lasting for her.

Venereal Diseases

The venereal diseases are hard to study, because there is always the problem of how accurate the reports will be. Getting gonorrhea in the field implies sexual relations with someone who carries the disease, most likely a member of the local group. There has never been a clear agreement among anthropologists on the norms and ethics of having sexual relations with the subjects of study in the field. Some do (Cesara 1982; Heinz 1979; Rasmussen 1976), some do not, and many do not say. After pretesting the questionnaire, I decided that the dangers of losing informants was greater than the value of the data obtained, and I gave up asking whether the researcher and/or members of the research group had engaged in sexual relations with local people during the research.

I did, however, add venereal diseases to the checklist of possible problems. Table 10.8 provides the responses. The table does not show the percentages of regionalists who had experience with the various diseases, because there are so few of them. Certainly venereal diseases are not unknown among researchers; neither are they frequently admitted (if contracted). Note that the most commonly reported—yeast infections—may be transmitted venereally, but might equally well have been brought from home or acquired in the field in some way other than by sexual contact. Yeast infections tend to flourish in the field due to poor hygiene and a lack of bathing facilities.

Table 10.8. Venereal Diseases

	N. America	Europe	L. America	India	Africa	Pacific	Total
Total	61	17	63	17	23	23	204
Gonorrhea							
Had condition, self	0	0	0	0	0	2	2
Others in group had it	3	0	1	1	0	0	5
Syphilis							
Had condition, self	0	0	1	0	1	0	2
Others in group had it	0	0	0	0	0	0	0
Herpes (genital)							
Had condition, self	0	0	1	0	0	0	1
Others in group had it	2	0	1	0	0	0	3
Chlamydia							
Had condition, self	0	0	1	0	0	0	1
Others in group had it	0	1	0	0	0	0	1
Yeast Infections (of vagina)							
Had condition, self	3	2	5	1	0	1	12
	5%	*12%*	*8%*	*6%*	*0%*	*4%*	*6%*
Others in group had it	5	3	6	1	1	6	22
	13%	*29%*	*17%*	*12%*	*4%*	*30%*	*16%*

AIDS

The most potentially dangerous of the diseases transmitted by intimate contact is undoubtedly AIDS. Public health officials warn us that this fatal disease is a worldwide epidemic that could wipe out whole populations of people. In parts of Uganda, Kenya, and central West Africa, it is said that the HIV antibody, which indicates exposure to the disease, may already be found in large segments of the population. And while the U.S. epidemic has primarily struck homosexual and bisexual men and intravenous drug users, it affects heterosexual and non-drug-using men and women in a broad area of central Africa.

While there are large numbers of AIDS cases among the U.S. population, and large numbers in parts of Africa, Haiti, and other areas, no anthropologists in the sample reported having contracted AIDS on the questionnaire, and no cases have been reported in this study. The *Anthropology Newsletter* of February 1989 reports that Kenneth W. Payne, a 1985 Ph.D. from University of California-Berkeley, died of AIDS in November 1988.

Miscellaneous Infectious Diseases

There are a whole string of infectious diseases that only a few people reported happened to them or someone in the research group. These include roseola (5), mumps (5), rubella (4), polio (2), measles (5), and chicken pox (7). Many of these diseases are endemic in developing countries, and occurred to children of field-workers. This report underscores the importance of maintaining a full range of immunizations for children as well as adults who go to the field, as standards of hygiene and the prevalence of the disease organisms in the local population are likely to make contracting these diseases more probable than at home.

Finally, we have a category of "odds and ends," infections that are frequent enough that they impact many research projects, that are unpleasant enough that they should be noted and fieldworkers should be prepared to deal with them, but which are not so serious or systematic that they represent a certain kind of threat to health and safety in the field. Table 10.9 presents the experience that the sample reported with these infectious diseases.

Some of these infections can be distressing and potentially disabling. Influenza, like colds, can be acquired anywhere, but may be more difficult to treat in the field.

Ear infections are much more prevalent in some research sites than others. The director of a field project in Belize, for example, reports that four students needed treatment for ear infections in 1985, and that they probably got their infections from swimming in a lagoon. A researcher in Honduras reports a chronic fungal and bacterial ear infection that persisted for three years and resulted in some permanent hearing loss. A researcher who worked in rural Uttar Pradesh India tells of having a severe ear infection in 1968 and getting it again when he returned to work there in 1974–75. Jane Buikstra (University of Chicago) got a persistent ear infection in the summer of 1986, with some loss of hearing and ringing in the ears. She noted that ear problems complicate airplane travel, especially for those who need to use small, unpressurized planes to get in and out of their field site. Injury to ears can also be a side effect of drug therapy for other conditions.

Eye problems among fieldworkers have also been reported. Conjunctivitis is endemic in many areas, and many fieldworkers as well as locals get it, but it is

Table 10.9. Miscellaneous Infectious Diseases

	N. America	Europe	L. America	India	Africa	Pacific	Total
Total	61	17	63	17	23	23	204
Sores (Staphylococci)							
Had condition, self	8	1	12	2	7	7	37
	13%	*6%*	*19%*	*12%*	*30%*	*30%*	*18%*
Others in group had it	9	4	6	1	2	2	24
	28%	*29%*	*29%*	*18%*	*39%*	*39%*	*30%*
Influenza							
Had condition, self	10	4	5	2	3	8	32
	16%	*24%*	*8%*	*12%*	*13%*	*35%*	*16%*
Others in group had it	3	5	8	2	0	0	18
	21%	*53%*	*21%*	*57%*	*13%*	*35%*	*25%*
Conjunctivitis (Eye Infections)							
Had condition, self	4	1	6	2	2	2	17
	7%	*6%*	*10%*	*12%*	*8%*	*8%*	*8%*
Others in group had it	5	4	7	1	1	1	19
	15%	*29%*	*21%*	*18%*	*12%*	*12%*	*18%*
Otitis (Ear Infections)							
Had condition, self	0	1	7	3	0	3	14
	0%	*6%*	*11%*	*18%*	*0%*	*12%*	*7%*
Others in group had it	3	2	6	1	2	3	17
	5%	*18%*	*21%*	*24%*	*8%*	*26%*	*15%*

usually readily controlled with neosporin ointment. Trachoma is also endemic in many areas of the world, but no one in the sample reported having contracted it. One person reported temporary blindness as a side effect of malaria medication, and another lost an eye in an accident.

The staphylococcus sores listed in Table 10.9 are only a small part of the multitude of skin problems that fieldworkers report. Blisters are experienced by 35% for self and 46% for anyone on their field team, with the highest rates reported by those who work in North America. Rashes are also reported by many, 28% for self and 43% for anyone in the group. Poison ivy (or poison oak) is reported for the majority of field groups in North America and is frequently reported by all researchers: 16% say that they have had it in the field, and 30% report it for anyone in the group. Cuts and sores are reported by more than half of the fieldworkers, but no one considered these problems major. For an account of an excruciating rash, and the role it played in fieldwork decisions, see Chagnon (1974:20–42).

In the next chapter, we will look at the hazards of degenerative disease in fieldwork.

CHAPTER 11   DEGENERATIVE DISEASES IN THE FIELD

When we consider the kinds of health problems that can arise during fieldwork, we should include the many sorts of medical emergencies and milder discomforts that cannot be "blamed" on the conditions or the locale of fieldwork. Health is not perfect at home either, and we wonder whether the sickness, disability, and death that occur in the field are merely proportional to the amount of time that anthropologists spend there, or whether fieldwork produces a higher level of problems.

In this chapter, we will look at the evidence of fieldworkers suffering from a range of ills that are degenerative rather than infectious, parasitic, or traumatic. Degenerative diseases are those problems that arise in the body as part of the process of aging or that are caused by "wear and tear" rather than microorganisms or larger forces. Some of the conditions discussed here are not diseases at all, but normal nondisease processes such as pregnancy and childbirth. Sherry Ortner of the University of Michigan registers a quite reasonable objection to placing these topics in a chapter on degenerative diseases, but they fit here better than elsewhere in this classification.

In North American society, we are used to considering the degenerative diseases, especially heart disease, stroke, and cancer, as the primary causes of death. And indeed a study of the obituaries suggests that these are the primary causes of death for anthropologists too, as well as for those who follow other occupations. Anthropologists differ from others in their rates of nondegenerative diseases, but resemble them in also experiencing the same major degenerative diseases, in and out of the field.

Degenerative diseases could conceivably be less prevalent among a group of anthropologists than in the general population, due to the occupational selection factor. Perhaps those who have debilitating degenerative diseases such as epilepsy, diabetes, multiple sclerosis, asthma, or heart disease do not choose to start training in anthropology, in anticipation of the difficulties they would face doing fieldwork. We have to ask whether there are any diseases that preclude fieldwork. If so, does chronic disease preclude all fieldwork, or just certain kinds of very strenuous, or very remote work? Are supervisors aware of the medical conditions of their students when the first fieldwork is being planned? Do supervisors attempt to influence the student in selecting fieldwork that is within their ability, or is the decision left entirely to the student, perhaps with the advice of a doctor?

These considerations apply to those who suffer from severe chronic degenerative disease, but to some extent, all fieldworkers run the risk of experiencing some degenerative disease in the field, mild or severe. Anyone can develop an allergy, get a toothache, or fall victim to a heart attack or stroke in the field. The special issues, then, are not so much prevention and avoiding the problem, but the need to provide for emergency response, access to medical care, evacuation to a hospital if necessary, and so on. As we consider the categories of degenerative diseases reported by the sample and by volunteers, no doubt we can think of ways to minimize the difficulties caused by degenerative disease in the field.

Although we will follow our standard technique of presenting the incidence of diseases and problems by the area of the world in which the reporting anthropologist specializes, we will note in this chapter that there are no strong trends in the area in which degenerative diseases occur. They can happen anywhere, and are probably proportional to the amount of time spent in various areas. Serious consequences of these problems, however, are probably more frequent in the remote areas of the world, where high quality medical care is not available, or is available only after a long trip.

Let us start with the normal functioning of the reproductive system. Men's problems with the reproductive tract are likely to be found under the heading of venereal disease, which we considered in the last chapter. Women are more likely to be affected, as we saw in Chapter 10, by relatively minor yeast infections, and also by the problems that arise with ovulatory cycling and from pregnancy. So the problems listed in this section are primarily those of women, although some men anthropologists demonstrated identification with their wives by claiming pregnancies as those of "self."

Dysmenorrhea

A few volunteers (2) reported problems with painful menstrual cramps in the field, just as some women do at home. Menstruation may be more difficult for some women in the field due to the absence of convenient bathrooms and drug stores to obtain supplies A male archaeologist reported that his female field assistants were "always having trouble with their periods" and having to go to town to see the doctor, which might be a better illustration of interpersonal difficulties dealing with employees than a particular medical complaint.

Normal Pregnancy, Miscarriage and Abortion, and Childbirth

Pregnancies can happen anywhere, and unwanted pregnancies may perhaps be somewhat more likely in the field, due to the same scarcity of bathrooms and drugstores, which makes effective contraception more difficult. The contrast between the norms and behavior of the anthropologists and the local people are often highlighted in the area of conception and contraception.

Table 11.1 shows the rates of pregnancy and of miscarriage and abortion in the field among the researchers in the sample.

We see six pregnancies among the primary informants, and a total of 28 informants, 14% of all the fieldworkers, who had one or more pregnancies on their expeditions. Volunteer informant Barbara Parker (University of Michigan) responded when told about this study, "Are they considering pregnancy? I know of several women who have become pregnant during their fieldwork period, myself included." A chairman, asked about deaths in the field to people in his department, replied that there had been two deaths, but at least three pregnancies to members of his department, so he feels that the life force is winning.

Table 11.1. Pregnancy and Termination in the Field

	N. America	Europe	L. America	India	Africa	Pacific	Total
Total	61	17	63	17	23	23	204
Pregnancy							
Had condition, self	2	1	2	0	1	0	6
	3%	6%	3%	0%	4%	0%	3%
Others in group had it	9	5	3	2	1	2	22
	18%	35%	8%	12%	9%	9%	11%
Miscarriage and Abortion (spontaneous or induced)							
Had condition, self	2	0	0	0	0	0	2
	3%						1%
Others in group had it	3	2	1	0	0	1	7
	8%	12%	2%	0%	0%	4%	4%

Two volunteer informants told me of incidents in which they had taken a young woman into the field to do some serious fieldwork, only to discover over the next month that she was pregnant and unhappy about it. In each case, the woman left the project to have an abortion, and returned later. A well-known archaeologist wrote to me, "I now require that any student (female) that is picked for a long-term field project is on the pill. Others may say that I haven't got the right to interfere with their personal lives in this way, but I say that's tough. After flying one crew member out of a remote area for an abortion, I refuse to repeat the experience."

Complications of pregnancies can, on occasion, develop into a dangerous situation. Sherry Ortner (University of Michigan) had a miscarriage in the field, and said, "I was lucky to be a short walk from a field hospital at that particular moment. If I were any further away I don't know what would have happened." Another woman got gestational diabetes during her second pregnancy, while she was in the field, possibly triggered by influenza, which she had halfway through the pregnancy. She had to leave the field, and had the baby back home.

Elizabeth A. Grobsmith (University of Nebraska) became pregnant while working with her husband in southeast Alaska with the Tlingit. She had previously experienced years of infertility and corrective surgery, so the pregnancy was very welcome but of high risk. She left the field to go to Los Angeles for care, returned to the field but had to leave again due to complications. She gave birth to twins at home in February 1982.

Not all of the 28 pregnancies reported necessarily ended in childbirth in the field, of course. Most leave the field before the baby is due. An account of "birthing in the bush" by Morton and Sheila Solomon Klass tells of having a baby in Trinidad in 1958, an event that was uncomplicated by problems and that was put to good ethnographic use in understanding the behavior and emotions of parents in that field setting. There were, however, difficulties in nursing the baby, and this led to new understanding of the importance of nursing for maternal and child health (Klass 1987:121–146).

Appendicitis

Appendicitis is a better example of a degenerative disease in the field. Probably the fieldwork has no causal relation to the illness, although it is possible that changes in the diet may trigger the inflammation. Although appendicitis is no longer the common cause of death it once was, before the advent of antibiotics and safe techniques in surgery, it is still a dangerous condition when one is far from sophisticated medical care.

Eight of the 204 informants report having experienced a crisis with appendicitis in the field; in four cases, it was the reporting anthropologist who had the problem (Table 11.2).

Emily Martin got appendicitis in Taiwan and was operated on successfully. Jane Granskog (California State University, Bakersfield) had an appendectomy at a clinic in Tuxla Gutierrez, a small town in Chiapas, Mexico, while doing field-work in 1970. "I once had an appendectomy while I was doing a video documentary in the city of Oaxaco in Mexico," wrote Michael J. Higgins (University of Northern Colorado). Mike Agar, working in India with Alan Beals and his family in the mid-1960s, had appendicitis.

Mary Leakey and Donald Macinnes each developed acute appendicitis on Rusingar (an island of Lake Victoria). They had to be rushed by boat to Kisumu Hospital, "rushed" being a relative term as the boat was delayed in each case by mechanical faults. Macinnes nearly died and was out of action for months (M. Leakey 1984:101). Louis Leakey later required Dian Fossey to have her healthy appendix removed before starting fieldwork, apparently at least in part as a test of her seriousness in wanting to do the fieldwork. Fossey wrote to Leakey, "Now I won't be spilling viscera all over the mountains" (Cole 1976:326). Appendicitis and its complications are common worries and common emergencies in the bush, but few surgeons would recommend removing a healthy appendix.

Ulcers

Stomach ulcers are a common problem in the field, causing pain and discomfort and interfering with proper nutrition and good general health (Table 11.3). They result from a chronic condition of acid in the stomach, which produces lesions in

Table 11.2. Appendicitis in the Field

	N. America	Europe	L. America	India	Africa	Pacific	Total
Total	61	17	63	17	23	23	204
Had condition, self	1	1	1	0	1	0	4
	2%	6%	2%	0%	4%	0%	2%
Others in group had it	1	0	2	0	1	0	4
	4%	6%	5%	0%	8%	0%	4%

Table 11.3. Stomach Ulcers

	N. America	Europe	L. America	India	Africa	Pacific	Total
Total	61	17	63	17	23	23	204
Had condition, self	0	0	3	1	0	0	4
			5%	6%			2%
Others in group had it	5	1	2	0	0	0	8
	8%	6%	8%	6%	0%	0%	6%

the stomach lining or the duodenum. These lesions are painful and interfere with enjoyment of eating and drinking.

An ulcer of the stomach can happen to people who work anywhere, but it may be harder to manage in some environments than in others. Ulcers seem to cluster among those who work in North and Latin America, Europe, and India. One wonders whether a spicy, chili-laden diet is related to this concentration.

Ulcers may sometimes be involved in drug reactions, which complicate other complaints. For example, Willis Sibley, now at Cleveland State University, was working as a Visiting Professor at the University of the Philippines in 1969 and did a brief period of fieldwork there. He contracted amebic dysentery, and was treated in the hospital with a medicine that included arsenic as one of its ingredients. This medication caused perforation of an ulcer, which in turn required treatment.

Kidney Stones and Bladder Stones

These painful conditions develop in middle age in a certain proportion of the population, especially those who do not drink frequently during the day and who have a low output of urine. Mineral deposits block the urinary tubes in severe cases. Surgery may be needed to remove the deposits, or sophisticated high technology treatments may be able to break up the deposit with ultrasound, avoiding the need for surgery. The condition usually develops over a period of weeks or months, allowing plenty of time to leave the field and reach the needed medical care. No one in the sample reported kidney or bladder stones as a field problem, although these problems are known to occur in the field.

Hemorrhoids and Anal Fissures

Hemorrhoids are commonly reported as a complicating problem of fieldwork. These dilated blood vessels on the anus develop quickly, often as a consequence of diarrhea and/or constipation. The anal irritation can be painful and difficult to treat, because the tissue of the anus is sensitive and the swelling is aggravated by bowel movements. No volunteers reported hemorrhoids, but about 15% of the sample reported hemorrhoids as a problem when asked about them. It was striking that absolutely no one reported hemorrhoids as a problem for other members of the research group, probably because sufferers do not talk about them.

Headaches, Migraine and Others

Another painful condition experienced in the field is headaches, especially severe migraine headaches (Table 11.5). Properly speaking, a headache is a symp-

Table 11.4. Hemorrhoids

	N. America	Europe	L. America	India	Africa	Pacific	Total
Total	61	17	63	17	23	23	204
Had condition, self	8	1	6	4	3	6	28
	13%	*6%*	*10%*	*24%*	*13%*	*26%*	*14%*

Table 11.5. Migraine and Other Headaches in the Field

	N. America	Europe	L. America	India	Africa	Pacific	Total
Total	61	17	63	17	23	23	204
Had condition, self	9	1	8	2	5	8	33
	15%	6%	13%	12%	22%	35%	16%
Others in group had it	17	6	14	0	7	0	44
	43%	41%	35%	12%	52%	35%	38%

Table 11.6. Toothache in the Field

	N. America	Europe	L. America	India	Africa	Pacific	Total
Total	61	17	63	17	23	23	204
Had condition, self	6	4	12	6	8	9	45
	10%	24%	19%	35%	35%	26%	22%
Others in group had it	11	3	9	1	3	2	29
	28%	41%	33%	41%	48%	48%	36%

tom rather than a disease. They can result from circulatory problems, excess sun and dehydration, allergies, drug reactions, stress, lack of sleep, or many other causes. The pain of a migraine is severe, and one may not be able to assure the silence and privacy under field conditions that the migraine sufferer typically wants. Including "other" headaches along with migraines, 54% of the sample reported experience with headaches in the field. Whatever else is brought in the medical chest, do not forget the aspirin.

Toothache

Many people in North America never experience the sustained pain of toothache, because their dentist is prepared to see them on an emergency basis the same day if a tooth starts hurting. So it was rather a surprise to find 36% of the sample reporting that someone on their expeditions had experienced a notable toothache. Table 11.6 shows the distribution.

As with hemorrhoids, people report toothache when asked about it, but it does not feature in the stories that come to mind when people are asked about the dangers of fieldwork. Toothache is painful and disorienting, but it is not dramatic or dangerous. These rates suggest that a pretrip visit to the dentist for preventive care is a good idea, and asking for suggestions for emergency field treatment of a toothache might well be in order. Many problems of tooth decay and pain can be prevented by a timely checkup before starting fieldwork in a remote location.

Allergies—Rashes, Hay Fever, Asthma, Anaphylaxis

Allergies can plague people anywhere in the world. They are common, and in addition they are blamed for a range of conditions, especially respiratory and skin problems, that are not clearly diagnosed or understood. One volunteer woman is apparently allergic to her field site, since each time she goes there she gets severe respiratory symptoms that only ease when she leaves. She has tried it five times, and each time was forced to leave—twice to go directly to a hospital. She is now seeking a new field site. She notes that her departmental colleagues were unsympathetic and unsupportive while she struggled to understand what was happening.

Allergies are highly localized, and certain pollens, dust, and mites may cause allergic reactions in many people. Given the great variability in localities for allergens, it is striking that the proportions reporting difficulty from allergies are so similar in all parts of the world (Table 11.7).

Asthma is a severe condition that can interfere with breathing. Sufferers need to carry special drugs for treatment in emergencies, and those who suffer from severe allergies that threaten anaphylaxis, such as those allergic to bee stings, must also carry special treatments and prepare others in the expedition to help them with such treatment.

Charles Keyes (University of Washington) developed asthma during fieldwork in Thailand in 1967, and only experiences it while working in Asia, most recently in 1986 in China. Robert Levy (University of California-San Diego) acquired an allergy to mold and mildew while working in the Philippines, which he suffers from to this day.

Marie Clabeaux Geise (State University of New York College-Buffalo) has developed an allergy to bone dust, and seems to have damaged her immune system, resulting in long-term disability. She is very ill, lives with severe fatigue and pain and weakness in any muscle used for more than a few minutes.

Arthritis

The aches and pains of arthritis are increasingly common with age, and arthritis sufferers tend to find that the limitations on activity increase as they get older. The unavoidable extremes of heat and cold, uncomfortable beds, and sitting on the

Table 11.7. Allergies in the Field

	N. America	Europe	L. America	India	Africa	Pacific	Total
Total	61	17	63	17	23	23	204
Allergies							
Had condition, self	14	4	13	3	6	5	45
	23%	*23%*	*21%*	*18%*	*26%*	*22%*	*22%*
Others in group had it	16	5	12	1	6	4	44
	49%	*53%*	*40%*	*24%*	*52%*	*39%*	*44%*
Rashes							
Had condition, self	14	3	15	9	10	7	58
	23%	*18%*	*24%*	*53%*	*43%*	*30%*	*28%*
Others in group had it	15	1	6	1	3	3	29
	48%	*24%*	*33%*	*59%*	*57%*	*43%*	*43%*
Asthma							
Had condition, self	0	1	6	0	0	2	9
	0%	*6%*	*10%*	*0%*	*0%*	*9%*	*4%*
Others in group had it	10	3	3	1	6	1	24
	16%	*24%*	*14%*	*6%*	*26%*	*13%*	*16%*

ground may encourage arthritis victims to curtail fieldwork if their condition worsens with age. It is common to find some experience of arthritis on expeditions—11% report problems with it. Several people reported it as their most serious and long-lasting health problem in the field.

Epilepsy and Convulsions

While the sample only reported hemorrhoids for themselves, they only reported epilepsy for others in their research groups. There were three cases where others suffered from epilepsy, two reported by North Americanists and one Europeanist. In one case, the anthropologist commented that he had no idea prior to the trip that the field assistant suffered from epilepsy, and was shocked to find that anyone would not inform others in advance; however, he also admitted that he would not have allowed the field assistant to go on the expedition if he had known.

A chairman reported that the wife of one of their graduate students had suffered serious convulsions while doing fieldwork on an island in the southern Pacific in the 1970s. She had to be evacuated by helicopter to a hospital, where she was successfully treated. The cause was never isolated.

Diabetes

Like epilepsy, diabetes is the kind of chronic disease that the potential fieldworker would ordinarily know about and take into account in making professional plans. Because it requires careful management of the insulin levels by diet and drugs, the flexibility needed for many kinds of fieldwork might not be possible for the sufferer. Eight percent of the sample reported experience with diabetes in their group. Table 11.9 shows that it is most prevalent among those who work primarily in North America and Europe, where medical care can usually be reached quickly in case of emergency. A volunteer informant reported that a field

Table 11.8. Arthritis in the Field

	N. America	Europe	L. America	India	Africa	Pacific	Total
Total	61	17	63	17	23	23	204
Had condition, self	2	0	2	1	2	3	10
	3%	0%	3%	6%	8%	12%	5%
Others in group had it	3	4	3	0	2	0	12
	8%	24%	22%	6%	17%	12%	11%

Table 11.9. Diabetes in the Field

	N. America	Europe	L. America	India	Africa	Pacific	Total
Total	61	17	63	17	23	23	204
Had condition, self	2	0	1	0	0	0	3
	3%		1%				1%
Others in group had it	6	2	4	0	1	1	14
	13%	12%	8%	0%	4%	4%	8%

assistant on an archaeology project in Peru in 1982 went into diabetic coma, and had to be taken out on an emergency basis.

Cancer

Cancer is a terrible disease, and anthropologists suffer from it heavily, as do other North Americans. Generally speaking, however, cancer develops slowly enough that even if it starts in the field, one has plenty of time to get out for medical treatment. Fieldworkers therefore report that cancer is a rare problem in the field, even though the obituaries for anthropologists as a whole show that it is a frequent cause of death (Table 11.10).

According to the obituary columns of the anthropological journals, at least 45 people died from cancer at less than 65 years of age during the past decade. Some of those who died from cancer include Eileen Basher, Martin Alexander Baumhoff, Hal Eberhart, Judith Friedman Hansen, Chester F. Gorman, Vera Mae Green, Robert Fleming Heizer, Chet S. Lancaster, Barbara Myerhoff, Maxine Letcher Nimtz, Vera Rubin, James P. Spradley, B. Allan Tindall, and Klaus Friedrich Wellman. Robert MacDougall of Cornell University died in 1987 at age 46 of cancer that began in the stomach and liver. His wife reported that "rightly or wrongly, our family and his colleagues believe that fieldwork had something to do with his illness."

A particular form of cancer that may be related to the risks of fieldwork through chronic overexposure to sunlight is a form of skin cancer called melanoma. At least one of those who died, archaeologist Chet Gorman, first developed melanoma while in the field, and left to seek treatment. James H. Vaughan (Indiana University-Bloomington) has experienced melanoma and its treatment, and encourages anyone with concerns about it to contact him to share information.

Heart Attacks and Strokes

Heart attacks can happen in the field, and sometimes happen during the hectic week of preparation for the field, on the trip to the field, or on the way back (Table 11.11). Stress increases the chances of heart attack for fieldworkers, and remoteness from medical care may increase the probability of death from a heart attack. The sample reports that heart attacks, strokes, and circulatory disease (for example, a blood clot in the leg) are relatively rare in the field. These events however, can be very serious.

Douglas Raybeck, 36, Hamilton College, suffered a preinfarction angina in Kuala Lumpur while he was doing fieldwork and teaching at the National Uni-

Table 11.10. Cancer in the Field

	N. America	Europe	L. America	India	Africa	Pacific	Total
Total	61	17	63	17	23	23	204
Had condition, self	0	0	0	1	1	1	3
				6%	*4%*	*4%*	*1%*
Others in group had it	1	0	0	0	0	0	1
	2%	*0%*	*0%*	*6%*	*4%*	*4%*	*2%*

Table 11.11. Heart and Circulatory Disease in the Field

	N. America	Europe	L. America	India	Africa	Pacific	Total
Total	61	17	63	17	23	23	204
Heart Attack							
Had condition, self	0	0	0	1	0	2	3
				6%		8%	1%
Others in group had it	1	2	1	0	0	0	4
	2%	12%	2%	6%	0%	8%	3%
Stroke							
Had condition, self	0	1	1	0	0	0	2
	0%	6%	2%	0%	0%	0%	1%
Circulatory Disease							
Had condition, self	1	1	0	0	1	1	4
	2%	6%	0%	0%	4%	4%	2%

versity. He was taken to the University of Malay hospital, where a massive heart attack hit him. Because he was in intensive care when it struck, he survived. He recuperated in Malaysia for some months before returning to the United States, but was unable to resume his fieldwork.

Frank Broiling, 37, director of the Office of Contract Archeology, University of New Mexico, died of massive coronary in the field in 1979.

Richard Frucht, 42, University of Alberta, died of a heart attack on campus March 1979. He was leaving in April for 18 months of fieldwork on St. Kitts.

Eleanor ("Happy") Leacock, 61, suffered two strokes in Samoa while doing fieldwork in 1987. She was airlifted to Hawaii where sophisticated medical care was available, but she died in the hospital.

Most of the deaths to anthropologists over the age of 65 are due to degenerative diseases, and very few of these have any direct connection to fieldwork. The connection to fieldwork of those below 65 in age is due merely to the extra stresses that fieldwork may generate, and the delays in reaching medical care for those who work far from a physician. The rate of deaths from degenerative diseases is almost surely higher among anthropologists in the field than among other social scientists, due to the absence of medical care, but the incidence of disease is probably very similar.

CHAPTER 12 MENTAL HEALTH AND ILLNESS IN THE FIELD

For some anthropologists, some of the time, fieldwork may require experiencing loneliness, isolation, sickness, fatigue, malnutrition, pain, and discomfort. This is not to say that there aren't also moments of great meaning, connectedness, and joy, but while fieldwork is rarely dull, it is also rarely continually smooth. Some live with constant worry about the expedition, the safety of personnel, and the intellectual issues of the fieldwork. It is no wonder that some individuals experience mental distress, and that the stress of fieldwork sometimes contributes to full-blown psychiatric illness.

Let us start by looking at the incidence of the most serious and clear-cut psychiatric illnesses, and then go on to look at the much more common and milder signs of psychic distress.

We start with a symptom, properly speaking, rather than a disease. Hallucinations are an overt sign of serious mental illness, usually schizophrenia. It is not a condition that would ordinarily allow one to continue to conduct research during an acute episode. Table 12.1 shows that only one fieldworker reports hallucinations in the field, but five others had other members of the research group, family, students, employees, or colleagues, who experienced hallucinations in the field. These few cases do not show any particular geographic pattern.

Manic States

Similarly, manic states experienced in the field would necessarily be very disruptive of fieldwork. They too are rare among primary fieldworkers, more common among the other members of the research team (Table 12.2).

We note that those who work primarily in Africa report a much higher incidence (17%) of manic states than those in other areas (average 3%).

Depression

Far more common among fieldworkers is the report of depression, a condition that might range from an extremely debilitating state of inability to talk, eat, and

Table 12.1. Hallucinations in the Field

	N. America	Europe	L. America	India	Africa	Pacific	Total
Total	61	17	63	17	23	23	204
Had condition, self	0	1	0	0	0	0	1
Others in group had it	1	0	2	0	1	1	5
	2%	6%	4%	0%	4%	4%	3%

Table 12.2. Manic States in the Field

	N. America	Europe	L. America	India	Africa	Pacific	Total
Total	61	17	63	17	23	23	204
Had condition, self	0	0	0	0	2	0	2
Others in group had it	1	1	2	0	2	1	7
	2%	6%	4%	0%	17%	4%	4%

Table 12.3. Depression in the Field

	N. America	Europe	L. America	India	Africa	Pacific	Total
Total	61	17	63	17	23	23	204
Had condition, self	6	1	10	3	3	6	29
	10%	6%	16%	12%	12%	26%	14%
Others in group had it	10	5	9	1	1	3	29
	26%	35%	30%	24%	17%	39%	28%

take care of oneself, to a mild sense of sadness and preoccupation with absent loved ones, with familiar places and things, and with worry about the success of the scientific work. Probably at least a mild degree of depression from time to time is to be expected during prolonged fieldwork, especially for those who leave their families behind when they go to the field (Table 12.3). We will look at the evidence on the role of families in the field on the health and safety of fieldworkers, including mental health, in Chapter 13. Here we merely note that depression is reported as an experience in the field by some 28% of the sample from time to time.

Table 12.3 shows that depression is basically like degenerative diseases that are equally distributed to all continents, but with somewhat higher rates for those who work in the underdeveloped and remote parts of the world, as we have commonly seen for infectious disease. In part, this may be because depression is often a product of sickness and accidents. In the extreme forms, depression and manic states are related in the form of affective disorders, so the two conditions should be considered together. Almost all of those who marked manic states also claimed experience with depression, for self or others.

Anxiety States

Anxiety, too, is common and in its milder forms perfectly normal. Indeed, one would wonder about the adjustment of an anthropologist who reports experience with snakebites, heart attacks, and vehicle accidents in the field, but reports never having suffered from anxiety (Table 12.4). Anxiety reminds one to mentally rehearse and prepare for the things that can go wrong. It can, of course, in extreme forms, also come to interfere with work and with adjustments to the situation.

Like depression, anxiety is more often reported from the Latin Americanists, Africanists, and the Pacific specialists, than from the "tamer" areas of North America, Europe, and India. Overall about a third of the sample report it. Anxiety tends to be more handicapping to researchers working alone and out of touch with

Table 12.4. Anxiety in the Field

	N. America	Europe	L. America	India	Africa	Pacific	Total
Total	61	17	63	17	23	23	204
Had condition, self	6	4	11	2	5	5	33
	10%	*24%*	*17%*	*12%*	*22%*	*22%*	*16%*
Others in group had it	9	1	11	2	3	4	30
	25%	*29%*	*35%*	*24%*	*35%*	*39%*	*31%*

Table 12.5. Culture Shock in the Field

	N. America	Europe	L. America	India	Africa	Pacific	Total
Total	61	17	63	17	23	23	204
Had condition, self	7	4	13	3	5	9	41
	11%	*24%*	*21%*	*18%*	*22%*	*39%*	*20%*
Others in group had it	7	2	14	3	4	3	33
	41%	*15%*	*44%*	*35%*	*39%*	*19%*	*36%*

their supporting people at home than for those who can share their worries, rational and irrational, with trusted others.

Culture Shock

Culture shock is, in some ways, the defining characteristic of anthropologists. Although they know more than others what to expect about experiencing another culture, that they voluntarily subject themselves to the process and the experience of culture shock, uncomfortable as it often is, is a guarantee that they are really confronting the reality of the other culture. There are a number of good descriptions of the experience of culture shock in the literature (Bowen 1964; Briggs 1970; Maybury-Lewis 1988). The sample here confirms that it is a common experience of fieldworkers (Table 12.5).

Alcoholism and Drug Abuse

Alcohol and drugs can lessen some of the psychological pain of culture shock, anxiety, depression, loneliness, and other stresses of fieldwork, but when used to excess they can interfere with the ability to adapt to the fieldwork setting and get on with the scientific work of the project. Indeed, this statement is probably the best definition of what we mean by the phrase, "used to excess." The sample more often attributed alcoholism and drug abuse to others on the expedition than to themselves (Table 12.6). Note that the drugs referred to here are primarily "recreational" drugs (marijuana, cocaine, heroin), but may also include some prescription drugs, such as sleeping pills or tranquilizers.

North America and Latin America seem to be the areas of highest incidence of reported problems with alcoholism or drug abuse. Both of these conditions are far more often reported for others in the group than for the self. We note that many more people in the sample reported in another part of the questionnaire that they

Table 12.6. Alcoholism and Drug Abuse in the Field

	N. America	Europe	L. America	India	Africa	Pacific	Total
Total	61	17	63	17	23	23	204
Alcoholism							
Had condition, self	0	0	1	0	1	0	2
Others in group had it	11	4	12	0	1	2	30
	18%	*24%*	*21%*	*0%*	*9%*	*9%*	*16%*
Drug Abuse							
Had condition, self	2	1	0	0	0	1	4
Others in group had it	8	1	6	0	1	2	18
	16%	*12%*	*10%*	*0%*	*4%*	*12%*	*11%*

"sometimes drink too much or too often" than report that they have had a personal problem with alcoholism in the field, as we would expect. And as we would expect, there is a high agreement among individuals in reporting these two indicators of problems with alcohol consumption.

Some cultures or situations may encourage the use of alcohol on a daily or frequent basis, and the anthropologist may feel pressured or required to participate in frequent drinking to the detriment of work, even if alcoholism is not a problem. E. A. Hammel, of Berkeley, while collecting data from scattered farmers across the hills of Peru, took advantage of the local beliefs of "hot" and "cold" foods to avoid daily consumption of the generous offers of locally made brandy when he came to interview. He simply rode into the farmyard eating a mango, an extremely "cold" food that would never be consumed with the extremely "hot" brandy. He didn't have to make any excuses or apologies for refusing brandy, it simply wasn't offered to him under the circumstances.

Other cultures may use drug or alcohol use as a test of manhood or an initiation into the culture. Melanie Dreher (Cassell 1987:162) tells of living with her children in a Jamaican village where *ganja* was an important element in the culture. She and the children were not expected to take part, but when her husband arrived he was pressed to consume large quantities of *ganja* and white rum, while the locals watched and were amused at the effects on him. Napoleon Chagnon tells of his experiences with *ebene*, a hallucinogenic herb (Chagnon 1968:211–213), which seemed to have played an important role not only in his understanding of the Yanomamö culture but also in differentiating him from the local missionaries in the eyes of the locals.

Few volunteers reported problems with drug use. A woman in the sample tells of interviewing at night in a big city, under conditions where it was difficult to sleep in the daytime. She started taking sleeping pills when she finally got home in the morning, which began a pattern of drug dependency which she has struggled with for twenty years. Another woman tells of struggling with dependency on the use of diet pills, which had influenced her fieldwork but seemed to be only incidentally related to it.

Loneliness and Lack of Acceptance

Life in the field is difficult for many observers. One of the members of the sample wrote in large letters "LONELINESS" across the questionnaire in response to the question "What was your most serious problem in the field?" Another spontaneously added "crippling loneliness" to the list of mental illnesses in the checklist. And in interviews, particularly around the topic of taking a spouse or other family members to the field, the subject of the isolation and loneliness of fieldwork came up again and again, volunteered by both men and women anthropologists.

Part of the difficulty comes from separation from loved ones in one's own society. One misses the presence of friends and family, and wishes to share in the events of their lives in the home society while fieldwork goes on. While few anthropologists stay in the field as long as ecologist Delia Owens (1984:168), her reaction to receiving the news that her father had died six weeks earlier may strike a chord of remembrance of pain in many fieldworkers:

> One of the hardest things to bear during our seven years in Africa was being away from home at such times. While we were gone, Mark's mother passed away, and his grandmother. And besides my father, I lost my grandmother. And I missed the marriage of my twin brother. We struggled with feelings of guilt because we were not at home to help our families through the difficult times, or to celebrate the good ones.

Another component of fieldwork pain comes from the difficulties of obtaining psychological support from new friends and acquaintances in the studied society. Jean Briggs, of Memorial University Newfoundland, who has written one of the most powerful accounts of the daily psychic reality of fieldwork (1970), tells of her 18 months of fieldwork in a small community among extremely isolated Eskimo fishers and hunters in northern Canada. In Golde's book, *Women in the Field,* Briggs tell us

> One of the questions I am asked most frequently about life at Back River is, "Were you accepted?" People seem to expect a straightforward yes-or-no answer, but in fact there is no such easy response. What is meant by "accepted?" What kind of communication, what kind of exchange of services, can be called "acceptance"? . . . When I left for the field, I, like my questioners, was naive enough to believe that "rapport" was something that was built up, gradually and painstakingly, over a period of weeks or months and then ran on its own momentum until the end of one's stay, barring untoward accidents or carelessness. I discovered, to my sorrow, that the situation wasn't quite so simple. [1986:20]

Briggs's detailed account of the daily stresses of life in her adopted family make gripping and exhausting reading. Her accounts of her own increasing irritability, resentments, and attempts to understand the behavior of herself and of the family members who provided her with a home are fascinating but rather frightening.

Mark and Delia Owens (1984:101) tell of becoming so needy for human contact after months alone together in the Kalahari studying lions and hyenas that they could barely carry on a normal conversation with the residents of Maun, Botswana:

> Shaking hands, I found myself holding on too long, grasping a friend's hand or lower arm with my left while pumping away with my right. We smiled so much our cheeks ached, and greeted everyone over and over again, repeating their first names several times. Then suddenly feeling foolish, I quickly sat down at a table and ordered a beer.

Many other anthropologists have reported failures to achieve "rapport" as a respected and admired inside-outsider. Bowen (1964) reports that she was placed in the category of "witch" for her offenses against proper Tiv behavior. Chagnon (1974:1–40) reports that he was forced in some communities into a choice between irrelevance and competition for leadership positions in the group.

Golde (1986:75) states frankly

I would like to be able to report that this situation [of experiencing discomfort in the field] was only transitory and that with time the people came to love and trust me completely, helped me sympathetically when I needed it, and freely opened their hearts and minds; the truth is far from that rosy ideal. I carefully had to calculate a strategy for almost every piece of information I gleaned, and I bartered, cajoled, and wheedled or bluffed knowledge I didn't have in order to get more. At times I deliberately exaggerated or distorted facts, counting on the people's need to defend the village by correcting my impressions. Sometimes I was petulant, saying "You say you want me to stay here, get married here, yet you won't even tell me what this means or why it is done."

Effects on Mental Health of Illness and Malnutrition

One of the saddest stories in the history of anthropology is that of Bernard Deacon, whose story has been told fifty years later by his fiancée, Margaret Gardiner (1984), from his letters of the 1920s when he did his fieldwork on the island of Malekula in the New Hebrides, and from her later interviews with people who knew him in the field.

Deacon and Gardiner met at a tea party in Trinity College, Cambridge, in 1925. He was a student of A. C. Haddon, at Cambridge, and prepared for the field by going to see Malinowski, another Haddon student, who told him how to make arrangements for a native mistress. (Gardiner: "This upset me. 'So what did you say?' I asked. 'Oh, I just took notes,' said Bernard.")

His letters from the field show the effects of health problems on his mental state.

In a climate like this you cannot go without civilization suddenly and adopt native life. Actually I should say the natives are much weaker and more diseased than the whites— they are constantly down with malaria, even though they take quinine, and yaws is universal. I had malaria badly about three weeks ago, but it hasn't recurred, and I think it is not going to. It's a wretched thing, anyway. (March 1926)

Sometimes, after rain, my island seems fantastically close . . . and I'm absurdly happy again. Then suddenly I'm back in Malekula again, with the heavy, heavy heat. It makes you feel as weak as a babe. (April 1926)

There is a strange quality in the light. Everything is a little inconsequent, a little contradictory: I have a bit of fever today and it is like a veil over the world. (May 1926)

I wish there were two of me, it is fearfully difficult to do any decent intellectual work with the constant pressure of physical existence. I haven't had fever for some time though I seem to have done lamentably little in the free interval. (May 1926)

I can't give up until I have finished here, another six months at least. I wish to God things would move faster, but there are blocks and hindrances every day. . . . I had a low fever all the forenoon, but it is gone now, and I am calm, just sweating gently (June 1926) . . . I am terribly overstrained, my work seems all to be going to bits. There seems nothing but Death—a man was dead in the village this morning of dysentery. . . . I've got to collect skulls for Haddon: a man said to me one day, "soon you (the white man) will be able to come and collect all our skulls: we won't bother you." (undated, probably July 1926)

Margaret Gardiner tells of her reaction to receiving these letters in Cambridge, where she was still a student (Gardiner 1984:35).

Even then it simply didn't occur to me that Bernard himself might be in any danger. After all, he was a white man and immune from most of the diseases that were killing the natives. I didn't recognize or understand the extent to which recurrent fevers and sores, the debilitating climate, the sheer difficulties of his physical existence and his doubts and despairs about his work were undermining his health.

Deacon himself writes good advice to any fieldworker as he continues to deal with his failing health in the months ahead, but seems not to take any of it, continuing to work long hours with inadequate food and continual infections.

Margou—I have been ill, and for the first time today feel nearly my normal strength back. . . . I have learned one lesson from it—that it is essential if you're going to live in the tropics never to let your strength go down. Knock off immediately—feed up and go steady until you do get it back. In a cooler climate where there is no fever, dysentery, etc. you can run for a long time on a tired body, gradually getting back strength but here unless you take steps quick you go lower and lower and then a bout of fever that you can't get rid of practically breaks you down altogether. (late July)

I wish we had been together here: it would have been a great deal easier, two than one. (September 1926)

Very lovely Malekula can be sometimes. I was perhaps unjust to it at first—I had a good bit of fever then, the last month or two it has finished. In fact altogether I'm very well—only sores are a trouble, but I bandage them decently. (October 1926) [1984:42]

During the period November to March Deacon and Gardiner wrote often, and negotiated an agreement that she would come to Sydney and marry him in April. He had planned to leave Malekula at the beginning of March, after 15 months in the field, but the steamer was late. Instead, on March 5 he became feverish again, and two days later his malaria turned into "blackwater fever," a common complication of malaria in the prechloroquine days. A missionary couple on Malekula nursed him as best they could, but he died March 12, about three months after his 24th birthday. Deacon died of a physical ailment, one that burdened him physically and mentally during his fieldwork. Although the death from malaria would not have to happen today, the mental consequences of illnesses—and we have seen that fieldworkers experience many illnesses—still occur.

Laura Nader (in Golde 1986:103) tells of her reaction to attempting to carry on with fieldwork after contracting two serious, but (at that time) undiagnosed, diseases:

Apart from the obvious fact that such illnesses are physically debilitating, I would like to draw attention to the mental state they produce vis-à-vis fieldwork and the people one is studying. When I first felt sick, I did not know what was wrong with me. . . . In the absence of "knowing" I began to consider the whole illness as psychosomatic. At the same time I became panicked because I was losing so many work days. I made myself go out to talk to people; I goaded myself to type up the materials I had collected; I tried to force myself to eat. Only after I had fainted one day while washing my hair in a public washing place did I begin to admit the possibilities of being sick. Fortunately, a medical doctor had been sent from Oaxaca to take care of an epidemic of measles. . . . I have often wondered what would have happened had the doctor not come along. I was in a completed depressed and debilitated condition, resenting these obstacles to my work. I couldn't stand being sick. I couldn't stand it (understand it) when an informant wouldn't "cooperate." I couldn't stand the Catholic priest and those self-righteous natives who encouraged his "persecution" of me.

Nader was diagnosed as having malaria, and was taken to Oaxaca City to stay in a hotel while she took a course of Aralen, an antimalarial medicine. After three weeks in the city she was still very sick, weak, and feverish. She continues:

Slowly I began to feel better, except that I was terribly depressed. I thought that the depression must be related to my not working and made arrangements to return to the Sierra. When the Land Rover came early one morning, I could not get out of bed. That day I forced myself to walk five blocks to see an American nurse living in Oaxaca. I will always remember those five blocks and how shameless I felt; when I couldn't walk, I simply sat down on the edge of the sidewalk. When the nurse saw my state, she said "Sick people can't know how to take care of themselves, I should know that." She put me in a taxi and sent me to a doctor. Upon entering his office, I burst into tears and said, "I don't care about being sick, but I want to know why I'm so depressed." It was he who told me I had hepatitis. [Golde 1986:103]

Nader lost three months of fieldwork all together, and virtually restarted her fieldwork when she returned to the village.

Renato Rosaldo, in personal communications (1986), tells of the difficulties of making decisions, both practical and scientific, in the field when illness, poor nutrition, and professional anxiety cloud judgment. Particularly in dissertation research, Rosaldo notes, anthropologists may be living with short supplies, a limited budget, only partial confidence in a brighter future, and a sense of desperation that if the valuable scientific data are not obtained quickly, there will not be any additional opportunities to collect them. Hence graduate students may be willing to make any sacrifice, including that of the health and well-being of themselves or their loved ones, to stay in the field and get the data. The book by Mark and Delia Owens (1984) illustrates this process fully.

Hazards of Seeking Approval from Locals

Marjorie Shostak (1981:36–37) illustrates the difficulties of wanting the friendship of the local people.

By the time I worked with Naukha and Kxaru, I had lived in the field for more than nineteen months, and frustration, rather than reasoned patience, characterized a good proportion of my reactions. The strain of having been away from home so long, the continual pressure of adapting to other people's ways, the hard work of collecting reliable information about the lives, and the demands of the physical environment had exhausted me. . . . I wanted immediate rapport, immediate understanding, immediate confidences. I was lonely and no longer felt capable of exerting the necessary effort to gain acceptance.

Aram Yengoyan warns of the dangers of wanting and needing to be liked by one's informants (1977:250). He tells a wry story of being perceived as a homosexual by the Mandaya (upland rice cultivators of the Philippines) because he was unmarried at the time and did not approach the local women, and also of being misperceived by locals who did not understand his tasks.

My initial desire to be accepted by the Mandaya evaporated soon after the debacle with the females and with the Muslim proselytizer. It was at this point that I realized that the ideal of being completely accepted by a particular group is a romantic myth. . . . The ethnographer who feels he is a special personality who must be accepted and "liked" by all the members of the group he is working with is fairly naive. No one is liked and accepted by everyone, even in his own culture, so there is no reason why he should be completely accepted in an alien society.

Yengoyan goes on to consider the efforts that ethnographers make to fit into the local culture and avoid making themselves conspicuous, even at considerable personal inconvenience or danger. His conclusions, based upon a lifetime of field research, should encourage young anthropologists who hesitate to refuse to drink dirty water, to wade through snail-infested swamps, or to insist upon use of safety belts in their vehicles.

This raises the question of going "native." The Mandaya and Pitjandjara recognized that I was racially and culturally different, and their expectations of my behavior were well established. They know that whites wear trousers and shirts, are not subincised, do not have totems, and do not believe in *asuwang* spirits.

Repatriation Stress

This rather clumsy term refers to the mental distress that some people feel at coming home again after spending time in the field. While it is not a phrase in common use in North America, no anthropologist seemed to have any difficulty understanding exactly what it means, and no one asked for an explanation. On the contrary, they reported that repatriation stress is a common hazard of the anthropological life.

We note in Table 12.7 that repatriation stress is much more commonly reported for self than for others in the research group. This is probably partly because most of us are more sensitive to our own emotions and feelings than to others', but also because repatriation stress doesn't develop until after leaving the field, so that the primary informant may be separated from the others and hence not know how they feel.

The sensation of repatriation stress seems to be primarily a sense of alienation and dislocation from one's own society, a sense that life doesn't make sense in the home society, and a judgmental sense of criticism of the society. One may be lonely for people, sights, sounds, smells, etc., from the studied culture, which have in some way replaced the home culture in one's affections. A few anthropologists sink into deep depression, and have a sense that they have ruined their life and ruined their membership in their own society. In most cases this sense is transitory, and it usually passes after some months. The previously noted tendency for anthropologists to wear tokens of the cultures they have worked with is an indicator of a permanently changed cultural identity.

Suicide Attempts and Gestures, Covert and Overt

Ruth Landes (in Golde 1986:123) tells us:

> Fieldworkers situated alone often feel private panic at being stranded in the oceanic vastness of a foreign people. One's concept of self disintegrates because the accustomed responses have disappeared; one seeks restoration through letters from home, addressed to the remembered personality. There are loneliness, uprooting, fears, true and marked physical hardships, diseases, lack of diversions to relieve tensions—all of these nurture melancholies and spiritual fatigue. I have known at least one person who toyed with the idea of suicide and another who actually committed it.

In the extremes of despair and psychic pain, many people consider suicide, and a minority of these may actually kill themselves. We saw under the heading of human hazards that some deaths in the field are difficult to classify without understanding the full motivation of the deceased person. Whether a death was caused by a suicide, murder or deliberately provoked murder may be difficult to

Table 12.7. Repatriation Stress

	N. America	Europe	L. America	India	Africa	Pacific	Total
Total	61	17	63	17	23	23	204
Had condition, self	3	2	7	2	5	4	23
	5%	*12%*	*11%*	*12%*	*22%*	*17%*	*11%*
Others in group had it	1	0	3	0	0	3	7
	7%	*12%*	*16%*	*12%*	*22%*	*30%*	*15%*

ascertain, and a death that follows deliberate or reckless behavior relative to sickness and accident may have a suicidal component to it.

Outside the field it is generally easier to tell whether deaths are caused by suicide. Probably most anthropologists can think of at least one acquaintance or colleague of their own who has died by suicide. At least seven anthropologists are said to have died by suicide in the past decade.

Mental Health Stresses on Graduate Students

Since repatriation stress is likely to be most severe after first fieldwork, and after prolonged fieldwork, it is particularly unfortunate that it hits graduate students hardest of all anthropologists.

Typically the graduate student has done relatively lengthy fieldwork, and typically he or she has become very deeply involved in the fieldwork, to the extent that one might feel very cut off from the home society. To then return to a situation of low status, often with marginal economic resources, with the daunting task of organizing the data collected and writing a Ph.D. dissertation from it, is a difficult set of demands. In a relatively high proportion of cases, the student will have dissolved personal and intimate ties during the fieldwork, and may be searching for a new attachment at the same time. Some have been sick or injured and need to recover from these physical problems. And this intersects with an ideology in anthropology that good anthropologists flounder in private until an intellectual framework for the research has been constructed, which denies the student the support of faculty and other students in many cases. A less psychologically supportive situation can hardly be imagined.

It is not easy to estimate how many of the students who go the field eventually finish the Ph.D. or become professionally employed without the Ph.D., on the one hand, and how many flounder in the attempt to write up the research and eventually fail. The question combines several factors, like the availability of jobs for new Ph.D.'s and the attractions of alternative career possibilities. But to have invested some years in classroom work and then at least a year in fieldwork before abandoning the attempt would seem to be an expensive mistake by anyone's standards.

Controlling Fieldwork Stress and Easing the Pain of Mental Distress

Yet most young anthropologists don't kill themselves or ''go crazy,'' or ''have a nervous breakdown'' as people used to say. Instead they flounder, they agonize, they withdraw from contact, and they stall, sometimes for several years, until ready to confront the data collected and turn it into an acceptable thesis. Some drop out, even after fieldwork, unable to bring the thesis to completion or to cope with the isolation and discouragement of the post-field period. (Unfortunately, this study cannot provide information on the rate, as the sample is drawn from workers at a later stage of their careers.) But most eventually solve their problems in private, and deny them in public. Eventually these people complete the thesis, get jobs in the established universities, and stand ready to replicate the system of training students by refusal to recognize and discuss the problems they faced.

How can we minimize the problems of mental distress and illness associated with fieldwork? Would minimizing the pain of the fieldwork experience also lessen the power of the confrontation between the anthropologist and the culture?

To minimize the distress, we can recognize that mental stress can be very great in the field, and that we will vary as individuals and at different times in our lives in our ability to accept and cope with these stresses. We need to entertain the possibilities of our own limits in deciding what fieldwork we can and cannot do. There is an endless array of researchable problems, and no one has to go work on leech-infested jungle trails, on high altitude mountains, or in urban slums if that is beyond their own psychic capacity. "Know thyself," we are advised, and that seems to be particularly wise advice in the case of someone planning fieldwork.

Second, we all have defense mechanisms that keep the corrosive effects of psychic strain away from us when it gets to be too much. Some of us read mystery stories, some write poetry, some sleep long hours, and so on. We need to recognize the defenses that work for us, and have access in the field to those "holidays" from stress when we need them. Some researchers feel that they have a lot to learn about situations if they are denied their escapes, and leave them behind, but one ought to allow, too, for the severe situation, and provide for an outlet when things get extreme.

A classic anthropologist's defense from the difficulties of fieldwork is to keep a fieldwork journal, in which one's honest and spontaneous reactions to the events of the day are recorded, even if these responses are impolite, impolitic, or even irrational. Recording and being conscious of one's reactions is a healthy defense against the stresses of the continually unfamiliar, and the improper impulse. One must learn to control behavior in the field, but it is too alienating to attempt to control even one's thoughts, hence the usefulness of the diary, especially for those who work alone with the local informants (see Golde 1986:75). Malinowski's *Diary in the Strict Sense of the Term* (1967) is the classic instance, and while it makes fascinating reading, the fact that it was eventually published poses a warning to contemporary anthropologists that their most private thoughts may eventually get back to those observed.

Psychically, most of us depend upon others and derive a great deal of comfort and satisfaction from those close to us. Indeed, we will see in the next chapter that this is a major reason why many anthropologists feel strongly about bringing their spouse and family members to the field. But there are two pitfalls of this dependency and shared closeness that we have to take into account.

First of all, the spouse and/or others who provide the support and comfort also have their own psychological needs, and the investigator will need to devote some attention to meeting these needs if the other comes along. The attitude that the fieldwork is paramount, that no one has the right to expect anything from the anthropologist in the field other than that the work is well done, is not only a dated survival of sexism, but more important, it just doesn't work in the long run. Nowadays, there are few relationships that will provide long-term support if the regard is not reciprocal.

Second, we have seen that not everyone can carry off all forms of fieldwork, and this consideration is just as true for other members of the research group, family, students, and colleagues, as it is for the primary researcher. If anyone in the group cannot stand the strain, they have to have an escape route. This implies that the researcher is not totally free to select a site and a problem, regardless of the wishes of the others involved in the group. Somehow the group has to be able to make decisions that take into account the basic needs of all the members. This is an issue we will examine in Chapter 13, "Families in the Field."

And finally, we have to develop some acceptance of the need, under some circumstances, to leave the field and seek rest, recreation, therapy, or just a change of scene when it gets to be excessively stressful. Too often researchers (especially graduate students) are working on a shoestring, and they feel that they cannot afford to leave the field, that they could never afford to come back and finish the fieldwork if they leave early, or that they will be laughed at and punished by non-support if they leave in response to massive anxiety, depression, or other signs of stress. Sometimes such a feeling is evidence of the loss of good judgment that accompanies severe stress, but of course it is also frequently true that money is in short supply, particularly on student research projects. And it may well happen—indeed we know it does happen—that colleagues and supervisors are not supportive or accepting of the need to take a rest from the continual stress of fieldwork.

In any case, if a person has to leave the field to regain mental stability, then they have to leave just as much as if they had contracted hepatitis or tuberculosis. I stress this point because I think it sometimes happens that exhausted and stressed researchers who cannot justify leaving early get sloppy with hygiene and precautions until sickness "forces" them to leave early, a way of "solving" the problem without taking responsibility for the decision to treat a mental problem seriously.

Renato Rosaldo (Stanford) suffered from fieldwork stress in his work with the Ilongot in the Philippines, even before the death in 1981 of his wife, Michelle Zimbalist Rosaldo. In conversation (1986), he urges attention to the problems that some fieldworkers will have maintaining mental health in the field. He urges us to accept and recognize that exhaustion, malnutrition, many infections, and some drugs can involve mental consequences of depression and anxiety. A person suffering from field-induced stress is not in the best position to recognize his or her own problem and take rational action, neither overreacting nor underreacting. It may be that a supervisor, fellow student, or other colleague may detect the developing problems from a distance. We should have some kind of an accepted procedure of monitoring mental health as well as physical health and accepting the need for treatment or rest when required. The financial problems are often very real, but maintaining health and good judgment in the field needs to be a primary goal, even if it means that the completion of the fieldwork will be delayed.

Rosaldo (1984, personal communication) points, too, to the prices of denial and distance as a means of maintaining mental balance in the field, paid in the quality of the anthropological work that is produced. What is the use of staying longer in the field if it means that one cannot afford the risk of getting close to the emotional content of the events going on around one? The task of confronting the complex realities of the life of a distant and exotic culture is enormously demanding. It is not clear whether many people, even many anthropologists, who have been selected for their abilities to comprehend cross-cultural events, can accurately and openly understand the emotional content of what is experienced in other cultures. But surely it must be an added burden and handicap if the observer who has traveled so far and endured so much in the effort to be in the right place to observe and understand is at the same time suffering from depression, anxiety, or culture shock.

CHAPTER 13   FAMILIES IN THE FIELD

We saw in Chapter 4 that in the case of India and Asia, between a quarter and a half of field trips consisted of the researcher going alone, while in other areas the majority of informants went with others—colleagues, students, or family members. From the point of view of logistics, larger groups are probably easier to manage, as the work of travel, maintenance, and settling in can be shared among more people. Larger groups represent more exposure to risk, but also provide more resources for prevention of problems, nursing, coping with problems that arise, and for emergency evacuation if needed.

When the others who accompany the researcher are family rather than colleagues or students, however, there are often special considerations. Research financing usually covers the expenses of the professional staff but not the expenses of family members, so that resources are likely to be stretched more thinly on a family trip. And while spouses who come along usually share in the work and responsibilities of keeping the expedition going, children usually do not. In fact, young children may greatly add to the work of the adults, in their need for food, comfort, supervision, play, education, and entertainment. Children are at least as much exposed to the risks of illness and accidents as adults are, and respond more dramatically to many forms of illness and injury. Thus, taking families to the field has both positive and negative implications for the researcher, personally and professionally, and for the family members.

In personal communications, researchers have told us that loneliness can be an overwhelming problem in the field, and that it is easier to maintain a sense of psychological well-being when the experience is shared with family members. Many anthropologists have reported that the fieldwork itself benefits when family members come to the field. One person said that especially when the lives of the two sexes are lived separately, it is extremely important to have a spouse in the field to report on what the other sex is doing and saying and thinking. Some spouses help with the work of data collection, or help by typing notes or labeling specimens. Most help with the everyday work of camp life, cooking and washing clothes. Nevertheless, the presence of the family may also take time away from the demands of data collection, introduce distance between the investigator and the local population, and constrain decisions about how the fieldwork will be done owing to special requirements of family members (such as competing work demands, preferences or phobias, allergies or illnesses).

Recently there has been interest in the issues of taking children to the field (Cassell 1987), and we will look at the experiences of our sample in this area shortly. First we will look at the reports of behavior and issues surrounding taking spouses to the field.

Spouses in the Field

The information in Table 13.1 differs from that we previously looked at (Table 4.2) in that it reports whether the investigator has at any time taken the spouse to the field, whereas Chapter 4 was reporting on the numbers who went on particular field trips. We see in Table 13.1 that taking the spouse is more related to working in distant and difficult environments (India and Africa) than it is to working in nearby and more convenient ones (such as Latin America and Europe), although the highest rates are among those who primarily work in North America, where access to the field by spouses is particularly easy. Respondents make it clear that spouses do not necessarily come for the whole field trip. Many report that they like to go alone and get settled, and then have the family come to share part of the experience. Others expect the family to come to the field only for brief vacations.

Taking the spouse seems not to be particularly related to taking students to the field: about 73% of those who ever take students have ever taken their spouse, while 27% of those who have taken students have not taken a spouse. Overall, only 20% report having taken students to the field—a fraction of those who have taken their spouse. Social-cultural fieldworkers (including linguists) are only slightly more likely (70.5%) to take a spouse than archaeologists (including physical anthropologists) (68.5%).

The 57 women in the sample report that 68% have taken their husbands, while 70% of the 147 men have taken their wives. These small differences may reflect differences in the percentage ever married, or in age structure of the men and the women. Table 13.2 shows the percentage of those who have taken a spouse to the field by age and sex groups.

We note in Table 13.2 that the proportion of those who have taken a spouse to the field is higher for the older groups, partly as a result of the cumulative nature of the question. But it is probable also that in recent years important changes in the nature of fieldwork and in the nature of marriage in North America have affected the custom of taking a spouse to the field. Among the older anthropologists, it was more acceptable and more frequently seen that the wife would subordinate her career interests and even her preferences to those of the husband, accompanying him for long periods of time to the bush if that was what he wished. The

Table 13.1. Percentage of Spouses in the Field

	N. America	Europe	L. America	India	Africa	Pacific	Total
Total	61	17	63	17	23	23	204
Spouse (or equivalent) ever came?	74%	65	67	76	74	61	70%

Table 13.2. Percent that Has Taken a Spouse to the Field, by Age and Sex

Age	Males	Females	Both Sexes	N
20–29	0%	100%	50%	2
30–39	62	60	62	52
40–49	76	72	75	80
50–59	64	63	64	39
60–69	75	100	78	23
70+	75	—	75	8
Totals	147	57	204	204
	70%	68%	69%	

older age groups not only have higher proportions who have taken their spouse to the field, but the spouse is reported to have spent more time in the field. Indeed about 40% of the sample over 50 years of age report that their spouse "always" or "almost always" goes along on fieldwork. The problems of spouses are somewhat different for the two sexes, so we will consider them separately.

Wives in the Field

One informant on the role of wives in the field is Betty Clark, wife of J. Desmond Clark (University of California, Berkeley), who has been working with her husband for nearly fifty years in Africa, India, Britain, and North America, in the field and at the university. Betty Clark told me early in this study of the necessity she perceived not only to hire a cook in the field but actually to check on the cook, especially in the early days of fieldwork but occasionally throughout the work, to make sure that drinking water was thoroughly boiled, dishes properly cleaned, fresh food prepared, and so on. As an active participant in the fieldwork research, and as camp manager, she has played an important role in maintaining the health and psychological equilibrium of students and colleagues as well as her husband and her children in the field. And it was striking to hear at a gathering in 1986 to honor Desmond Clark, after fifty years in the field of archaeology, that he is notable not only for the accomplishments of his scientific work but also for never having a death on one of his expeditions. The credit for that record goes not only to him but also to Betty Clark—for care in planning, for a cool head in emergencies, and for maintaining the day-to-day health and safety of the fieldwork teams.

Another informant on the role of "wives in the field" is Nancy DeVore, who has accompanied husband Irv DeVore (Harvard) through years of fieldwork in Africa, the Pacific, and Australia. The range of field skills she has mastered—bush cooking, truck driving, hut construction, first aid, shopping for months at a time, entertaining visiting colleagues, teaching her children when they were young, recording animal observations, and typing correspondence—is impressive and at the same time quite unreasonably expected of anyone in this role. Watching her cope, one wonders how colleagues who do not have such a competent spouse manage to survive.

Other accounts of what it was like to be a wife on an archaeological expedition during the past fifty years can be seen in Linda Braidwood's (1953) account of fieldwork in Iraq, and in the charming account by Agatha Christie of her adventures while accompanying her husband, Max Mallowan, on his expeditions in Iraq and Syria (Christie 1946; see also Morris 1978 and Hibben 1983). Social anthropologists' stories are told by Theodora Kroeber (1970). For an account of an unhappy partnership, see the wonderfully rich, even outrageous tale of Carobeth Laird's work with John Peabody Harrington (Laird 1975). Nathalie Woodbury, editor of the "Past is Present" section of the *Anthropology Newsletter,* reviewed books by wives of anthropologists in the November 1985 edition.

Among younger anthropologists, it more often happens that the spouse has his or her own career requirements that may conflict with the demands of fieldwork. One pattern is that of the marriage of two anthropologists, both doing professional fieldwork.

The pattern is not new, although it is probably more common among the younger people. We think of Margaret Mead and Gregory Bateson or, earlier, Margaret Mead and Reo Fortune (Mead 1977). Louis and Mary Leakey provide another example from the older generation. One can think of dozens of examples of couples who have collaborated in their professional work, and one frequently observes marriages among graduate students. There are obvious advantages to this: they both have an understanding of the scientific-professional requirements of the work; they are able to work together toward important career goals in the field; and ideally they can share the burdens of the housekeeping and scientific tasks. When asked, in the questionnaire, whether they would take their family to the field in the future, seven of the 204 noted that their spouse is also an anthropologist and goes as a fellow professional. This arrangement eases the financial strains of taking families to the field on funded research, as both can have a stipend and their expenses are covered.

When couples have children, however, they sometimes find that the partnership in fieldwork cannot be sustained. Bonnie G. MacDougall, of the South Asia Program of Cornell University, writes (1987)

> There was a period in our lives (at the end of the '70s) when we would take turns parenting and going to South Asia. One of the reasons we did not travel to the field as a family was because we felt our field sites and methods of operations to be too risky. By that time we were familiar enough with instances in which fieldworkers had lost children to meningitis, rabies, and so on.

Other couples are seen in which both are professionals but not both anthropologists, and these couples seem to have a difficult time managing to go to the field together, at least for any long period of time. When the wife is a doctor or lawyer, business executive or artist, couples seem to face the same problems synchronizing their assignments and their lives as couples in which it is the wife who is the anthropologist and the husband who has other career commitments. And clearly, the frequency of marriages in which the wife has substantial professional commitments has increased in the past decade.

Husbands in the Field

For women anthropologists, one pattern is to have an anthropologist husband in the field with her: at least a half dozen among the 57 women in the sample were living this pattern. Both being professionals does not solve all of the potential problems of families in the field, however. There may still be conflicts of site and problem selection, of work sharing, and of their personal life.

A second pattern is one in which the wife needs to go to the field, but the husband has career commitments which do not permit him to go to with her, except perhaps for a few weeks at a time as a visitor. Joan Cassell tells something of the constraints on fieldwork of this kind of marriage (Cassell 1987:3) and the difficulty she had getting advice about her arrangements for simultaneously doing fieldwork and taking care of her two children, six and nine, without the help of her physician husband or her usual societal supports.

> When (fieldwork in) Jamaica was discussed, I took it for granted that, as a married woman with two children, I would be unable to go . . . I knew no female professors or anthropologists with young children. My male professors with children had wives who stayed home to care for them. . . . My adviser, when asked, assured me that lots of people did fieldwork with children. . . . (After a few weeks in Jamaica alone) I started awakening in the middle of the night, wondering whether I had made a terrible mistake. It occurred to me that all the people my adviser knew who had done fieldwork with children were probably researcher-husbands, whose wives cared for the children, ran the household, typed the husband's fieldwork notes, and studied the local women on the side.

The third pattern is that in which the husband has lower career achievements, and/or less education, than the anthropologist-wife. In two cases that I know of, the husband is also somewhat younger than the wife. The husband's contributions to fieldwork may lie primarily in the areas of camp management, vehicle maintenance, working with crews of locals, and so forth. This pattern is said to have substantial advantages for the woman anthropologist, in that the husband's priorities are not so likely to conflict with her needs to carry out fieldwork and accomplish research goals. Marriages, however, are rarely made to order, and the obvious advantages of this pattern for the wife do not necessarily increase its frequency. Nor do they guarantee a successful marriage; the divorce rate seems to be as high in these marriages as in others.

Strains on the Relationship

Fieldwork seems to cause strains on marital relationships both for those couples who go to the field together and for those who are separated by fieldwork. Table 13.3 shows the answers to the question of whether fieldwork caused problems for the relationship with the spouse (or equivalent).

Asked if fieldwork caused any problems in the relationship, about 30% replied that it had. Among those who said there were no relationship problems, were those who had no spouse, or who left the question about spouse blank. About 92% of those who took a spouse to the field, ever, reported problems in the relationship caused by fieldwork. Some of the remarks made were even more pointed: "Of course there were problems," one person said, and another said, "Only until we got a divorce." All of the fieldworkers who took family members to the field reported special health and safety problems because of doing so, although many also noted the health and safety advantages of families: more caution, taking better care of health from day to day, and a concerned helper in an emergency.

Most of the strains seem to come from the relationship of the spouses and the requirements of fieldwork, but others may come from the complicating attitudes and behaviors of the local people. Locals do not necessarily welcome spouses and attempt to make their stay pleasant. Wives tell of loneliness and a sense of uselessness in the field in situations where lack of the local language or difficulties for women in moving freely restricted their activities. Some hate aspects of fieldwork, such as discomfort, insecurity, living with insects, inability to keep clean personally or to keep the house or kitchen clean, to get a decent meal. And the spouse doing fieldwork may or may not be sympathetic or helpful in dealing with these problems of adjustment. Certainly it happens that some are distinctly unsympathetic, are unappreciative of the sacrifices that the spouse is making, and merely want to be left alone to get on with the work (Laird 1975).

Not surprisingly, these strains affect marriages. Some spouses find that they cannot tolerate the life, and return home earlier than expected. Others grit their

Table 13.3. Relationship Problems Caused by Fieldwork

	N. America	Europe	L. America	India	Africa	Pacific	Total
Total	61	17	63	17	23	23	204
Caused relationship problems	31%	18	30	24	35	35	30%
In future, would you take family?	63%	35	57	71	65	57	59%

teeth and bear it during the scheduled fieldwork, but refuse to plan additional trips. Quite a substantial proportion of couples who return from the field divorce within a year or two. Whether the rate of divorce is higher for those who do field-work than those who do not cannot be answered with available data, but it seems likely that the rate is high.

Strains of Separation

Other couples avoid the stresses of shared fieldwork by separating, so that the anthropological member of the team goes to the field while the spouse stays be-hind to maintain the usual family home and his or her own career requirements. The difficulties of separation are obvious: many find other sexual partners during the separation, and even among those who do not, the failure to share important life events increases distance and stresses the marriage.

Forming Intimate Relations with Locals during Fieldwork

One solution to the problem of loneliness in the field and the difficulty of taking one's spouse along is to take another (or a first) spouse from among the local population. If the population studied is truly remote, the researcher may expect that consequences of this choice may not impinge on family and professional life at home. Many anthropologists have formed more or less serious, more and less long-term and committing ties in the field.

Most anthropologists are hesitant to discuss this kind of situation. One excep-tion is Hans J. Heinz, who tells a curious love story in his account of his pseudo-marriage to a !Ko Bushman woman (1979). Manda Ccsara (1982) tells of her sexual and other adventures in the field. Another informant is Peggy Golde, who rejected forming such a tie in the field. She says of the local Mexican villagers she was studying:

> They found it hard to understand how, I, so obviously attractive in their eyes, could still be single. The obvious remedy was to suggest that I marry in the village. They certainly recognized that I could not work in the fields, wash clothes, grind corn, make tortillas, or haul firewood, but they assured me that, if I did marry a village boy, my future mother or sister-in-law would do all that for me. . . . The important thing was to get me safely married so that I would cease being an anom-aly. . . .
>   (After telling about a man who came to her house drunk one night and tried to break in) If I had needed it, this event would also have served as a reminder of the inadvisability of intimate involve-ments on my part. Even if the professional and ethical norms of restraint hadn't been communicated to me as a graduate student, with the warning that intimate relations could result in the loss of the capacity for objectivity . . . my very inability to predict the short- and long-term repercussions of such relations, either for myself or for the people, would have acted to brake any impulses I might have had to move closer. [Golde 1986:85]

Marriage to a local person involves whole sets of norms and assumptions that may or may not be shared between the anthropologist and the local people. For example, Robert Dentan (1988:627) tells, in a discussion of violence among the Semai:

> . . . there is some evidence that a young man among the culturally similar Temiar blowpiped a poisoned dart into the eye of an ethnographer who refused to allow him sexual access to the eth-nographer's Temiar wife, even though the affinal tie between the wife and the supposed murderer was one in which Temiar custom encouraged sexual dalliance and even marriage (Noone and Hol-man 1972).

It is also possible to have a child with one of the local people, which some peoples would welcome as an opportunity to cement ties with the anthropologist. Golde tells of the attitudes of the villagers in Mexico where she worked:

> One man said he hoped that I would have a child in the village, whom I would leave behind when I returned to the States. It was his belief that such a child, having some of my blood, presumably would be fair, strong and wise because of it. [Golde 1986:85]

Golde did not fulfill this fantasy of the local peoples, but there are several well-known cases of anthropologists who have had a child with a member of the informant population. Some of the early Arctic explorers and investigators had children with local women, and a 60-year-old descendent of one of these researchers recently visited paternal relatives in the United States, an event reported in a feature article in the *New York Times*. Relying upon the remoteness of the study population to protect one from the consequences of such arrangements is unrealistic, as no populations are so remote that they can hold an interesting secret indefinitely.

Illness of the Spouse during Fieldwork

Spouses, like the anthropologists themselves, are subject to all the risks to their health and safety that are posed in that environment. Dozens of volunteer informants tell of illnesses and injuries to their spouses, including altitude sickness, boating accidents, malaria, hepatitis, dog bites, car and truck accidents, and heart attacks. The illnesses of one's spouse, like illnesses to one's self, can be complicated by the difficulties of obtaining proper medical care, not knowing the local language, and financial problems caused by the medical bills. There are many cases of field seasons delayed or terminated early because of the illness or accident of a spouse. For instance, a volunteer reports, "In 1973, my then-wife developed double pneumonia, which is a rarity in the jungle, and this took some time to diagnose and cure."

Death of the Spouse during Fieldwork

In an interview by Burton Pasternak in *Current Anthropology* (29:640), the Chinese anthropologist Fei Xiaotong discusses the death of his first wife, a fellow student, in the field in 1935.

> . . . I prepared to leave for fieldwork in Guanxi, at Yao Mountain. I had a girlfriend at the time, Wang Tonghui, and we agreed to go into the field together. But of course we had to get married to do that. . . . So we married, and after a few weeks we began our journey. It was 108 days from the wedding to her death.

A footnote provides the details.

> On a remote trail, Fei walked into a tiger trap and was badly injured by falling rock and timbers. Unable to release him, his wife set off in search of help. The next morning, despite great pain, Fei managed to extricate himself from the trap. He crawled for most of the day and was finally found late in the afternoon by . . . local tribesmen. Several days later they found his wife's body floating in a mountain stream (Arkush 1981:66–67). [Pasternak 1988:640]

Fei was unable to walk, even with a stick, for six months or so. During his recuperation he wrote his first book, based upon their field notes, and published it under the name of his deceased wife.

Any death in the field to a member of the research group is a difficult situation, but when it is the spouse of the anthropologist who has died, the problems may be overwhelming. Several cases are reported of a spouse who became ill or injured in the field, was transported back home, and then died. At least under those circumstances the surviving spouse does not have to transport the body out of the field area or otherwise make special arrangements for burial.

Renato Rosaldo lost his wife, Michelle Zimbalist Rosaldo, in a fall from a mountain path in the Philippines, while both were working with the Ilongots. Rosaldo's difficulties in managing the situation were complicated by the remoteness of the field site, and the additional responsibilities of caring for his two small children, who had accompanied their parents to the field (Rosaldo 1984).

Children in the Field

Taking children to the field is a complicated enterprise—one that was little discussed in any public form until the publication of a fascinating book edited by Joan Cassell (1987), *Children in the Field, Anthropological Experiences.* It includes accounts of birth and death of children in the field, several detailed accounts of the experience from children's point of view, and a fascinating essay by Jonathan Wylie, who had been taken to the field as a child in the 1950s, and who took his own child in the 1980s. This book is strongly recommended to anyone who contemplates taking children to the field.

Such a person can also get advice from a wide range of colleagues, as taking children to the field is very commonly done. Table 13.4 shows the percentage of respondents who ever took any of the children, and their responses to the question whether in the future they would take their children and other family members (including spouse) to the field.

Taking children is most common among those anthropologists who also report taking a spouse. Overall, about 20% of the fieldworkers report never having taken either spouse or children, 34% have taken spouse but not children, 46% have taken both spouse and children, and less than 1% have taken children but not the spouse.

The need for caretakers for young and dependent children may be another problem for fieldworkers. In some areas of the world (India and southern Africa come particularly to mind), the tradition of hiring servants to help manage children is well established, and childcare might actually be easier for parents of young children than it would be at home. But in many other parts of the world, there is no such tradition of hired caretakers, and a child's kin are expected to do everything required.

Young babies and toddlers may need so much care under unfamiliar conditions that their presence would seriously interfere with fieldwork. Older children, of course, can take care of themselves in some way, but parents nevertheless report

Table 13.4. Frequency of Taking Children to the Field

	N. America	Europe	L. America	India	Africa	Pacific	Total
Total	61	17	63	17	23	23	204
Children ever came?	64%	38%	39%	53%	45%	28%	47%
In future, would take family	63%	35%	57%	71%	65%	57%	59%

that even these children change many aspects of the fieldwork situation by their presence. It is easiest to manage one or a small number of children if both parents share the responsibility. The experiences of Joan Cassell (Cassell 1987:1–27), who took two children, 6 and 9, to Jamaica without the help of her husband, and of Melanie Dreher (Cassell 1987:149–171), who took three children, 7 years, 4 years, and 9 months old to the field, are rather unusual among fieldworkers. Jonathan Wylie took his 19-month-old daughter to the field without his wife, but his case is almost unique (Cassell 1987:113–120). It may be, however, that the increasing independence of spouses from one another, and the increasing incidence of single mothers in all occupations will lead to an increase in cases of children being taken to the field by one parent. Where there is only one parent to care for children, the dangers to children include illness of the parent, who might be hospitalized or unable to care for the child.

Psychological Stress on Children from Fieldwork

Parents report that children often find what Nancy Scheper-Hughes (University of California-Berkeley) calls "the radical otherness" of fieldwork to be stressful. Indeed, their parents, too, often or usually find it stressful—and they have chosen this path while the children have not. Again, Scheper-Hughes puts it well: "Family members may or may not share the anthropologist's affinity or enthusiasm for "basic strangement," and the children especially may have been more often drafted than have willingly volunteered for the "foreign service" (Scheper-Hughes 1987:218).

Some of the stresses on children are merely those that any child faces when moved to a new home—the need to make new friends, learn a new environment, and deal with the family under conditions of isolation. Jonathan Wylie (Wylie 1987:91–120) recalls his childhood field experience in several French villages. He tells of the forced intimacy of family life in the field, which may come at an awkward time for growing children. He recognizes some of the difficulties his mother had in the long periods they spent in the field, and has sensitive suggestions as to how her life could have been made more endurable for her. And he tells something of how difficult it is for a child to learn a new language, attend a new kind of school system, find children to play with, and adjust to a difficult culture. This was in a French village—surely one of the easier cultures for an American child to master.

Several parents tell of the benefits but also the difficulties of their children's love for pets and small animals, ranging from the pleasures of feeding a lamb a bottle for Jonathan Wylie's daughter, to the fun of keeping lizards, monkeys, and toucans for the Hugh-Jones's children in the jungle of Colombia, and chickens for the three Scheper-Hughes children in Brazil. But relations to animals are also cited as object lessons for children about the differing standards of behaviors in the studied culture. American children seem frequently to criticize the local cultures for cruelty to animals, and children have been shocked by cockfights (Scheper-Hughes 1987:227), the stoning of a dog to death (Scheper-Hughes 1987:227–228), killing and eating a monkey (Cassell 1987:49), and the death of a dog in a fight with other dogs (Cassell 1987:166). Many of the children are reported to be upset by the scarcity or absence of familiar food and experience deep anxiety over hunger for themselves and the people they see around them. Many endure illnesses, serious or trivial, and are disturbed by them. The letters and diaries of children quoted in Cassell's book seem frequently to center on issues of illness of self and siblings and the lack of good things to eat.

Several of the children are reported to have become so depressed and upset over their situation that they refused to eat (Dreher 1987:156; Scheper-Hughes 1987:227). Others (or the same child at another stage of coping) refused to talk or to interact with anyone outside the family (Dreher 1987:154–156; Scheper-Hughes 1987:229). None of the children described in Cassell's book were taken out of the field by their parents in response to their social and psychological difficulties, but other anthropologists have told me of the need to do this.

Illness of Children in the Field

Illness of children during fieldwork is commonly reported by volunteers. They are subject to most of the risks of fieldwork that adults experience, and in some cases they may be more exposed (because little children put everything in their mouth, for example) or may be exposed to more serious consequences (because of smaller body size, for instance).

The one-year-old daughter of a worker in American Samoa contracted a severe diarrheal disease while the family was working on an island served by a boat that came only once a month. Fortunately, the boat arrived unexpectedly, off schedule, and the family took advantage of its arrival to get to the hospital, where the child arrived with a fever of 104 degrees and severe dehydration. The child could easily have died without transport.

Another volunteer reports, "My three-year-old son suffered severe bouts of gastrointestinal infection with high fever, during which he refused to eat or drink and was unable to keep his medication down. We were living in Quito Ecuador at the time, and fortunately we could take him to hospital where he got medication by suppository or injection."

Several parents tell of children unable to absorb medication by mouth during severe illness, so that treatment by a physician was essential. An archaeologist was horrified when a 12-year-old girl lost one-third of her body weight in a few days from severe vomiting and diarrhea, and could not keep down medication.

The oldest son of an anthropologist working in Tanzania developed vestibular neuronitis, a disease not reported by anyone else in this study. He was hospitalized for eight weeks in Africa and continued to have symptoms of the illness for more than a year after he returned to the United States.

Jonathan Wylie developed appendicitis while in the field in France with his family in the 1950s, and had his appendix removed—a frightening experience, although no more dangerous in France than in the United States.

Deborah Gewerz (Amherst College) tells that her five-year-old daughter got pneumonia in New Guinea in 1974. The roads to the capital were washed out at the time, so she was taken to a small subprovincial hospital, six hours away. Because of a shortage of penicillin there, the child was given chloromycetin, a drug that could have caused serious side effects to the child's bone marrow. Eventually she was flown to the district capital, where she received good care and recovered.

Bernice Kaplan tells of taking her two children on a year of fieldwork in Peru many years ago. The baby suffered from eczema, skin rashes, and digestive troubles. Kaplan writes:

Family and friends believed us "mad" to take a 3-month-old and a 21-month-old to Peru. My view
was that "people have babies there too." What I did not know until we were well into data gathering, and which might have affected my decision had I known, was that at that time, 1955, 50%
of local infants died before reaching two years of age.

Other parents expressed regret that their children had been forced to endure extremely frightening experiences, even if they were not hurt or sick. A woman
archaeologist and her four-year-old child were kidnapped by guerillas in Peru and
then abandoned in the desert to walk back to town. And a single mother working
in Indonesia became very sick and could not care properly for her child due to her
coma and delirium.

Deaths to Children in the Field

As much as parents would like to avoid thinking about it, children do die in the
field. As one such parent, I can testify that the reality is very stark. The best account of such a death is by Patricia Hitchcock, entitled "Our Ulleri Child," (published originally in *Redbook* magazine and reprinted in Cassell 1987:173–183).
Their one-year-old son, Ben, died in Nepal, in his sleep, of a sudden respiratory
illness. Patricia Hitchcock speaks of issues that all parents who consider taking
their children to the field must face.

As always, relatives tried to dissuade us. They would look at year-old Ben and remind us how fast
dysentery can dehydrate a baby. But I would see a headline in a local newspaper, "Child Drowns
in Family Pool," and hope that—in some ways—we would be taking him to safety. We all had
very real needs that could be met only if we stayed together. The children needed a father. Two
years spent apart would bring John home a stranger; none of us would be able to understand what
he had been through or what he was thinking or writing about. To me, this would not be a marriage.
[Hitchcock 1987:175]

Donald Messerschmidt, formerly of Washington State University, and his wife
adopted a child while conducting fieldwork in Nepal in the early 1970s. That
child, Krishnan Lal, died in the field at age six months, from complications based
on an acute attack of intestinal peritonitis and diarrhea.

Nancy Howell's twin sons went to the Kalahari with their father in the summer
of 1985. They suffered a truck accident during the long trek into the field site, and
Alexander Lee, age 14, died alongside anthropologist Melissa Knauer, both from
head injuries caused by falling from the top of the moving truck when a tire blew
out. A child of Bob Laughlin (Smithsonian Institution) was drowned in a swimming pool in Chiapas, Mexico. The child of Eugene Hunn (University of Washington) died of bronchitis, also in Mexico. The daughter of the late Ralph Beals,
of the University of California, Los Angeles, died in Mexico about 40 years ago.
Louis and Mary Leakey lost a daughter in Kenya to dysentery at three months.
For each of these families, and others unnamed, the pain of losing a child has
been a substantial element in their fieldwork experience.

Pros and Cons of Taking Children to the Field

Not only children, but also parents experience real stresses when children are
taken to the field. Melanie Dreher comments that she had less physical care of her
children in the field than at home because of the availability of help and the centrality of children in all parts of the culture. She points out that it is not so much

the demands of childcare as the demands of doing fieldwork well that make it difficult to combine the roles.

> One of the features that distinguishes fieldwork from other kinds of sociological research methods is its pervasiveness. It is a 24-hour, seven-day-a-week job. I had never thought much about this until my husband innocently asked, ''Are you finished work now?'' or ''What time will you finish work today?'' How do you explain fieldwork to nonanthropologist husband and children? That it is ongoing, never complete? That concepts of time off and time on are irrelevant? . . . That the only time the work stops is when you physically remove yourself from the fieldwork situation. [Dreher 1987:168]

Researchers point out that rapport with local people may be improved by taking children, who in a sense testify to the normalcy of the parents by their presence. Some people find a gratifying degree of affection and warmth being expressed toward their children that they themselves had never experienced from the local population. Cassell warns, however, that there are messages about the power relations between the anthropologists and the subjects of study that are expressed in their behavior toward the anthropologist's children (1987:270). Indeed, the conclusion to her book is extremely thought provoking on this account.

Fieldwork can be very stressful for spouses and children. However, one has to make trade-offs—choices among available alternatives, among various kinds of fieldwork, or none at all. We have to learn to make distinctions between individuals, whether children or adults, family members or professionals, with regard to their susceptibility to various kinds of fieldwork hazards; and we need to make distinctions between various fieldwork sites in terms of the hazards that will be encountered there and the alternative ways we can anticipate those hazards and be prepared to respond to them if they strike members of our research groups.

Some parents feel that no matter how much suffering is involved for children, they are being done a favor in the long run by going to the field, as they will never be as provincial, complacent, or spoiled with possessions as the typical American child of the second half of the 20th century. And some feel that for every danger in the field, there is a corresponding danger in North American society that is being avoided, so that all in all the child might be safer going to the bush. One trades the risk of snakebite for the risk of the drug pusher, the risk of malaria for the risk of teenage suicide. It is difficult to quantify these risks precisely, but probably the risks of mortality are much higher for fieldwork than for staying home. The magnitude of the scale of the risks depends very much on where the fieldwork research is done, how far the group is from medical care in case of emergency, and whether there is safety equipment and an emergency evacuation procedure.

For families that are close and loving, going to the field means being together and sharing some of the most intense experiences of life. Many would argue that it is not desirable to avoid risks, for oneself or for one's children, but almost no one would argue for running unnecessary or pointless risks, which contribute nothing to the value of the research or the quality of life. The question of when risks are worthwhile is a central concern for all anthropologists, and one that would repay more sharing of experiences and opinion, more analysis and research.

CHAPTER 14   PRACTICING MEDICINE IN THE FIELD

We have seen the need for medical care, and the considerable distances that many researchers have to travel to obtain it. It is not surprising, then, that many anthropologists become part-time "barefoot doctors," using medical techniques to the best of their ability to treat themselves, their families, students, colleagues, employees, and even the local population.

Some anthropologists believe that it would be impossible to carry on fieldwork without practicing medicine for the locals, and some believe it would be immoral to do so. At least a few of them have found themselves floundering about in situations considerably beyond their medical skill. Some are troubled by "playing God" with the local people—selectively allocating scarce medical supplies to some and denying them to others. Some anthropologists worry about the ethics of using medical care to alter the power relationship between student and studied—that is, using the awe generated by successful medical treatment to build rapport.

In this chapter, we will look at the responses of the sample to questions about whether they took care of the health of themselves and others—who their "patients" were, what kinds of medical conditions they treated, what techniques they used, and what the outcomes have been.

Table 14.1 shows that about three-quarters of the anthropologists treat themselves for medical problems in the field, and this proportion does not vary much between continents. In other categories, the proportions vary by the need for medical treatment, which is otherwise unavailable to local people, and by the presence of others among the research group, family, students, and local employees who might need or request treatment.

The issues of practicing medicine in the field are neatly introduced by Peggy Golde (1986:72) with a story about the remote village in Mexico where she was starting her fieldwork:

Table 14.1. Practicing Medicine in the Field

	N. America	Europe	L. America	India	Africa	Pacific	Total
Total	61	17	63	17	23	23	204
Treated self	70%	71%	71%	65%	78%	74%	72%
Treated local people	25%	23%	32%	35%	56%	48%	34%
Treated group (includes family)	33%	41%	38%	29%	56%	22%	19%
Treated students	20%	41%	19%	12%	26%	9%	10%
Treated local employees	8%	0%	11%	12%	22%	0%	10%

It wasn't ten days (from the time Golde arrived) before I had my first request for medical aid. A wizened, toothless old woman, extremely agitated, brought her infant grandson wrapped like a cocoon in her *rebozo*. He screamed in terror at the sight of me. Through gestures and an occasional Spanish word, I discovered that a dog had bitten him on his penis. Since I could see that the skin hadn't been broken, after debating with myself about the wisdom of acting as a nurse, I decided to take the risk and painted his little penis crimson with mercurochrome. The old woman left, highly contented with this flamboyant treatment, and after that my house became the village pharmacy and first-aid station.

I was somewhat surprised at the Indians' assumption that I was competent to treat them medically. I discovered that in the past they had been given injections and medications by public-health nurses and schoolteachers; they therefore expected me, as an educated foreign woman, to do the same. Every morning there would be at least two or three people waiting in my yard until I awoke and could minister to their needs in my "nurse's uniform" of gaily striped men's pajamas, which they found laughable but not immodest. They always asked, "how much?" I began to charge an egg (even though they often managed to forget to pay), since I otherwise had trouble finding eggs to buy. I did what I could within the limits of my ability and of my supply of aspirin, Alka Seltzer, burn ointment, and Bandaids, and when a difficult problem presented itself, I would send or accompany the people to the clinic in Iguala, which they had never used.

David McCurdy (1976) is also a good informant on the problems of medical practice in the field. He found that when he did fieldwork in India in 1962, providing medical care for the population was an obligation that he accepted in exchange for the information they gave him. But gradually, he found his practice moving from dispensing aspirin, to taking someone to a clinic, to attempting to start a clinic, and finally to providing a range of medical services. Simultaneously, the time commitment increased from a few minutes a day to many hours. He got so that he hid from the villagers several hours a day in order to get any of his own work done. Eventually he trained a local assistant to practice the same "medicine" that he knew.

In rural areas of Africa, at least until recently, the expectation that anyone of European descent would be qualified and willing to provide some medical care was so prevalent that Mary Leakey (1984) never explicitly mentions the practice of medicine in the field, but includes a photo captioned "My assistant, Mike Tippett, tending a Masai woman and her child during the daily clinic at Olduvai camp." If such "daily clinics" are part of the responsibilities of the anthropological role, some attention to training and examination of the duties involved would seem to be in order.

The sample provides us with some information on how a cross section of anthropologists handle problems of practicing medicine in the field. One question we wonder about is whether the anthropologists are practicing medicine because the locals and the researchers cannot reach trained medical help easily, or whether there are other factors. Table 14.2 shows the proportions who have treated members of various categories, by the distance that they reported from their most important field sites to the nearest doctor or hospital.

Table 14.2 provides data to support the belief that anthropologists practice medicine on themselves and each other in part due to the absence of locally available medical care. But we also note that while the proportions are somewhat higher for those farther from medical care, substantial proportions are reported even for those who are within a few hours of a doctor, a clinic, or a hospital. It is likely that there are many cases where researchers do not trust the hygienic standards of the local hospital or clinic. The treatment of locals is much more related to the distance from alternative care, and the rate is substantially higher for those otherwise remote from medical care.

Table 14.2. Proportion Practicing Medicine by Distance to the Nearest Doctor
(Note that columns do not sum to 100%, and researchers may treat
members of various groups)

Travel to Doctor	Easy (2 Hrs or Less)	Effort (2–8 Hours)	Remote (8 Hours +)	Total
Total	91	56	57	204
Treated				
Self	69%	68%	79%	72%
Locals	21%	32%	56%	34%
Research group (includes family)	37%	32%	39%	36%
Students	23%	13%	23%	20%
Locally hired employees	7%	11%	12%	9%

Table 14.3. Used Particular Medical Treatments

	Treated Locals $N = 69$	All Fieldworkers $N = 204$
Ever take local people to the hospital?	65%	22%
Ever give penicillin or other prescription drugs?	57%	19%
Ever give an injection?	26%	9%
Ever lance or cut skin to treat an ailment?	29%	10%
Ever apply a tourniquet?	22%	8%
Ever treat a snakebite?	14%	5%
Ever deliver a baby?	13%	4%
Ever stitch or suture a wound?	13%	4%

We wonder whether the medicine being practiced is, like that described by
Peggy Golde, a mild version of first aid, depending upon Band-Aids and aspirins,
or whether more dramatic and heroic medical ventures are being attempted. The
sample answered a series of questions about whether they had ever carried out
some medical procedures. Among the 69 who report that they treated the local
population when asked to do so (some actually held a regular clinic) the following
proportions answered yes to the question of whether they had ever used certain
techniques.

Table 14.3 seems to suggest that those who become involved in treating the
locals may be called upon to attempt some difficult medical procedures. It is re-
assuring to note that the single most frequently taken action is to take local people
to the hospital. The other procedures all involve some risk to the patient, and we
see that except for prescription drugs only a minority of those "practicing" have
tried them.

The same conclusion is reached by asking the respondents for the worst medical
problem they encountered while treating people in the field. Most anthropologists
may wish to confine their "medical intervention" to simple problems like colds
and headaches, but they report that much more serious conditions came their way.

Fifty-nine of the 69 who report having treated locals gave a brief account of
their worst or most challenging case. These include a miscarriage, complications
of a birth, and what was called a septic birth. Diarrhea and dysentery were the
worst problems encountered by five investigators, another had to deal with cholera, someone found dehydration the worst, and another described a crisis with a

sick child who died. Accidents were brought for treatment to 17 fieldworkers, including two who developed gangrene, one gunshot, a mauling by a bear, a scorpion sting, a snakebite, two burns, a case of trauma, and five cases described as "wounds," including a knife wound from a stabbing, a severed toe, and a head injury. Someone had to deal with a ruptured spleen. Parasites were the worst problems for some, including a case of elephantiasis and four cases of malaria. Infectious diseases named as the worst problem included cholera, measles, pneumonia, and tuberculosis. Degenerative diseases named included chest pain, diabetic coma, epilepsy, and a psychotic episode. Minor problems mentioned included a rash, a request for birth control pills, and a sprain. This list may be useful to those planning fieldwork who wonder how much training in first aid or emergency medicine they should acquire before going to the field. The problems listed here are not such that an ordinary Red Cross first aid course would prepare one to treat in the absence of a physician.

The degree of medical preparation that our respondents brought to the field varies widely. Two members of the sample are M.D.'s as well as Ph.D.'s, and another was a nurse before she got her Ph.D. in anthropology. Presumably such people are far better prepared to treat others than most of us are. I recall thinking while in the field that I should have gone to medical school so that I could be of some real use to the !Kung rather than bringing them a professional expertise in sociology that they could easily do without. Among the Kalahari research group we have the unusual case of an anthropologist, Mel Konner, who actually went through medical school after his first fieldwork. He is now a physician as well as an anthropologist (see *Becoming a Doctor*, 1987) although he does not practice clinical medicine in North America. No doubt he finds his skills of considerable use when he is working in the Kalahari.

It is difficult to know how useful the researcher's medical skills are to the locals. While few researchers had taken a first aid course in preparation for fieldwork, most did claim to take a "serious first aid kit," and most of those who did not take one worked where medical care was available. It may be that over the years, the researchers have picked up a great deal of useful knowledge and skill from observing physicians, reading, and trial and error in the field, and that they are actually making major contributions to the health of the local populations by their activities, but this is not certain.

Respondents were asked several questions about their successes and the difficulty of their medical practice. Table 14.4 presents their answers to the following questions: (1) Were you comfortable in the role of medical provider? (2) Was this a time-consuming responsibility, or a minor and occasional one? (3) Did you ever feel that someone was made worse by your treatment? (4) Did you ever feel that

Table 14.4. Success and Failure in Medical Practice in the Field

	N—"yes"	Treated Locals N = 69	All Fieldworkers N = 204
1. Were you comfortable in role?	31	45%	15%
2. Was it time consuming?	17	25%	8%
3. Did you ever make someone worse?	2	3%	1%
4. Did you ever save a life?	30	43%	15%
5. Did you ever have a patient die?	17	24%	9%

you probably saved a life by your treatment? and (5) Did you ever have a death of a sick person you were treating? Since these questions apply primarily to those who treated the local population, the table presents the percentage who said "yes" to the question for the segment who offered medical care to the locals only ($N = 69$) and for the whole group ($N = 204$).

Table 14.4 provides a basis for believing that practicing medicine in the field is an only partly satisfactory part of the anthropological role for those who do it. The majority of those who dispense medicine are not comfortable in the role, but three-quarters report it is only a minor or occasional duty. While a substantial proportion have had one of their "patients" die, the same could surely be said of well-trained physicians. They frequently feel that they used their skill to save a life, and rarely feel that any mistake they made caused someone to get worse.

Is this report plausibly true? Is it so easy to save lives? It probably is true: anyone with access to antibiotics can save the lives of people with a range of bacterial infectious diseases who would be otherwise seriously threatened. Since the development of antibiotics, any literate person with them is a more powerful healer than the most skilled and dedicated physician of the pre-antibiotic world. Anyone with chloroquine can provide relief to a victim of malaria. And even access to cheap and safe rehydration solution can save victims of diarrheal diseases who would otherwise die.

Why then is there any concern about anthropologists practicing medicine in the field? Physicians, national government spokespeople, and ethicists raise objections to the practice. What are the problems of practicing backwoods medicine?

There are dangers to the patients in doing so. The medical establishment has a simple rule: First of all, do no harm. With the best of intentions, untrained medical care providers can allow their ambition to outrun their ability, and harm patients. Antibiotics are indeed wonder drugs for most people. But others are allergic or hypersensitive to them, and the reactions to the drug may end up doing more harm than the untreated disease would have. In the press of necessity, while dealing with a seriously sick patient, anthropologists may be tempted to take more drastic steps than they are really prepared to carry out safely. No one should learn to give intramuscular or intravenous injections by trial and error. The errors can be too great. No one should do a tracheotomy on a choking patient because they saw it done in a movie, even if the alternative is watching the person choke to death. We need to evaluate our level of skill and expertise in advance of an emergency, and decide what our limits are.

Physicians also express concern that "bush doctors" may harm the public health of the local people even while helping certain individuals. For instance, antibiotics kill bacteria, but also allow those mutant strains that happen to be resistant to the antibiotic to flourish, so that a widespread administration of pills to sick people may result in a population plagued by microorganisms that can resist the available treatments. This phenomenon has been widespread in the case of malaria, and the alternative drugs available, like Fansidar, are much more dangerous and unpleasant than the originals. Physicians are better trained to manage this problem than amateurs.

National governments may object to the practice on the grounds that it is illegal for anyone not licensed to practice medicine. Amateur operations may interfere with the maintenance or establishment of a national medical system. And anthropologists may influence the expectations of the local population for the quality and quantity of the care that they need and demand.

And from a psychological point of view, there are dangers to the anthropologist from the power of life and death that medical practice suggests. In fact, the individual can take little personal credit for the abilities at hand, but some people find that the power is heady, and may lead to a loss of good judgment in the situation.

Practicing medicine can become thoroughly entangled with other issues of the research: is the investigator accepted, liked, respected? Are some people friends and others enemies? Is information to be endlessly demanded without any form of reciprocity, or can the anthropologist give something back to the community? All these are important, indeed essential, questions that need to be brought into consciousness lest their unconscious answers influence life and death risks to the population.

If one is going to practice medicine in the field, there is an excellent guide to first aid and treatment of illness and injuries, entitled *Where There Is No Doctor* (Spanish version, *Donde No Hay Doctor*), by David Werner (1985), a guide designed for use in Latin America by "village health workers," people who attempt to practice public health and treatment medicine with the help of a well stocked first aid kit but without formal medical training. The bibliography of this report includes a section of reference books for health and safety in the field, all of which would be appropriate resources for a departmental library shelf. If one can plan in advance what medical problems are likely to arise in the field, and who will be included among those treated, rational plans for medical care can be made. If courses need to be taken, if skills need to be acquired and practiced, and if supplies of drugs and equipment will be needed, provisions can be made before the beginning of fieldwork. If one learns in the field that more skills are needed, the rational course is to take patients to the nearest doctor or try to persuade the nearest doctor to come to the patients.

CHAPTER 15   MAKING FIELDWORK SAFER

We have seen in this report that there are real and present dangers associated with fieldwork. There are substantial numbers of deaths in the field from a variety of causes, there are a wide variety of kinds of threats reported by the survivors, and substantial suffering and loss of time and energy are involved in these accidents and illnesses. We have tried to specify what these component dangers are, how serious they are, and how frequently they occur to people who do their fieldwork in various parts of the world.

Summarizing the Dangers of Fieldwork

In the material we have looked at, we have seen many of the dangers of fieldwork, one by one, but we have not yet quantified what kinds of fieldwork are dangerous compared to others. For that we have to shift the focus from the experience of individuals with specific hazards to somehow summarizing the various hazards that people face. Unless we do so, we can't be sure whether the risks of one area (such as altitude sickness) are alternatives to the risks of another, or additional to them.

There are 180 categories of risk listed on pages 6 and 7 of the questionnaire form (see Appendix). No one checked experience with them all: the highest number claimed was 56 (and that by a senior anthropologist who has spent many years in the field in countries all over the world). Others (just a few) claimed experience with zero while most reported several to dozens of hazards. Figure 15.1 shows the distribution of the number of hazards reported for self.

Looking at the hazards listed, one might question the wisdom of summing them. Some are as minor as colds and mosquito bites and some as serious as airplane accidents and hepatitis B. But looking at the individual returns, the concern is seen to be not so serious. Virtually everyone checks a half dozen or so minor complaints—insect bites, respiratory and intestinal infections, blisters, and/or sunburns. Those who check off more problems are almost always those who experience the more serious hazards, even if the weights of them are not equal. The mean number of hazards reported is 13.4, and the standard deviation is almost exactly 10. To summarize the hazards, then, the distribution is divided into three sections: low (0–9), medium (10–19), and high (20 +).

One set of questions that we wanted to ask is whether archaeologists and physical anthropologists suffer any more (or less) than social-cultural anthropologists (including linguists). The answer by these measures is clear: there is no difference. Almost 40% of both groups are in the low hazard category; about 40% are in the middle; and about 20% in the high hazard group. Similarly there are no substantial—certainly no statistically significant—differences between the sexes

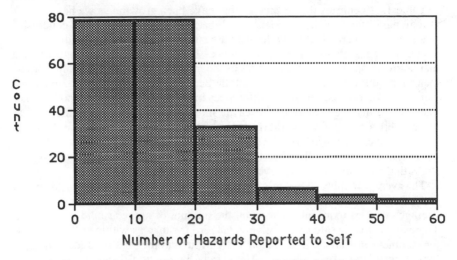

Figure 15.1. Sum of Hazards Reported to Self, by 204 Fieldworkers

Table 15.1. Level of Hazards Experienced in the Field, by Area

	N. America	Europe	L. America	India	Africa	Pacific	Total
Total	61	17	63	17	23	23	204
Level							
High (20+ Hazards)	4	3	15	7	10	7	46
	7%	18%	24%	41%	43%	30%	23%
Medium (10–19 Hazards)	29	6	25	5	4	10	79
	48%	35%	40%	17%	29%	43%	39%
Low (0–9 Hazards)	28	8	23	5	9	6	79
	46%	47%	37%	29%	39%	26%	39%
Average Number of Hazards	10.2	10.6	14.5	16.0	16.7	15.9	13.4
Standard Deviation	7.5	7.8	10.9	10.1	11.6	10.0	10.0

in the numbers of hazards encountered in the field, although a few of the hazards listed are only experienced by one sex or the other.

Two variables are significantly related to the number of hazards reported. The first is the amount of time that the researcher has spent in the field. Up to one year of exposure, about three-quarters of researchers have experienced less than ten forms of hazard, and are in the low-experience category; by two years of accumulated exposure, the low category is down to about half; and by three years of accumulated field experience the proportion in the low-risk category is down to about a quarter, where it stays thereafter. There are some differences between individuals in caution or preparation that persist through all durations, but the duration itself is still the major factor.

The second variable is area of research, which will surprise no one after observing the ways that hazards vary by area when examined individually. Table 15.1 shows the pattern.

Table 15.1 confirms the suspicions that have been growing as we have looked at regional differences in experience with hazards in this report. The conclusion that seems to emerge is that while there are substantial hazards in fieldwork any-where, there are also substantial differences between areas in the kinds of risks that fieldworkers take. Africa emerges as the most hazardous continent from these measures, followed by India, Asia and the Pacific, and Latin America. We don't want to make too much of small differences in numbers of hazards reported, as it may well be that the hazards of Africa are more finely enumerated in the list than those of other areas of the world (based upon my own African fieldwork). Still, I think that the impression from Table 15.1 that European and North American fieldwork are substantially safer than other areas is accurate, although we also stress that there are some risks everywhere.

The average number of hazards experienced by the fieldworkers who specialize in an area substantiates that conclusion. The standard deviation attached to that average provides more information on the amount of range around the average. There are relatively safe and relatively dangerous subareas within each of the ma-jor continentwide areas, just as there are careful and reckless (and lucky and un-lucky) fieldworkers in each area. The standard deviation is larger for the more dangerous areas: Africa includes downtown Nairobi and Addis Ababa as well as Omo, the Kalahari, and the Ituri forest. Asia and the Pacific includes New Zea-land as well as highland New Guinea, Hong Kong as well as Bali and Borneo. There are great differences between the inherent risks of these sites, and field-workers need to take them into account in their evaluation of the problems of health and safety working there.

Recall too that we saw in Chapter 4 that those who specialize in distant and dangerous research areas tend to go to the field less often than those who special-ize in nearby and convenient sites. Although the trips to distant parts may last somewhat longer, on the average the fieldworkers have spent considerably less time in the field, exposed to the dangers. So finding that more hazards are expe-rienced in those areas reinforces our impression that the probability of hazards are considerably higher per unit of time.

Raising Consciousness of the Dangers of Fieldwork

Ultimately, it is the decisions made by fieldworkers in the course of their re-search that will determine whether the dangers of fieldwork can be reduced. But we have seen that only a minority of fieldworkers go to the field in any one year, and the majority are engaged in teaching and other research most of the time. Yet all of us can participate in the process of reducing risks.

Simply ending the tradition of denying, explicitly or implicitly, that dangers exist and that research decisions often must be made in response to these dangers would help to bring the issues of health and safety in anthropology out into the open. Where illness or accidents changed the course of research plans, this can be acknowledged, in publications and in lectures, even if it is not appropriate on that occasion to go into any detail about the problems. This kind of acknowledg-ment would be especially helpful to graduate students who are making decisions about the course of fieldwork without the guidance of experience, or without the detailed advice of research supervisors. In order to preserve the tradition of in-dependence of graduate students in the field, it seems to me, it would be helpful for senior scholars to acknowledge more openly the difficulties they have encountered and the steps they have taken to adjust to them.

Taking Action on the Dangers

Having established some of the facts of the dangers of anthropological fieldwork, the question arises of what should be done about it. It is easy to conclude that anthropologists should be more careful, or more rigorously prepared for dangers in the field, but such a vague conclusion ignores the important fact that anthropology is an activity of independently minded scholars, governed neither by bureaucracy nor by professional review committees. Anthropologists carry out their work far from supervision, from formal rules of procedure, and far from interference. It is widely understood and accepted that only the anthropologist is on the scene, only he or she can make the day-to-day decisions of what should be done. Anthropologists reveal only what they wish about their experience in the field, and no one considers himself to be in a position to evaluate another's expertise until the written report on the research is submitted for publication.

Rather than appealing to anthropologists one at a time to improve the safety record in fieldwork, one may consider the influence of the various institutions that are concerned with fieldwork—funding agencies, professional associations, universities and their departments, museums and government agencies that employ anthropologists. Each of these has some ability to influence fieldworkers, although none has total control. And it is both a strength and a weakness of appealing to such groups for leadership in improving field health and safety that the people who staff the institutions are the same people who carry out fieldwork and who teach anthropology in the universities. Although no one has the power to change anyone's behavior except their own, participation on both the individual and institutional level can contribute to raising awareness of the problems of field safety, and to forging a cultural, normative response to the problems.

Hence in this chapter we will consider actions that can, in principle, be taken by individuals in their capacities as fieldworkers, teachers of future fieldworkers, reviewers and evaluators of their own and others' fieldwork reports and proposals, and participants in departments, universities, funding agencies, and professional associations. The task of this chapter will be to suggest actions and to share information about actions that others have taken, in a spirit of raising consciousness rather than laying down the law.

Anticipating the Dangers of Fieldwork

For the purposes of making fieldwork safer, it seems, fieldworkers must become more conscious of the risks of the areas where they contemplate working and the factors that make that area dangerous. Some of the dangers of sites are inherent to their location: altitude, temperature, sunlight, precipitation. Other dangers are a function of the isolation of the site, and can be overcome by technical means (methods of communication and transportation). These dangers are the negative side of isolation. For some purposes, isolation may be a positive feature of a site for a researcher, when it is important to study a subject undisturbed by outside influences. Some individuals simply enjoy the experience of being far from the telephone and the signs of commercial organization. Each person has to weigh the intellectual needs of the research, the health and safety issues of the research team, and their preferences when picking a field site. Probably everyone has times in their life when they are in maximally good condition, unrestricted by other responsibilities, and ambitious to tackle problems that can best be seen in remote, or inherently dangerous or risky settings. And probably most of us have other periods of life when we can work but need to avoid the most difficult field sites. By picking the questions to fit the sites, and the sites to fit our current abilities, a lot of difficulties could be avoided.

Anticipating Dangers of the Site

Many of the dangers can be anticipated by consulting readily available sources of information. The CDC annual manual *Health Information for International Travel* lists the countries where a wide range of infectious and parasitic diseases are found and not found. The United Nations *Demographic Yearbook* lists mortality by cause for countries, and one can assume that there are risks to fieldworkers from any disease that kills the citizens of the country. The questionnaire in the Appendix lists 180 risks that might possibly be found, and that list might be useful in focusing upon what might and might not be a hazard at a particular field site. In case of questions those planning research might want to consult others who have worked in that area, their physician, or write or phone the CDC with a specific question.

With a list of potential risks, decisions can be made to reduce those risks to the minimum, and to make a clear-cut decision to run those remaining risks. Special training courses for some members of the group might be needed in specific situations—to learn to run an outboard motor, repair a truck transmission, dig a latrine, or test water for bacterial contamination.

Obtaining Appropriate Medical Training

Those who intend to work far from medical assistance may want to take a medical course, and one needs to be realistic about the conditions in the field when deciding what course to take. For many the standard Red Cross first aid course (including CPR) will be enough, but others may feel that they have to acquire skills that go far beyond the temporary measures taught in such courses, to include skills such as giving injections, suturing wounds, and prescribing antibiotics.

Reading some of the health manuals listed in the bibliography will provide a basis for drawing up a list of the levels of skills that may be needed in the field, depending upon whether one has a hospital nearby, whether one intends to treat the local people, whether one knows that members of the research group have specific medical problems, and so on.

If one feels the need to learn to give subdural or intramuscular injections, administer oxygen or pain-killers, or pull rotten teeth, for instance, it will surely take some organization to make the arrangements, as such skills are not ordinarily taught to nonlicensed people. Other forms of preparation for health and safety in the field include seeing one's physician early in the process to plan the needed inoculation schedule and planning the medical kit and pharmacy that one intends to have in the field.

Emergency Communication and Transportation

Fieldwork could be made safer by an explicit consideration of the methods to be used for emergency communication and for evacuation of all or some of the members of the research team in case of need. Modern technology permits communication from anywhere to anywhere, if the equipment and the staff can be provided. Most of us cannot take along satellite communication disks or pay for a 24-hour staff to monitor our calls, but solutions to the problem of isolation can be found at much more modest cost.

Two-way radios are appropriate for many locations, but of course the technology must be learned if they are to be helpful. Several informants in this study told of buying two-way radios but never taking them out of the box, as the procedure for setting it up seemed too complicated. In at least one emergency, a two-way radio that could have saved lives sat in its packing materials, unusable. Radios can be time-consuming to operate and monitor, and arrangements for reception on a regular basis may be needed. Much simpler and less expensive emergency beacons are an alternative. The kind I have seen demonstrated are designed for boats, and consist of a coded transmitter that operates on a 50-hour battery. When triggered, the operator has a minute or two to cancel the call for help, before the rescue process begins. The beacon then sends a message to a satellite (STAR-SAT), which reroutes it to the nearest rescue center, which sends out a vehicle. The beacon itself is not expensive but the rescue might cost a fortune.

There are many locations in the world where cellular (cordless) telephones could be used, for calls in as well as calls out (as strange as the thought of pulling a ringing telephone out of one's backpack in the Amazon or the New Guinea Highlands might be).

The problem of what communication method is best for a particular setting is a technical question, and consulting a communications engineer may be necessary to find the best solution at the lowest cost. The Army, the Peace Corps, and missionary societies find methods of communications with their people in remote locations; anthropologists who must do so in order to ensure the safety of team members can solve this problem, too.

Similarly lives may depend upon the means of transportation to a hospital. If there are emergency vehicles in the country—planes, helicopters, ambulances—this information needs to be obtained before the need arises. One may need to establish credit in advance in order to be able to call upon them. There are few parts of the world so remote that help cannot be obtained if there is money to pay for it.

Influencing the Funding of Fieldwork to Improve Health and Safety

Recommending technological solutions to problems of health and safety may be simultaneously correct and useless, correct in that the solution could solve the problem but useless if there is no way to pay for the technology.

Observers of the funding of anthropological research note that fieldwork is already chronically underfunded. There is no surplus money in the foundations or the government research organizations to pay for any safety equipment, new training programs, emergency evacuation, or technological support. Foundation directors only shrug when the question of the funding of increased safety standards is raised: the money would have to come out of the existing research sources.

It is difficult to know how to recommend increased funding to improve safety in anthropology, as it is already the custom that research funding proposals do not cover all of the expenses of carrying out the research. It is common for proposals to describe intellectual goals that are not reflected in the funds requested. In other sciences, it is considered unprofessional to underestimate the legitimate expenses of research in order to increase the probabilities of obtaining a grant, but the practice is common in anthropology, where underfunding is chronic and low expectations are legion. Not only do researchers commonly absorb regular costs, but unexpected price rises, contingencies in the field, changes in the value of currency and other expenses are often their responsibility. Funding agencies commonly expect researchers to advance substantial amounts of their own money at the beginning of a field trip, to buy trucks for instance, in the expectation that they will recover the costs through a combination of monthly allowances and the value of the vehicle at resale when the research is done. Researchers rarely find universities or museums prepared to advance this money for them. Knowing these circumstances, one hesitates to recommend spending yet more of an individual's money to improve safety, provide insurance, and so on.

In the longer perspective, it might be appropriate for the American Anthropological Association to make the case to funding agencies for all anthropologists that the costs of safety in the field have not been built into the funding of anthropological research, and that procedures and guidelines should be established for doing so. Perhaps a source of temporary resources might be found to bridge into the practice of asking for and expecting to obtain the full costs of fieldwork.

In any case, the costs of fieldwork from grants are only provided for the professional members of the research team, whose participation can be justified. When anthropologists take their families and friends to the field, the personal costs of research to the researcher can become very high. The proprieties and implications of the use of expedition funding for the support of the family seems to be a sticky situation, and one that would probably have to be clarified in order to make a strong case for increased funding of health and safety equipment. The assumption that the scientist is alone and unencumbered is unrealistic in the case of anthropology, where the "laboratory" may be thousands of miles from home and the expected stay may be measured in months rather than hours. Making families and dependents "second-class citizens" ineligible for the benefits of the grant-provided facilities, or diluting the facilities to cover far more people than originally intended are both problematic implications of the usual accounting procedures for research grants. Both the foundations and the researchers would benefit from some realistic consideration of these special problems of anthropologists.

Students in the Field

Consciousness especially needs to be raised in the universities that have Ph.D. programs and especially in the twenty or so universities that teach and train the vast majority of the Ph.D. students, where graduate students need some acknowledgment of their need to master practical aspects of fieldwork as well as the theoretical background.

Margaret Mead (1972:142) discussed in detail the peculiarities of the training of anthropologists:

> The style, set early in the century, of giving a student a good theoretical orientation and then sending him off to live among a primitive people with the expectation that he would work everything out

for himself survives to this day. In 1933, when I gave a girl student who was setting out for Africa some basic instruction on how to cope with the drinking habits of British officials, anthropologists in London sneered. And in 1952, when I arranged for Theodore Schwarz to spend a year learning the new technologies that we intended to use in the field, his professor at the University of Pennsylvania thought this was ridiculous. Men who are now professors teach their students as their professors taught them, and if young fieldworkers do not give up in despair, go mad, ruin their health, or die, they do, after a fashion, become anthropologists.

A special situation exists when anthropologists take undergraduates to the field as a part of the student's substantive studies. While graduate students are generally seen as fully adult, entitled to take their own responsibility for risks, like faculty, undergraduates, who may be under the age of legal majority, are more the responsibility of the university. The university needs to be sure that their health and safety is protected in the best available way, and that the students and the university are insured against the costs of hazards.

All participants in fieldwork—faculty, graduate students, undergraduate students, assistants, and family members—might be required to put some kind of statement in writing about their current health, their understandings of the risks of the enterprise, and the locus of responsibility for accidents, illnesses, and financial liability. If the individual has instructions for others in the case of serious illness, accident, or death, these instructions should be spelled out, and copies made available to others. The more explicit such agreements are, the less the likelihood of misunderstandings later.

It is a strong tradition in anthropology that a department should not have a required course in teaching students how to cope with the practical side of anthropology. Still, a course might offer students planning research an arena in which to carry out some systematic planning. Students recently back from the field might help to keep the discussions focused upon a useful level, professors might admit that they become concerned with the practical details of fieldwork—shopping, food preparation, and accommodations—from time to time, and admit that they were not born knowing how to carry out all these elaborate arrangements. Students going to the field might be encouraged to plan rationally and consciously, rather than simply close their eyes, grit their teeth, and jump in.

Probably few professors, no matter how experienced or distinguished, can teach all of the skills that might be needed in a group of students going to the field. Students must be encouraged to get their expertise from experts outside anthropology where that is appropriate, and encouraged to share the results and contacts. It will be useful for students to observe their professors also approaching the problems of field safety from a rational perspective, as they jointly and separately plan future research.

One of the problems that arise when anthropologists contemplate teaching field skills to their students is the possibility that the older generation will teach the younger a lot of bad information and advice: "pour whiskey on snakebite"; "if you get diarrhea, drink more of the dirty water until you get used to it"; "never wear a seat belt, it could kill you if you needed to get out of the truck quickly." More than a few anthropology professors insist that the germ theory of disease is merely a superstition of Western cultures, and assert that those who suffer from field illnesses and accidents are giving in to weakness and ought to reconsider their commitment to the field. Graduate students gathering field wisdom from their professors will have to be prepared for the possibility that they are contacting the exotic subculture of their discipline without necessarily processing all the contents as ''facts.''

Regional Sharing of Health and Safety Information

The second kind of group that can usefully share the process of raising consciousness of field health and safety is the group of people who work in the same region or district. Whether or not there are intellectual issues for discussion, those who work in the same region and adapt to the same environment have a lot in common and a great opportunity to help one another.

The region is a natural unit for shared problems and solutions. An example can be drawn from the California Archeological Society, who have prepared reports and shared information on Valley Fever and Lyme disease through their newsletter (Loofbourow and Pappagianis 1985).

In some circumstances, a research group may provide information and help to one another. The Pygmy Research Group, for instance, led by Bob Bailey and Irven DeVore, has written a detailed health and safety manual covering topics from the most highly recommended brand of canvas shoes for the Ituri Forest, to the probable course of the disease in microfiliariasis. Anyone planning research in that area should contact the researchers to obtain their advice, but perhaps this group is more useful to most of us as an example. Many areas of the world have had sufficient density of investigators that a substantial amount of information could be collated to help regulars and newcomers to the area.

The sharing of health and safety information for a region requires a certain trust and confidentiality among researchers—some of the statements made (critical of local medical facilities, for instance) might be embarrassing if repeated in the wrong circles. And as is the case for graduate students, it is entirely possible that some of the advice offered will be wrong, and will need to be critically evaluated. But the information can be invaluable, and trial and error is such a painful and inefficient way of learning anything, that the need to develop a moral commitment to protect such documents from disclosure is overwhelming.

Departmental Responses to Improving Health and Safety

In departments, various steps can be taken to improve standards of health and safety. A department might want to invest in some of the health guides cited in the Bibliography for a general library shelf provided for those planning research. Even the smallest department might want to get the annual CDC *Health Information for International Travel* each year.

Departmental colleagues can show an intelligent interest in the planning of future research by colleagues and students, and in the accounts of things that went wrong of completed research. Many of the informants of this study, in the sample and among the volunteers, have mentioned that colleagues seemed disapproving when they spoke of accidents and illnesses, and offered little in the way of moral support for the almost inevitable difficulties that people experience when reentering their usual positions after long periods of fieldwork. We might find ways to provide more comfort and understanding for one another within departments.

One of the purposes of my letters to the chairs of departments in 1987 was to ask whether the department had a formal policy on health and safety. General policies were found only for government agencies—both U.S. and Canadian—especially those involved in archaeology, which often had detailed plans for servicing vehicles, keeping logs of accidents and unusual incidents for the use of others who work in the area. It is general in such agencies to provide two-way emergency communication with field crews. Departments might consider establishing similar procedures, especially when the department maintains vehicles or equipment for local use by students and researchers. But few have the facilities or staff.

Academic departments generally reported that it was their policy that the academic supervisor should advise graduate students about health and safety, if necessary. Most departments had or have no policy and no formal training in the subject for students. A few offer some kind of a seminar for advanced graduate students in which special topics in fieldwork are considered, which is or could be a vehicle for explicit consideration of preparations for field safety. Particularly when students work in the same (or nearby) field sites as their professors, departments could play a supportive role in sharing information on risks, local facilities for special training to reduce hazards, local medical resources to cope with the consequences of field problems, and so on.

University Responses to Problems of Health and Safety

Many universities in North America have been blind to the problems of fieldwork hazards to date, although most accept some responsibility for health and safety on campus, and may regularly monitor procedures in chemistry laboratories, artistic studios, and the athletic fields. Universities have the special motive of financial responsibility for the activities of their employees, and the threat of lawsuits provides a special urgency to action on the university level.

Some universities have already formulated a response to the hazards of fieldwork, or are in the process of doing so. A number of universities require a signature on a waiver of responsibility drawn up by the university lawyers from students and faculty who travel abroad on university research. The desire to avoid financial risk can be combined with the desire of the university to assure that the researchers are aware of the risks being taken. The University of Toronto, for instance, appointed a high-level university advisory committee on health and safety policy in 1986, under the leadership of ex-President James Ham, who had previously been professionally concerned with the Canadian policies on safety in asbestos exposure. The committee made a number of recommendations to insure that all participants acknowledge awareness of the hazards, their own responsibility for maintaining health and safety in the field, and the limitations of the university's liability. A copy of the university policy on health and safety in fieldwork can be obtained from the Office of Research Administration, University of Toronto. Other universities might want to emulate this procedure as well as its conclusion.

Most universities already have established policies and procedures on oversight of protection of the rights of subjects in research. To add procedures for the protection of rights of researchers, especially to health and safety in fieldwork, should not be excessively difficult. The fact that such procedures may help to shield universities from liability in case of lawsuits arising from accidents and illnesses helps to reinforce the probabilities that such policies will be adopted. Note that such policies are not confined to anthropologists but apply to all fieldworkers at the university.

Professional Association Responses
to the Problems of Health and Safety

And, finally, there are some sorts of actions that anthropologists can take to improve field health and safety that need to be addressed on the level of the profession, through the professional association (AAA 1971). Some problems that are individual burdens—or tragedies—when experienced one at a time show up clearly as classes of problems, with very different kinds of appropriate responses, from the point of view of the profession. The professional association could appoint a task force to investigate and make recommendations in these areas if that seemed useful.

I would suggest that this study has drawn our attention to three specific topics that present frequent and serious problems to anthropologists: (1) malaria, (2) hepatitis, and (3) vehicle accidents. Reduction of risk for these three problems would make a substantial contribution to the safety of field research.

Malaria affects large numbers of fieldworkers and causes massive discomfort and loss of field time. Prevention and treatment of malaria is a complex medical and technical problem, increased in difficulty by regional differences in the malaria species and in the evolution of drug-resistant strains of the microorganism. When asked what forms of prevention and treatment they followed, a large proportion of the volunteers indicated that they knew neither what the available drugs were, nor the pros and cons of the various alternative therapies. Anthropologists need to be educated about malaria in a serious and systematic way. We need authoritative sources of information, medical centers that will take our problems both of prevention and treatment seriously, and opportunities to share and update information as it becomes available. Taken on an individual level, the task is daunting and the probability of success is relatively low. But as a concerned work group, representing the thousand or so researchers who are exposed to malaria each year and the hundreds who contract the disease, the task becomes more supportable. A professional association-sponsored task force on malaria education, prevention, and treatment is needed.

Hepatitis continues to be a major burden on fieldworkers, and the dynamics of its transmission and disease process seem not to be well understood in the field. Fieldworkers need to understand the role of unclean water sources and the need for hygiene in the kitchen to prevent the spread of hepatitis. The price is too high to pay for a little carelessness and an unwillingness to appear critical of the standards of hygiene of the locals.

The third area in which incidence and fatalities need to be reduced is vehicle accidents. In and out of the field, far too many anthropologists are dying in car, truck, and motorcycle accidents. We know how to reduce the fatalities, as competent large-scale research has been done by the various Traffic Safety Councils. The keys are drivers' training, reducing speed, and especially the use of seat belts. It is not the custom in many parts of the world where fieldwork is done, to use seat belts now as it was not the custom in the United States to use them just a few years ago. But wherever they are adopted, fatalities are greatly reduced and drivers quickly become used to them. Knowing that, it seems to me, we have the obligation to use seat belts to protect ourselves and the people in our care.

And finally, on the general level, there are all the other hazards detailed in this report. In this context, it seems that perhaps the professional association could help us define our medical needs, both before and after fieldwork, and help people in all regions of the country to find medical practitioners who are knowledgeable and sensitive to the special problems of anthropologists. From time to time we need tropical medicine experts, parasitologists, diagnosticians, and psychiatrists who understand the special problems of fieldwork and the people who do it. On a national and local level, it would be very helpful to have channels for sharing information and obtaining reliable advice quickly in case of need.

Conclusion

Some segments of the anthropology profession are opposed to considering what can be done to reduce illness and accidents. I think such people are concerned that the attempt may lead to a lot of rules and interference in how fieldwork is done, without really contributing to health or safety. There may even be people who do not want to reduce the risks, feeling that anthropology is made dramatic and valuable by the risks that are taken and the injuries and deaths that occur. These people are addressed by Claude Lévi-Strauss in the following passage from *Tristes Tropiques:*

> Adventure has no place in the anthropologist's profession; it is merely one of those unavoidable drawbacks, which detract from his effective work through the incidental loss of weeks or months. . . . The fact that so much effort and expenditure has to be wasted on reaching the object of our studies bestows no value on that aspect of our profession, and should be seen rather as its negative side. . . . We may endure six months of traveling, hardships and sickening boredom for the purpose of recording (in a few days or even a few hours) a hitherto unknown myth, a new marriage rule or a complete list of clan names, but is it worth my while taking up my pen to perpetuate such a useless shred of memory or pitiable recollection as these (memoires)? [1984:11]

I think it is true and important that the value of anthropology lies in its intellectual achievements, not in the suffering it costs to do it. The worth of the enterprise will not decline if it is done more safely.

In any case, I think the fear that the activity will be tamed and diluted is misplaced. Fieldwork in many parts of the world is inherently dangerous, inherently unpredictable, inherently risky. After we make it as safe as we can, eliminating all of the avoidable hazards, there will still be hazards. It is the job of anthropology to venture into the unknown, to expose oneself to the experiences of other people, and to ask questions even when there are no obvious answers. The less this is done blindly, the less energy and health that is wasted on needless suffering, the more the task will prosper.

REFERENCES CITED

American Anthropological Association
  1971 Statement on Ethics. Washington, D.C.: American Anthropological Association. [Also published as appendix to Ethics and Anthropology: Dilemmas in Fieldwork. Michael A. Rynkeiwich and James P. Spradley, eds., 1976. New York: Wiley.]
  1977a Guide to Departments of Anthropology, 1976–77. Washington, D.C.: American Anthropological Association.
  1977b Annual Report, 1976–77. Washington, D.C.: American Anthropological Association.
  1987 Guide to Departments of Anthropology, 1986–87. Washington, D.C.: American Anthropological Association.
Auerbach, Paul S.
  1986 Medicine for the Outdoors: A Guide to Emergency Medical Procedures and First Aid. Boston: Little Brown.
Bowen, Elenore Smith (Laura Bohannan)
  1964 Return to Laughter. Garden City, N.Y.: Doubleday.
Braidwood, Linda
  1953 Digging Beyond the Tigris. New York: Schuman.
Briggs, Jean L.
  1970 Never in Anger: Portrait of an Eskimo Family. Cambridge: Harvard University Press.
  1986 Kapluna Daughter. In Women in the Field: Anthropological Experiences. Peggy Golde, ed. Pp. 19–46. Berkeley: University of California Press.
Capron, André, J. D. Dessaint, M. Capron, J. H. Ouma, and A. E. Butterworth
  1987 Immunity to Schistosomes: Progress Toward Vaccine. Science 238:1065–1072.
Cassell, Joan, ed.
  1987 Children in the Field: Anthropological Experiences. Philadelphia: Temple University Press.
Cavalli-Sforza, Luigi Luca
  1986 African Pygmies. Orlando: Academic Press.
Centers for Disease Control (U.S. Department of Health and Human Services, Public Health Service)
  1987 Health Information for International Travel: 1987. Washington, D.C.: U.S. Government Printing Office.
Cesara, Manda
  1982 Reflections of a Woman Anthropologist: No Hiding Place. London: Academic Press.
Chagnon, Napoleon A.
  1968 Yanomamo: the Fierce People. New York: Holt, Rinehart & Winston.
  1974 Studying the Yanomamo. New York: Holt, Rinehart & Winston.
Christie, Agatha
  1946 Come Tell Me How You Live. New York: Dodd Mead.
Cole, Sonia Mary
  1975 Leakey's Luck: The Life of Louis Seymour Bazett Leakey, 1903–72. New York: Harcourt Brace Jovanovich.
D'Andrade, Roy, E. A. Hammel, D. L. Adkins, and C. K. McDaniel
  1975 Academic Opportunity in Anthropology: 1947–90. American Anthropologist 77:753–773.
Dentan, Robert Knox
  1988 On Reconsidering Violence in Simple Human Societies. Current Anthropology 29:625–629.
Dillman, Don A.
  1978 Mail and Telephone Surveys: The Total Design Method. New York: Wiley.

Dreher, Melanie
1987   Three Children in Rural Jamaica. *In* Children in the Field: Anthropological Experiences. Joan Cassell, ed. Pp. 149–172. Philadelphia: Temple University Press.
Forbes, Malcolm
1988   They Went That-A-Way. New York: Simon & Schuster.
Freilich, Morris, ed.
1977   Marginal Natives at Work, Anthropologists in the Field. Cambridge: Schenkman.
Gardiner, Margaret
1984   Footprints on Malekula: A Memoir of Bernard Deacon. Edinburgh: Salamander Press.
Golde, Peggy, ed.
1986   Women in the Field: Anthropological Experiences. Berkeley: University of California Press.
Goldenweiser, Alexander
1941   Recent Trends in American Anthropology. American Anthropologist 43:155–163.
Harris, Marvin
1968   The Rise of Anthropological Theory, a History of Theories of Culture. New York: Crowell.
Hatt, John
1985   The Tropical Traveller. London: Pan Books Ltd.
Heinz, Hans J.
1979   Namkwa. Boston: Houghton Mifflin.
Hesser, Jana
1987   Hepatitis: Risks and Prevention for Fieldworkers. Paper presented at the American Anthropological Association meeting, Chicago.
Hibben, Eleanor B.
1983   In Outer Places: Adventures with Franc C. Hibben. Santa Fe: Sunstone Press.
Hinsley, Curtis
1968   Cushing and Fewkes in the American Southwest. *In* Observers Observed. George Stocking, ed. Pp. 13–52. Madison: University of Wisconsin Press.
Hitchcock, Patricia
1987   Our Ulleri Child. *In* Children in the Field: Anthropological Experiences. Joan Cassell, ed. Pp. 173–184. Philadelphia: Temple University Press.
Howell, Nancy
1986   Occupational Health and Safety: An Issue in the Culture of Anthropology. Anthropology Newsletter, May, p. 2.
1988   Health and Safety in the Fieldwork of North American Anthropologists. Current Anthropology 29:780–787.
Hugh-Jones, Christine
1987   Children in the Amazon. *In* Children in the Field: Anthropological Experiences. Joan Cassell, ed. Pp. 27–64. Philadelphia: Temple University Press.
Jacobsen, Margaret
1983   Honors thesis, University of Cape Town.
Johanson, Donald, and Maitland Edey
1981   Lucy: The Beginnings of Mankind. New York: Warner Books.
Kaplan, Bernice A.
1986   Conventions of Conventions. Anthropology Newsletter 27:8, 28.
Klass, Morton, and Sheila Solomon
1987   Birthing in the Bush: Participant Observation in Trinidad. *In* Children in the Field: Anthropological Experiences. Joan Cassell, ed. Pp. 121–148. Philadelphia: Temple University Press.
Konner, Melvin
1987   Becoming a Doctor: A Journey of Initiation in Medical School. New York: Viking.
Kroeber, Theodora
1970   Alfred Kroeber: A Personal Configuration. Berkeley: University of California Press.
Kuper, Adam
1983   Anthropology and Anthropologists: The Modern British School. London: Routledge & Kegan Paul.
Laird, Carobeth
1975   Encounter with an Angry God: Recollections of My Life with John Peabody Harrington. Banning, Calif.: Malki Museum Press, Morongo Indian Reservation.

Landes, Ruth
    1986   A Woman Anthropologist in Brazil. *In* Women in the Field: Anthropological Experiences.
            Peggy Golde, ed. Pp. 119–142. Berkeley: University of California Press.
Larcom, Joan
    1983   Following Deacon: The Problem of Ethnographic Reanalysis, 1926–1981. *In* Observers Ob-
            served: Essays on Ethnographic Fieldwork. George Stocking, ed. Pp. 175–195. Madison: Uni-
            versity of Wisconsin Press.
Leakey, Mary
    1984   Disclosing the Past, An Autobiography. Garden City, N.Y.: Doubleday.
Leakey, Richard
    1983   One Life. London: Michael Joseph.
Lévi-Strauss, Claude
    1984   Tristes Tropiques. New York: Atheneum.
Loofbourow, J. D., and Demosthenes Pappagianis
    1985   Coccidioidomycosis: An Occupational Hazard for Archaeologists. Special Report No. 2.
            Fullerton, Calif.: Society for California Archeology.
MacCurdy, G. G.
    1919   Academic Teaching of Anthropology in Connection with Other Departments. American An-
            thropologist 21:49.
Malinowski, Bronislaw
    1967   A Diary in the Strict Sense of the Term. New York: Harcourt, Brace & World.
Maybury-Lewis, David
    1988   The Savage and the Innocent. 2d edition. Boston: Beacon Press.
McCurdy, David W.
    1976   The Medicine Man. *In* Ethics and Anthropology: Dilemmas in Fieldwork. Michael A. Ryn-
            kiewich and James P. Spradley, eds. Pp. 4–16. New York: Wiley.
Mead, Margaret
    1959   Writings of Ruth Benedict, An Anthropologist at Work. New York: Avon, Equinox Books.
    1972   Blackberry Winter, My Earliest Years. New York: William Morrow.
    1977   Letters from the Field 1925–1975. New York: Harper & Row.
Morris, Ann Axtell
    1978   Digging in the Southwest. Santa Barbara, Calif.: Peregrine Smith, Inc.
Mowat, Farley
    1987   Virunga: the Passion of Dian Fossey. Toronto: McClelland and Stewart.
Nader, Laura
    1969   Up the Anthropologist—Perspectives Gained from Studying Up. *In* Reinventing Anthro-
            pology. Del Hymes, ed. Pp. 284–311. New York: Pantheon Books.
    1986   From Anguish to Exultation in Mexico and Lebanon. *In* Women in the Field: Anthropolog-
            ical Experiences. Peggy Golde, ed. Pp. 97–116. Berkeley: University of California Press.
Nash, June
    1979   We Eat the Mines and the Mines Eat Us. New York: Columbia University Press.
National Academy of Sciences
    1982   Summary Report—1982 Doctorate Recipients from United States Universities. Office of
            Scientific Engineering and Personnel. Washington, D.C.: National Research Council.
New York Times
    1987   80 Years Later and a World Away, Eskimo Sons of Explorers Meet U.S. Kin. 7 June, page
            25.
Opler, Morris
    1987   Response to Dr. Farrar. Anthropology Newsletter, March, page 3.
Owens, Mark, and Delia Owens
    1984   Cry of the Kalahari. Boston: Houghton Mifflin.
Pasternak, Burton
    1988   A Conversation with Fei Xiaotong. Current Anthropology 29:637–662.
Preston, Samuel H., Nathan Keyfitz, and Robert Schoen
    1972   Causes of Death: Life Tables for National Populations: New York: Seminar Press.
Rasmussen, Knud J. V.
    1976   The Netsilik Eskimo: Social Life and Spiritual Culture. New York: AMS Press.
Rosaldo, Renato
    1984   Grief and a Headhunter's Rage: On the Cultural Force of Emotions. *In* Text, Play and Story.
            E. Bruner, ed. Pp. 120–141. Washington, D.C.: American Anthropological Association.

Scheper-Hughes, Nancy
    1987   A Children's Diary in the Strict Sense of the Term: Managing Culture-shocked Children in
        the Field. *In* Children in the Field: Anthropological Experiences. Joan Cassell, ed. Pp. 217–236.
        Philadelphia: Temple University Press.
Shostak, Marjorie
    1981   Nisa: The Life and Words of a !Kung Woman. New York: Random House.
Silverman, Harold
    1986   Travel Healthy: The Traveler's Complete Medical Kit. New York: Avon Books.
Silverman, Sydel
    1981   Totems and Teachers: Perspectives on the History of Anthropology. New York: Columbia
        University Press.
Society for California Archeology
    1979   Health Alert: Valley Fever. Society for California Archeology Newsletter 14:34.
    1985a Coccidioidomycosis: An Occupational Hazard for Archaeologists. Society for California
        Archeology. Special Report No. 2. Fullerton, California.
    1985b Health Alert: Lyme Disease. Society for California Archeology Newsletter 19:4.
Stinchcombe, Arthur
    1986   Stratification and Organization: Selected Papers. New York: Cambridge University Press.
Stocking, George W., Jr., ed.
    1974   The Shaping of American Anthropology, 1883–1911: A Franz Boas Reader. New York:
        Basic Books.
Stocking, George W., Jr.
    1983   Observers Observed: Essays on Ethnographic Fieldwork. Madison: University of Wisconsin
        Press.
University of Toronto, Governing Council
    1988   Policy on Safety in Field Research. Toronto: Office of Research Administration.
Werner, David
    1985   Where There Is No Doctor: A Village Health Care Handbook. Palo Alto, Calif.: The Hes-
        perian Foundation.
Wilkerson, James A.
    1985   Medicine for Mountaineering. 3d edition. Seattle, Wash: The Mountaineers.
Wiseman, John
    1986   Survive Safely Anywhere: The Special Air Service Survival Manual. New York: Crown
        Publishers.
Wolff, Kurt H.
    1964   Surrender and Community Study: The Study of Loma. *In* Reflections on Community Stud-
        ies. Arthur J. Vidich, Joseph Bensman, and Maurice R. Stein, eds. Pp. 233–264. New York:
        Wiley.
Wylie, Jonathan
    1987   "Daddy's Little Wedges": On Being a Child in France. *In* Children in the Field: Anthro-
        pological Experiences. Joan Cassell, ed. Pp. 91–120. Philadelphia: Temple University Press.
Yengoyan, Aram
    1977   Open Networks and Native Formalism: The Mandaya and Pitjandjara Cases. *In* Marginal
        Natives at Work, Anthropologists in the Field. Morris Freilich, ed. Pp. 217–253. Cambridge:
        Schenkman.

BIBLIOGRAPHY: HEALTH AND SAFETY GUIDES
USEFUL FOR FIELDWORKERS

Auerbach, Paul S., M.D.
  1986 Medicine for the Outdoors: A Guide to Emergency Medical Procedures and First Aid. Boston: Little Brown.

  For leaders of camping trips and other outdoor activities. Assumes that the user has taken a formal first aid course, such as those offered by American Red Cross, Outward Bound, and the American Heart Association CPR training. Expects that in a serious emergency, you can get to a hospital within a few hours. Good diagrams, covers a range of accidents and exposure risks, plus the early stages of illnesses.

Berkow, Robert, editor
  1986 Merck's Manual of Diagnosis and Therapy. 13th edition. West Point, Penn.: Merck-Sharp-Dohme.

  A technical manual of all the things that can go wrong with the human body, more useful for translating from medical jargon to English than for trying to take care of sick people. For most people, it assumes too much medical knowledge.

Centers for Disease Control (U.S. Department of Health and Human Services, Public Health Service)
  1987 Health Information for International Travel: 1987. [Available from Superintendent of Documents, U.S. Government Printing Office, Washington, DC 20402]

  This annual publication should be in every university and college library for consultation by those who intend to travel abroad, and in the office of every physician who treats and advises patients going abroad. It gives the most up-to-date and useful information on inoculation regulations and recommendations, country by country, and outlines the risks to health and safety, and gives good advice about their management. Your physician should reach for this book when you consult him (or her) before going to the field. Cost (in 1987) $4.75 each prepaid from Superintendent of Documents, 25% discount on 100 copies or more. Phone (202-783-3238) for up-to-date ordering information.

Loofbourow, J. D., and Demosthenes Pappagianis
  1985 Coccidioidomycosis: An Occupational Hazard for Archaeologists. Special Report No. 2. Fullerton, Calif.: Society for California Archeology.

  A guide to the risks and treatment of "Valley Fever," the serious lung disease caused by a fungus found in the soils of the central valley of California and some other locations in the western United States. Available for $1.00 from the Society for California Archeology, Central Business Office, c/o Department of Anthropology, California State University, Fullerton, CA 92634.

Sakmar, Thomas P., M.D., Pierce Gardner, M.D., and Gene N. Peterson, M.D.
  1986 Passport's Health Guide for International Travelers: How to Travel and Stay Well. [Passport Books, 4255 West Touhy Avenue, Lincolnwood, IL 60646-1975]

  Designed for the planning of international travel, covers much of the same ground as the CDC manual, but adds discussion of special medical problems of young children, pregnant women, and travelers' with special medical problems. This guide raises the question of whether it is sensible for persons with chronic medical problems (such as diabetes, asthma) to do fieldwork in remote locations. Advice in this guide is focused primarily upon the perils of the trip to the field, rather than long-term

198

stays. Good advice and information on obtaining medical care and contact with reliable doctors abroad. Gives a suggested list of medical kit contents for various degrees of isolation and risk.

Silverman, Harold, M.D.
  1986   Travel Healthy: The Traveler's Complete Medical Kit. New York: Avon Books.

A small inexpensive paperback that is good on exposure conditions, gives useful advice on packing a medical first aid kit, and has an 85-page appendix giving foreign brand names of U.S. drug products.

Turner, Anthony C., M.D.
  1985   The Traveller's Health Guide. 3d edition. [Roger Lascelles, 47 York Road, Brentford, Middlesex TW80QP, Britain]

Written originally for the BOAC personnel, and now addressed more widely, this guide concentrates upon problems encountered in airplanes, hotels, and other tourist places. Includes a good guide to obtaining treatment abroad.

Werner, David
  1985   Where There Is No Doctor: A Village Health Care Handbook. [The Hesperian Foundation, P.O. Box 1692, Palo Alto, CA 94302]

This low-cost 400-page guide to saving lives without a doctor's presence is just what you would want and need if you were taking care of the health of the local people. The language of the guide is either Spanish (Donde No Hay Doctor) or English (or you can send away for translations into Portuguese, Tagalog, French, Swahili, and Arabic. There is also an English edition adapted for use in India). The descriptions of illness and injury are vivid and direct, and frequently illustrated by cartoon-like drawings. The advice given is sensible and adapted to difficult conditions.

Wilkerson, James A., M.D.
  1985   Medicine for Mountaineering. 3d edition. [Published by The Mountaineers, 306 Second Avenue West, Seattle, WA 98119]

Focused primarily upon environmental hazards (altitude sickness, hypothermia, etc.) and traumatic injuries, this useful handbook assumes that you can get medical care in an emergency but that you will be reluctant to do so unless it is necessary. Hence it is very valuable in a short-term emergency situation, but not sufficient for taking care of yourself and others for months on end. All of the advice comes from physicians, and strikes a nice balance between technical information and the low level advice many of us need to respond to even a minor problem like bandaging a cut. A necessity for those working at high altitudes.

Wiseman, John
  1986   Survive Safely Anywhere: The Special Air Service Survival Manual. [Published by Crown Publishers, Inc., 225 Park Avenue South, New York, NY 10003]

A "survivalist" guide to outdoor living, disasters such as floods and hurricanes, and for natural and man-made disasters. The author gives advice on emergency shelter, living off the land, boiling and condensing water, flashing a rescue signal to a plane with a mirror, and so on. Some people love reading this sort of thing, others can't bear to think about all the terrible things that can go wrong. Collecting birch sap and constructing fish hooks from bits of wire seem unlikely to meet the kinds of emergencies that anthropologists encounter, but no doubt there is a lot of useful information in this book.

World Health Organization
  1967   International Medical Guide for Ships. Geneva, Switzerland: World Health Organization.

A clearly written guide for a ship's officer, not medically trained, to cope with medical emergencies, sicknesses, and injuries, in the days, weeks, or even months it may take before a ship comes to port and the patient can be seen by a doctor. Hence the account is serious and detailed, and it could provide useful guidance to someone faced with dealing with a broken leg, a suddenly unconscious patient, or even a toothache. Provides guidance on communicating with a physician at a distance by radio or telephone, gives proper vocabulary for describing symptoms.

APPENDIX: QUESTIONNAIRE FORM

ADVISORY PANEL ON HEALTH AND SAFETY IN FIELDWORK
American Anthropological Association
Members

| Jane Buikstra, U. of Chicago | Melvin Konner, Emory U. | Renato Rosaldo, Stanford U. |
| Maxine Kleindiest, U. of Toronto | Robert Netting, U. Arizona | John Yellen, N. S. F. |

March 23, 1987

Chairman Nancy Howell
2120 Cowper Street
Palo Alto, CA 94301
415-321-5823

Dear Colleague:

A rash of recent fieldwork-related deaths have set some people thinking about the dangers of fieldwork, and whether anything can be done to make it safer. Until the present study, no one has kept track of the fieldwork we do, or the problems that arise while we do it. Of course we will never manage to eliminate all risks of fieldwork in the future, but a first step in making it safer is to find out how dangerous fieldwork has been, in what ways, in the past and present. During the next year, I will be applying my skills as a demographer and my experience of two years of fieldwork in the Kalahari desert to the study of occupational hazards in anthropology, to try to increase our understanding of the risks of fieldwork.

Your name has been drawn in a small random sample from the listings in the AAA's, *1986-87 Guide to Departments* , to represent the experiences of all anthropologists. Everyone listed there had an equal chance of being selected for this sample. I hope that you will be willing to contribute your experience and your perspective to the study. Even if you have not done fieldwork, or if you have not had any problems in doing fieldwork, your response is needed to obtain an accurate picture. And even if you have already contributed to this study through the survey of Departments or have volunteered information on your experiences, your questionnaire is needed to link the parts of the study together in a framework in which we can estimate the probabilities of problems for categories of anthropologists.

All of the questions can be answered briefly except for the history of your fieldwork, on page 3. Some of the questions are bound to be somewhat subjective, so just use your existing information to answer the questions as best you can. Don't stop to inquire from all the people who were in your research group if they ever had problems. The questionnaire is designed so that you can finish it in less than a half hour (many can do it more swiftly). If you are willing to give the information but don't like to fill out questionnaire forms, please check the "phone" line on page 8 of the questionnaire and return it. I will phone you at your convenience (mornings and weekends are especially inexpensive times), or you can phone me at the number above.

Your participation is voluntary, you are free to withdraw your consent and discontinue participation in the study at any time. Your name will not be used in connection with this study without your consent. Your responses will be tabulated with those of the others in the group to provide an accurate description of the experiences reported. If you have any questions about this research feel free to phone me at 415 - 321-5823. If you have additional concerns, especially about disclosure of this research, you may ask questions or report grievances - anonymously, if desired - to the Human Subjects Coordinator, Sponsored Projects Office, Stanford University, Stanford , CA 94305 (or by phone to 415- 723-3638.)

After you have filled in the questionnaire, you might want to contribute more detailed information about accidents, injuries and sickness that occurred to you in your fieldwork. If you know of any anthropologists who have died in the field or as a result of fieldwork, I hope you will add a note to let me know the person's name, age, position, and the year and place of the death, so that I can make an accurate list of all such cases. In addition, your comments and ideas on the general problems of fieldwork safety and the best ways to increase it will be very welcome. Some of volunteers of detailed accounts feel that their story might harm themselves or others and so their identity will not be known in association with the events. Make it clear which alternative you prefer on your volunteered remarks, and your wishes will be respected. In any case, the answers you give on **this** questionnaire will be entirely confidential.

Thank you for spending a half-hour or so of your time, and for trusting me with personal information about your experiences. I hope you will join in this study, and join in the movement to make fieldwork safer for all of us.

Sincerely yours,

Nancy Howell, Ph.D.

Background questions. In this section, we establish the characteristics of the anthropologists giving information on this study. (Keep in mind that some basic information about you may be available from the *Guide*).

1. **Length** of career: Please give the **year** of:
   - Entry to graduate school _____
   - Your first professional job _____
   - Yourbirth _____
   - Your first fieldwork experience _____
   - What year do you count as the start of your career? _____

Do you consider yourself primarily: _____ an archeologist _____ a physical anthropologist
_____ a social-cultural anthropologist _____ a linguist
_____ other (specify) _____

2. Thinking about the **parts of your career** as an anthropologist, **check** each of the following components that has been a **substantial** part of your work. By substantial, we mean taking up about ten hours a week of your time for a year, or equivalent over a shorter or longer period. In case your work has changed over the course of your career, there is a space to indicate the beginning of your career, in the middle, and recently. If there hasn't been much change, just use the first column and leave the others blank.

	BEGINNING	MIDDLE	RECENTLY
Teaching, graduate and undergraduate			
Publications , editing			
Administration, of university or business			
Museum work, curator			
Consulting, government, applied anthropology			
Research on campus, laboratory, library			
Fieldwork - off campus, excavation, survey, ethnography			
Unemployment, retirement			
Sick leave (include maternity leave)			
Other (specify)			

3. Have you ever wanted to do any of the preceding career activities (teaching, etc.), but been **unable to** because of:
   - _____ poor health
   - _____ political instability in other countries
   - _____ lack of skills
   - _____ family responsibilities
   - _____ personal problems
   - _____ inability to get a grant
   - _____ no jobs available
   - _____ too dangerous
   - _____ family objections
   - _____ financial need

   If this factor prevented you from doing **fieldwork** that you wanted to do, please double-check it.

4. Has **training students on how to do fieldwork** been a part of your career? If yes, check **all** relevant:
   - _____ Teaching a course on fieldwork preparation.
   - _____ Taking the student to his/her own site.
   - _____ Letting the student work entirely alone.
   - _____ Taking students with you to **your** research site.
   - _____ Teaching or administering a field school.
   - _____ Other (specify) _____
   - _____ Advising students before they go to the field.
   - _____ Providing moral support and advice in letters, etc.
   - _____ Visiting a student in his or her field site.
   - _____ Reading and commenting on students' field notes.
   - _____ Writing to colleagues, arranging grants, etc.

5. **Current health and characteristics:** Compared to others you know, please put one check on each line placing yourself closer to one end or the other, or in the middle of the continuum.

Healthy	_____	Chronically ill
Fit and athletic	_____	Limited in physical activity
Over weight	_____	Normal weight
Smoker	_____	Non-smoker
A cautious and careful person	_____	Enjoy taking some risks
Often disorganized	_____	Usually efficient and well organized
A moderate or non-drinker	_____	Sometimes drink too much or often
Cheerful, even-tempered	_____	Depressed or anxious
A loner, need time to yourself	_____	Sociable, have many friends

2

Fieldwork Experience:

6. Please fill in the following information about **all** of the fieldwork experiences you have had. Please include your experiences as a student as well as those as a professional, short as well as long trips, those unfunded as well as those formally funded, and those close to home as well as those in exotic locations. (If you have done a great deal of fieldwork and survey work, you may have to omit any sites where you worked very briefly, where you were visiting others in the field, or where your primary purpose was not fieldwork.) The purpose of this list is to provide the basic information on how much exposure to risk of danger anthropologists have from their fieldwork. If you have a list in your vita or elsewhere, feel free to include it and I will extract the information needed. Or just jot down a name for each of your main sites, and go ahead and finish the questionnaire. Then check the "phone" line on page 8, and I will call you to get the details. This is a difficult question for some anthropologists but an important question for this research.

You do not need to list your fieldwork in the order in which you did it. Most people seem to find it easier to list it first by country and then by site, putting in the dates of their various trips last. Use any method that is convenient for you.

COUNTRY	SITE (can be a large or small area)	DATES (starting and ending)	N. IN GROUP (include families)	SOURCE OF FUNDS (national, private, univ.)

7. To summarize the history of fieldwork above, how many distinct **fieldtrips** have you gone on? _____

8. Again, to summarize your experience, roughly how many **months** (or weeks or days) have you spent doing fieldwork, all together? _____Just thinking about **1986,** January 1 to December 31, how many days during that year were you doing fieldwork? _____

9. **Now,** looking at your list of fieldwork experiences above, **choose the three sites which have been most important to your research.** You will be asked a series of questions about the conditions of work and life at up to three <u>sites</u> in the next section. Two areas in the same part of the world which share similar conditions can be treated as one site for these purposes. If, however, you worked at an urban and rural location in the same country, you should treat it as two sites because the living and working conditions would be so different.

Now, give a name for the three sites you have selected, the country in which each is located, and the years in which you worked there, on the following lines. In case conditions have changed radically at the site since you started working there, give only the years here that you will be describing.
Site 1: _____

Site 2:_____

Site 3: _____

Please note that if you haven't done any fieldwork, the questionnaire is finished. Please return it now in the enclosed return envelope. Thank you for your cooperation.

3

Characteristics of Field Sites. Most researchers find they can describe all their trips to a single field site together. If the conditions changed radically from one field trip to another to the same site, give the dates you are describing on page 3. The **research group** may include just you, or include your family, or your close co-workers, and their families, if present. Do not try to answer for large numbers of others, just for those who shared living conditions with you. The research group may have changed from one trip to another but answer for **all** that apply to any of your fieldtrips to that site.

All of the questions about your fieldwork sites are on this page and the next. It is probably easiest to answer all the questions for site 1, then circle back to answer them for site 2, and then site 3 (if any). Do it however it works best for you.

	Site 1	Site 2	Site 3
10. You (and the research group) slept in: (check **all** that apply)			
European-type houses (or hotel)	_____	_____	_____
Huts	_____	_____	_____
Tents	_____	_____	_____
Outside, no roofed shelter	_____	_____	_____
In truck, van, travel trailer, caravan	_____	_____	_____
Other (specify) _____	_____	_____	_____
11. You (and the research group) slept on: (check **all** that apply)			
beds with mattresses	_____	_____	_____
beds without mattresses	_____	_____	_____
mattress (or air mattress) on ground	_____	_____	_____
camp cot	_____	_____	_____
hammock	_____	_____	_____
directly on ground (on ground sheet, animal skin)	_____	_____	_____
Other (specify) _____	_____	_____	_____
12. Drinking water was obtained from (check **all** that apply)			
a piped system, with purification	_____	_____	_____
a piped system, no purification	_____	_____	_____
a well (dug or natural)	_____	_____	_____
collected rain water	_____	_____	_____
a stream or river	_____	_____	_____
a lake or pond	_____	_____	_____
Others (specify) _____	_____	_____	_____
13. This water was usually drunk after being:			
distilled	_____	_____	_____
boiled	_____	_____	_____
filtered	_____	_____	_____
chemically treated	_____	_____	_____
just allowed to settle	_____	_____	_____
untreated; just as it comes	_____	_____	_____
Other (specify) _____	_____	_____	_____
14. The research team used the following systems for **disposal of urine and feces:**			
flush toilets	_____	_____	_____
portable, chemical toilets	_____	_____	_____
dug an outhouse, latrine	_____	_____	_____
used existing outhouses, latrines	_____	_____	_____
buried excrement each time	_____	_____	_____
used fields or woods, followed local custom	_____	_____	_____
Other (specify) _____	_____	_____	_____

4

15. The **food was prepared** by (check **all** that apply)

	Site 1	Site 2	Site
the researcher alone	___	___	___
members of the research team	___	___	___
a restaurant or inn	___	___	___
family members	___	___	___
a hired local person, a cook	___	___	___
local people, not hired	___	___	___
Other (specify) _____	___	___	___

16. The **food** of the researchers was **provided by** : (check **all** that apply)

bought at modern supermarket, restaurants or hotels	___	___	___
bought in a distant town or city , and hauled in	___	___	___
local market, bought by self or research group	___	___	___
bought at market, by cook or local employee	___	___	___
grown by local people, not for sale	___	___	___
grown by self or research group	___	___	___
locally hunted or gathered	___	___	___
hunting, by a member of the research group	___	___	___
Other (specify) _____	___	___	___

17. **Transportation** in the field was provided by: (check **all** that apply).

trucks, bought	___	___	___
trucks, rented for short periods	___	___	___
passenger cars	___	___	___
airplane	___	___	___
helicopters	___	___	___
motor cycles	___	___	___
bicycles	___	___	___
motor scooter	___	___	___
walking, hiking	___	___	___
buses, public transport	___	___	___
motor boats	___	___	___
canoes or other small boats	___	___	___
dog sled	___	___	___
Snowmobile	___	___	___
horseback riding	___	___	___
Other (specify) _____	___	___	___

18. **Medical care** needed by researchers in the field was provided by:

local hospital, local doctor	___	___	___
local nurse or paramedic	___	___	___
self or members of research group	___	___	___
local, non-medical treatment (magical, herbal, etc.)	___	___	___
Other (specify) _____	___	___	___

19. Travel to **nearest hospital** :
Site 1: distance _____ travel time _____
Site 2: distance _____ travel time _____
Site 3: distance _____ travel time _____

20. Check the **items of equipment** that you usually had with you in the field:

	Site 1	Site 2	Site 3
two way radio	___	___	___
a serious first-aid kit	___	___	___
a gun or guns	___	___	___
extra vehicle in case of breakdown	___	___	___
spare parts for vehicles	___	___	___
injectable antibiotics	___	___	___
snakebite kit	___	___	___
water purification equipment	___	___	___
Other (specify) _____	___	___	___

5

THE QUESTIONS ON THIS PAGE REFER TO YOUR EXPERIENCE, ON ANY FIELD TRIP, OF PROBLEMS FROM VARIOUS RISKS TO HEALTH AND SAFETY. Please use the following code to indicate your degree of experience with each of these risks to health and safety:

    0. If this was not a risk at any of the places you have done fieldwork.
    1. If it was a risk, but you and your immediate research group did not suffer from it.
    2. If one or more members of your research group (or family) suffered from this problem, but you personally did not.
    3. If you personally suffered from this problem (whether or not others in your group also did).
    ?. If you don't know about this risk.

21. Parasites:

_____ malaria	_____ ascarasis (roundworm)
_____ amebiasis	_____ tapeworm
_____ leishmaniasis (river blindness, elephantiasis)	_____ hookworm
_____ schistosomiasis (Bilharzia)	_____ filariasis (microfiliarisis)
_____ trypanosomiasis (sleeping sickness)	_____ trichiniasis

22. Intestinal ills:

_____ travellers diarrhea	_____ giardiasis
_____ E. coli infections	_____ amoebic dysentery
_____ bacillary dysentery	_____ cholera
_____ salmonella	_____ typhoid - enteric fever
_____ paratyphoid	_____ typhus, epidemic or endemic
_____ brucellosis (Malta fever)	_____ stomach ulcers

23. Respiratory :

_____ pneumonia	_____ bronchitis
_____ tuberculosis (t.b.)	_____ asthma
_____ allergies,	_____ anaphylaxis,
_____ colds,coughs	_____ diptheria
_____ tonsillitis	_____ sore throat, strep throat
_____ coccidioidomycosis ("Valley fever")	_____ whooping cough

24. Liver,urinary:

_____ hepatitis A (infectious)	_____ hepatitis B (serum hepetitus)
_____ hepatitus, type unknown or other	_____ yellow fever
_____ jaundice - leptospirosis	_____ cirrhosis
_____ kidney disease	_____ urinary track infections

25. Genital,reproductive:

	_____ syphilis
_____ gonorrhea	_____ herpes
_____ AIDS	_____ chlamydia
_____ yeast infections, other infections	_____ genital lice
_____ pregnancy, childbirth	_____ miscarriage, abortion
_____ mastitis (breast infection)	_____ vaginitis (vaginal infection)

26. Infectious :

_____ measles	_____ mumps
_____ poliomyelitis (polio)	_____ smallpox
_____ chickenpox	_____ plague
_____ rubella	_____ roseolla
_____ Dengue fever	_____ Rocky Mountain spotted fever
_____ meningitis	_____ encephalitis
_____ Lassa fever	_____ leprosy
_____ influenza	_____ tracoma
_____ conjunctivitis (eye infections)	_____ otitis (ear infections)

27. Other illness: These are universally present as a risk, so just use codes 1, 2 and 3 ,for fieldwork illnesses only.

_____ cancer	_____ heart attack, angina pain
_____ stroke	_____ circulatory disease
_____ diabetes	_____ severe weight loss
_____ malnutrition, anemia	_____ food poisoning, salmonella, etc.
_____ headaches, migraine	_____ food poisoning, manioc, toxic foods
_____ epilepsy	_____ arthritis
_____ appendicitis	_____ hemmorhoids
_____ toothache, broken tooth	_____ broken bones

6

28. **Skin:**

_____ ulcers	_____ skin cancer
_____ cuts	_____ sores
_____ boils, abscess	_____ rashes
_____ poison ivy , oak, sumach	_____ Athletes' foot or other fungus
_____ blisters	_____ skin allergies, hives
_____ burns, peeling skin	_____ staphylococcal infections

29. **Snakes, insect bites:**

_____ scorpion bite	_____ snakebite
_____ mosquitoes	_____ spider bites
_____ tsetse flies	_____ fleas
_____ black flies	_____ lice
_____ chiggers	_____ sandfleas
_____ bee stings	_____ ticks
_____ army ants	_____ wasps, hornets
	_____ black ants

30. **Animal** bites or injuries : (give species), _____
_____ rabies
_____ anthrax   _____ tetanus

31. **Injury accidents:**

_____ car	_____ truck
_____ motor bike	_____ motorcycles
_____ bicycle	_____ helicopter
_____ airplane	_____ explosion
_____ guns	_____ knives
_____ traps	_____ local weapons
_____ falls	_____ avalanche, buried
_____ broken limbs	_____ cave in
_____ fractured skull	_____ severe bruises
_____ spinal injuries	_____ cuts and bleeding
_____ bullet wound	_____ electric shock
_____ sprain of ankle, thumb, etc.	_____ dislocation of shoulder, knee, etc.

32. **Exposure:**

_____ cold, hypothermia	_____ heat stroke , heat exhaustion
_____ sun burn	_____ fire, burns
_____ hit by lightning	_____ frostbite
_____ altitude sickness	_____ dehydration

33. **Water hazards:**

_____ poisonous fish	_____ sea-snakes
_____ boat accidents	_____ swept away, tidal wave, undertow
_____ drowning, hypothermia	_____ motion sickness
_____ poisonous stings (jellyfish, coral, stingray)	_____ leeches

34. **Assault:**

_____ robbery, or attempted robbery	_____ rape, or attempted rape
_____ murder or attempted murder	_____ suicide or attempted suicide
_____ abandonment	_____ fighting
_____ beating	_____ assault, attack

35. **Political:**

_____ political turmoil	_____ hostage-taking, kidnapping
_____ military attack	_____ suspicion of spying
_____ arrest	_____ factional conflict

36. **Mental** illness:

_____ anxiety	_____ depression
_____ alcoholism	_____ drug abuse
_____ culture shock	_____ repatriation stress
_____ hallucinations	_____ manic state

37. **Other** (please specify) _____

7

38. Which of these conditions **continued to cause problems after your return** from the field?
_____
Were **delays** in diagnosis and treatment part of the problem? _____ Where and when did you finally get the medical care
you needed? _____

39. Did you ever spend any time **recuperating** after you left the field? _____Explain: _____
Do you (or did you) suffer any **restriction of your activities** due to the problems that arose in the field? _____What were
they? _____

40. Which of the following **precautions** have you taken before going to the field?
_____ medical check-up   _____ innoculations, Gamma Globulin
_____ checking your health insurance coverage   _____ checking health insurance of others in the field group
_____ buying or checking life insurance   _____ making a will
_____ visiting scholars in the country for advice _____ meeting the local medical practitioners and asking advice
_____ taking or reviewing a first-aid course   _____ obtaining manuals for the vehicles you will use
_____ dental check-up   _____ establishing an emergency evacuation plan
_____ registering at your government's consulate in the country you are visiting

Did you take anti-malarial medication for prevention in the field? _____ What kind ?_____
Did you take any other medication on a preventative basis? _____ What kind? _____

41. Did you **treat medical problems** in the field:
_____for yourself?   _____ for members of your group?
_____for students?   _____ for local employees?
_____for the local people?   _____ check here if you are a physician.

If you treated medical problems for local people:
What was the most difficult problem a local person ever presented to you to treat? _____
Did you ever have a death of a sick person you were treating? _____
Did you ever feel that someone was made worse by your treatment? _____
Ever feel that you probably saved a life by your treatment? _____
Were you comfortable in the role of medical provider? _____
Was this a time-consuming responsibility, or a minor and occasional one? _____
_____ Did you ever have to lance or cut skin to treat an ailment? _____ Did you ever give an injection?
_____ Did you ever give penicillin or other prescription drugs? _____ Did you ever deliver a baby?
_____ Did you ever treat a case of snakebite?   _____ Did you ever stitch or suture a wound?
_____ Did you ever apply a tourniquet?   _____ Did you take local people to the hospital?
Do you have any favorite medical guide or text that you recommend to your students? _____
Author and name: _____

42. Was your spouse (or equivalent person) ever with you in the field? _____ How long? _____
Were any of your children ever with you?_____What ages were they then? _____
Were there special health and safety problems caused by having your family with you? _____
Were there special health and safety advantages of having the family with you? _____
Were there any problems caused in your relationship with your closest people, family or others, by fieldwork, whether they
came with you or you were seperated? _____
If you had it to do over again, knowing what you know now, would you take your family with you or leave them behind ?
_____

IF YOU WOULD LIKE TO BE PHONED TO COMPLETE THIS QUESTIONNAIRE, TO CLARIFY YOUR
ANSWERS, OR TO PROVIDE FURTHER DETAIL, CHECK HERE: _____

The best phone number for weekday mornings is _____
The best phone number for weekends is   _____

Thank you for your help and cooperation. Please return your questionnaire now in the enclosed postage paid envelope. If
you would like to provide further information on health and safety issues, please send your comments to the same address.

8

207

INDEX

Abortion in the field, 143, 144
Academic year, effects on fieldwork, 50
Acceptance in the field, 156, 157
Accessibility to medical care, 59, 60, 178
Accounts of fieldwork, 7, 162, 189
Accusation, of spying, 98; of witchcraft, 156
Advice to parents, 171–175
Africa, numbers of field trips to, 51, 52
African sleeping sickness, 119
Agar, Michael, 135, 146
Age, at finishing graduate school, 36; at first
    professional job, 37, 38; and sex of sample,
    32; at starting career, 39; at starting
    fieldwork, 37; at starting graduate school, 35
Agreements, on field safety, 189
AIDS, 139
Air-borne infectious diseases, 129–131;
    parasites, 125–127
Airline accidents, 108, 109
Alberta, University of, 136, 151
Alcohol, consumption, 42, 43; and hepatitis,
    135; and hypothermia, 73; management, 155;
    pressure to consume, 15; and snakebite, 82
Alcoholism, 43, 44; in the field, 154
Alienation, 159
Allergies, 147; to bone dust, 148
Altitude sickness, 69–71
Altmann, Stuart, 95, 118
Ambulance services, 187
Ambush, 8
Amebiasis (protozoa), 121, 122
Amebic dysentery, 122
American Anthropological Association, AAA,
    1, 186
American Association for the Advancement of
    Science, AAAS, 1
American Ethnological Society, 1
American Folklore Society, 1
American Museum of Natural History, 117
American trypanosomiasis, 119
Amherst College, 173
Amoebic, see Amebic
Anal fissures and hemorrhoids, 146
Anaphylactic shock, 8, 83
Angel, Lawrence, 136
Animals, hazards, 79–88; transport, 59; in
    vehicle accidents, 103
Annis, Elgen, 108
Anopheles mosquitoes, malaria, 115
Ant stings, 84

Anthropological Society of Washington, 1
Anthropologists, definition of, 9; health status,
    142; prototypical, 5
Anthropology, occupational risks, 8; and
    sociology, 2
Anthropology Newsletter, 42, 140, 166
Antibiotics, emergency equipment, 60; as
    treatment, 178, 186
Anticipating hazards of sites, 186
Antimalarials (drugs), 118
Anxiety, of fieldworkers, 152, 153; of
    respondents, 44
Appendicitis, 144, 145, 174; operations for,
    145; precautionary removal, 145
Aralen, 158
Archaeology, in anthropology, 2; hazards of,
    110; special hazards, 110–112
Archeological Institute of America, 1
Arizona State University, 102, 123
Army ants, 84
Arrests in the field, 96
Arsenic, 148
Ascariasis (roundworms), 123
Aspirin, 146, 147; and sunburn, 67
Assassination, 99
Assault, 91–93
Asthma, 148; and ascariasis, 123
Attempted rape, 93
Audience for anthropology, 9

Bacillary dysentery (shigellosis), 133;
    prevention, 134
Bacteria, 128
Bailey, Bob, 120, 190
Base camp, 46
Basher, Eileen, 150
Bateson, Gregory, 77, 166
Baumhoff, Martin Alexander, 150
Beals, Alan, 5, 123, 135
Beals, Ralph, 174
Beating, 91
Bedwell, Stephen, 74
Bee stings, 8, 83, 84
Benedict, Ruth, 2, 94, 95
Bernard, H. Russell, 74, 135
Bicycles, 106
Bilharzia (schistosomiasis), 120, 121
Birth in the field, 144, 169, 170
Bites from animals, 86, 87
Black flies, 85

Blackwater fever, 118, 158
Bladder stones, 147
Blame, 89, 100, 142
Blindness, 141
Blisters, 141
Blood transfusions, and Chagas' disease, 119; and hepatitis B, 136
Boas, Franz, 2, 3, 95
Boats, 74, 80, 87
Bohannan, Laura, 154, 156
Boiling water, 56; bacillary dysentery, 134; diarrheas, 132; giardiasis, 122, 123
Booth, Angus, 87
Boots, 80–83
Bovine tuberculosis, 130
Braidwood, Linda, 166
Brandeis University, 135
Breakbone (dengue) fever, 137
Brennan, Ellen R., 102
Bribes, 96
Briggs, Jean, 5
Brigham Young University, 111
Broiling, Frank, 151
Broken bones, from falls, 112; from vehicle accidents, 113
Bronchitis, 129, 130
Brown, Peter, 117
Brucellosis (undulent fever), 138, 139
Brush fires, 72
Buchbinder, Georgeda, 112
Buikstra, Jane, 142
Bull sessions on fieldwork, 6
Burns, 71,72
Bus or transport accidents, 107
Bush, fires, 72; medicine, 129; pilots, 10, stories, 6, 7; survival skills, 7
Bush, Steven, 109

Calgary, University of, 126
California Archeological Society, 138, 190
California State University (Bakersfield), 145
California State University (Fresno), 126
California, University of (Berkeley), 117, 136, 140, 166, 172
California, University of (Davis), 109
California, University of (Riverside), 135
California, University of (San Diego), 123, 140
Cambridge University, 2
Camp manager, 166
Camping, 71
Cancer, 151; and sun exposure, 66
Car accidents, 101; and alcohol, 103; deaths, 101, 102; nonfatal, 102; to students, 102
Carnegie Foundation, 54
Carneiro, Robert, 117, 118
Cars, in the field, 58
Case Western Reserve University, 92
Cassell, Joan, 164, 167, 171, 172, 175
Cavalli-Sforza, L. L., 88
Cave-ins, in archaeology, 111

Centers for Disease Control, 119; *Manual*, 119, 188; *see also* U.S. Centers for Disease Control
Cerebral malaria, 118
Cesara, Manda, 169
Chagas' disease, 119
Chagnon, Napoleon, 5, 7, 69, 80, 82, 91, 92, 95, 109, 141, 155, 156
Chartoff, Joe, 126
Checklist of hazards, 61, 186, 201–208
Cheerfulness of respondents, 44
Chemical insecticides, 85
Chemical treatment of water, 56
Chicago, University of, viii, 118, 123
Chicken pox vaccine, 128
Chigger bites, 86
Childbearing, in the field, 144; with locals, 170
Childcare, from locals 171
Children, choices, 172; deaths in the field, 174; depression, 173; effects on fieldwork, 172; in the field, 164; and mosquito nets, 84; pets in the field, 172; pros and cons, 174; relations to locals, 174, 175; scorpion bites, 83; stress in the field, 172, 173
Children in the Field: Anthropological Experiences, 171
Chlamydia, 139
Chloromycetin, 173
Chloroquine, 116–119
Cholera, 133; vaccine, 128
Choosing fieldwork sites, 185, 186
Christie, Agatha, 166
Circulatory disease, 151
City University of New York (CUNY), 136
Clark, Betty, 166
Clark, Geoffrey A., 123
Clark, J. Desmond, 120, 166
Cleveland State University, 135, 146
Clothing, protection from insects, 85, 86
Coccidioidomycosis (valley fever), 125, 126
Cohen, Ronald, 98, 103, 104, 135
Cold hazards, 72, 73
Colds, 129, 130
Cole, Sonia, 74
Columbia University, 1, 2, 23, 24, 112
Commercial airlines, 109
Companions in the field, 53
Conjunctivitis (eye infections), 140; treatment of, 141
Consequences of accidents, 113
Consulate registration, 64
Contagious diseases, 128
Contract research, 54
Control over others, 184
Convulsions, 149; and ascariasis, 123
Cooking in the field, 57
Cooks, 57, 166
Copley, Joanna, 8, 88
Corwin, Lauren A., 135
Courses, in field safety, 189

Cowgill, George, 135
Cows, 130
CPR (coronary-pulmonary resuscitation), 74, 186
Craig, Royna, 102
Crew, Harvey, 102
Criminal assault, 88, 89
Criminal interpersonal hazards, 89
Crocodiles, 87
Croxton, Ruth, 108
Culture shock, 155
Cutler, 118
Cuts and sores, 141

D'Andrade, Roy, 235
Dangers of fieldwork, 182
Dangers of practicing medicine, 180
Dangers to children, 174; of anthropology, 8; of other sciences, 8
David, Nicholas, 121
Days in the field in 1986, 50
Deacon, Bernard, 118, 157
Death, auto accidents, 101; degenerative diseases, 142; by drowning, 74, 75; from elephant and rhinoceros injuries, 88; helicopter accident, 108; help from consulate, 64; murder, 93, 94
Deer, and ticks, 137
Defense mechanisms, 162
Degenerative diseases, 142
Dehydration, 66, 68, 69, 106, 133; cause of death, 69; and diarrhea, 132; and kidney disease, 69; and seasickness, 75
Delaware, University of, 136
Delivering a baby, 178
Demographic Yearbook, 186
Dengue fever (viral disease), 137; and mosquitoes, 137
Denial of dangers, 184
Dental checkups, 62, 63
Dentan, Robert, 169
Dentist, 62, 147, 186
Departments of anthropology, 2, 3, 190, 191; safety programs and policies, 190
Dependency in the field, 7; on spouse, 162
Depression, 44, 152, 158, 159, 172, 173; and families, 153; and sickness, 153
Derry, David, 104
Desensitization to allergies, 84
DeVore, Irven, 71, 120, 135, 166, 190
DeVore, Nancy, 166
Diabetes, management, 140; coma, 150
Diarrheal disease, 132, 133; amebiasis, 121; treatment of, 133
Diary in the Strict Sense of the Term, 162
Diet in the field, 76–78; and malnutrition, 75
Diet pills, 155
Dietary deficiency diseases, 75
Dillman, D. D., 29
Diphtheria, 129; vaccine, 128

Dislocation, 159
Dissertation fieldwork, 47, 50
Distance to medical care, 59
Divale, William, 75
Diving accident, 113
Divorce and fieldwork, 164–175
Dogs, 87; and dog bites, 88; and ticks, 137
Dorner, Clarice J., 93
Douglass, Ron, 108
Downward mobility, 25
Dreher children, 173, 175
Dreher, Melanie, 155, 172, 175
Drinking behavior, *see* Alcohol
Drinking water, 55, 56
Drivers' training, 103, 192
Drowning, 74, 75
Drug abuse, in the field, 154
Drug smuggling charges, 96
Drug use in the field, 155; side effects, hallucinations, 152
Duodenùm ulcers, 145, 146
Duration of field trips, 47, 53
Durham, Bill, 109
Dysentery, 133, 134
Dysmenorrhea, 143

E. Coli infections (diarrheas), 118, 132
Ear problems, hearing loss, 140; and plane travel, 140; and swimming, 140
Eberhart, Hal, 150
Eczema, 173
Electric eel, 80
Electrocution, 112
Elephantiasis, 120
Emergencies, 82; communication, 187; evacuation plans, 63; medical treatment, 103; procedures, 114; rescue, 102; transport 173, 187
Emory University, 106, 117, 159, 179
Employees, in accident, 103; robbery by, 91
Employment of sample, 25
Endemic diseases in the field, 140
Epilepsy, 149
Epinephrine, for allergies, 84
Evacuation plans, fires, 72; to hospital, 59; political crisis, 96
Expeditions, *see* Fieldwork
Eye injury, 112, 113
Eye problems (conjunctivitis), 140; and malaria medication, 141

Factional conflict, 98
Faculty jobs, 3
Falls, 111, 112; as a cause of death, 112; injuries from, 111
Families in the field, 153; cooking, 58; frequency, 164; influences on fieldwork, 166; life in the field, 173; objections to fieldwork, 34, 35; responsibilities, 34
Fansidar, 117

Faulkner, Arthur, 93
Fecal contamination, ascariasis, 123; giardiasis, 123; of water, 57
Fei Xiaotong, 170
Field initiation, 155
Field Museum, Chicago, 92
Field schools, 35, 111
Field stress, 163
Field trip, to continents, 51; features, 51; number of, 46; as units, 51
Fieldwork, centrality of, 4; and chronic disease, 142; comfort, 5; cumulative time, 48; dangers, 6; destinations, 51, 52; establishes rank, 5; group size, 51, 52; kinds of, 5; on lawyers, 5; living conditions, 55; self-funded, 54; as a trial, 4; in urban society, 5
Fieldworkers' "uniform," 4; protective clothing, 73, 81, 184
Fighting, 91
Filariasis, 120
Filtering of water, 56, 123
Financial costs of emergencies, 63
Fire hazards, 71, 72; bush or brush, 72; in trucks, 72
First aid courses, 60, 103, 114
First aid courses taken, 62, 63
Flea bites, 86
Florida, University of, 104, 135, 137
Fonseca, Cesar, 109
Food in the field, 57, 58
Food poisoning (salmonella), 131, 132
Food preparation, 57
Food-borne infectious disease, 132; parasitic disease, 124, 125
Ford Foundation, 54
Formal organization of anthropology, 2
Format for tables, 65, 66
Foss, Hal Charles, 102
Fossey, Dian, 7, 87, 91, 95, 99, 145
Foundations, funding, 187
Freilich, Morris, 4, 6, 47
Frostbite, 73
Frucht, Richard, 151
Fryxell, Roald, 102
Fuller, Melanie, 95
Funding of fieldwork, 34, 53, 54; for increased safety, 187; private sources, 54; for research, 187
Fungus disease, histoplasmosis, 125; valley fever, 125, 126

Gallin, Bernard, 136
Gangrene, 82
Gardiner, Margaret, 157
Gardner, Ed, 108
Geertz, Hildred, 136
Geise, Marie Clabeaux, 148
Gender, and employment, 25, 26; and fieldwork, 48, 49; and highest degrees, 26; and subdisciplines, 28

Genital herpes, 139
Geographical distribution, of fieldwork, 51; of hazards, 8, 184
Germ theory of disease, 129
Gestational diabetes, 144
Gewerz, Deborah, 173
Giardiasis, 123
Gibson, Thomas, 122
Giving injections, 178
Going native, 159
Golde, Peggy, 157, 170, 176, 178
Gonorrhea, 139
Gorman, Chester F., 150
Government, agencies' policies, 62; funding of fieldwork, 53; policies on health and safety, 191
Graduate programs, 3
Graduate students, 3; accidents, 102; resentments of, 7; supervision of, 35, 188–190
Grady, Mark Allen, 102
Grana, Cesar, 102
Granskog, Jane, 145
Grants, as a reason for not doing fieldwork, 34
Grave robbery, 96
Green, Jim, 123
Green, Vera Mae, 150
Greenfield, Jennifer Beth, 102
Grobsmith, Elizabeth, 126, 144
Growing food in the field, 57
Growth of anthropology, 2
Guerilla warfare, 97
Guides to Departments, 1
Guns in the field, 60, 88, 109, 110

Haddon, A. C., 157
Hale, Mary C., 102
Hallucinations, drug reactions, 152
Ham, James, 191
Hamilton College, 150
Hammel, E. A., 155
Hanson, Art, 137
Hansen, Judith Friedman, 150
Harrington, John Peabody, 166
Harris, Alfred, 122
Harris, Jack, 69
Harvard University, 24, 135, 136
Having a child in the field, 170
Hawaii, University of, 112
Hawkes, Kristen, 91, 105
Hazards, by continents, 183; by exposure to field, 183; numbers reported, 182; raising consciousness, 184; by subdiscipline, 182
Headache pain, 147
Headland, Thomas, 48
Health, insurance, 63; manuals, 186; and safety policy, 191; status, 40
Health Information for International Travel, 134, 186
Heart attack, 150, 151

Heat exhaustion or stroke, 67, 68
Heinz, Hans J., 170
Heizer, Robert Fleming, 150
Helicopters, accidents, 108; in the field, 58
Helmets, head protection, 106
Hemorrhoids, 146
Hepatic diseases, 134; amebiasis, 122; amebic, 122
Hepatitis, 134, 136, 158, 192; type A, 135; and local cooks, 135; and dengue fever, 137; type B, 135; B vaccine, 128; type non-A, non-B, 136; and blood transfusions, 136; and malaria, 137
Herpes (genital), 139
Herzog, Harold, 95
Hesser, Jana, 134
Hides, and brucellosis, 138, 139
Higgens, Jon B., 102
Higgins, Michael J., 145
High altitude sickness, 69; encephalopathy (HAE), 70; pulmonary edema (HAPE), 70
High risk occupations, 8
High risk pregnancy, 144
High "tech" transportation, 59
Highest degree, of the sample, 26, 27
Highway robbery, 92
Hill, Kim, 105, 110
Histoplasmosis, 125
Hitchcock, Patricia, 174
Hitchhiking for help, 105; as transportation, 58, 59
HIV, see AIDS, 140
Hookworm, life cycle, symptoms, 125
Hopkins, Michael S., 124
Horseback riding in the field, 59
Hostage-taking, 99
Hotel rooms, 90
Housing in the field, 56
Howell, Nancy, 80, 81, 174
Hugh-Jones, Christine, 78
Hugh-Jones, Leo, 78, 172
Hugh-Jones, Tom, 78, 172
Human attacks and rapport, 88, 89
Hunn, Eugene, 174
Hunt, Robert, 72
Hunting accident, 110
Hunting and gathering food, 57
Hurtado, Magdalena, 110
Husbands in the field, 167, 168
Hypothermia, 73; treatment, 74

Ikels, Charlotte, 92
Illinois, University of, 109
Illness, of children, 173; and mental health, 157; of spouse, 170
Images, of anthropology, 5; of danger in anthropology, 9
Immune globulins, 128
Immunizations (inoculations), 128
Indiana Jones, 9, 79

Indiana University, Bloomington, 24, 106, 150
Infectious disease, causes of, 128; miscellaneous, 140; prevention, 128
Infectious hepatitis, 135
Influenza, 141; and pregnancy, 144; vaccine, 128
Injections, 186; antibiotics, 60; epinephrine, 84
Injuries from accidents, archaeological digs, 111; car accidents, 101–103; cumulative, 114; in explosion, 100; from falls, 112; hunting accidents, 110; from "local weapons," 110; from tools, 111; trench collapse, 111; truck accidents, 105
Inoculations for infectious diseases, 140; for cholera, 133; for pneumonia, 131; precautions, 62, 63; schedules, 128, 129; for travelers, 128; for typhoid fever, 133
Insect repellents, 85
Insect-borne diseases, 136, 137; parasites, 115–120
Insecticide, poisoning, 85; prevention of Chagas' disease, 119
Insurance precautions, 63
Internal consistency of answers, 114
Interpersonal stress, 100
Isaac, Barbara, 120, 136
Isaac, Glynn, 69, 120, 136
Isolation, 152, 157; and anxiety, 153; and loneliness, 155, 156

Jacobsen, Margaret, 87
Jaundice, 135
Jellyfish, 79, 80
Jenkins, Bruce, 108
Jensen, Anne, 93
Jobs in anthropology, 2; by gender, 26; for new Ph.D.s, 4
Johanson, Don, 96
Jones, Kevin, 105
Jones, William, 94
Jones-Jackson, Patricia, 102
Journal of fieldwork problems, 162

Kaplan, Bernice, 42, 72, 136, 173
Kaufulu, Zefe, 106
Kelley, Jane, 126
Keyes, Charles, 123, 148
Kidnapped for ransom, 99
Kidney disease, 69; stones, 146
Killer bees, 84
Killoran, Annaliese H., 93
Klass, Sheila, and Morton, 144
Knauer, Melissa, 105, 174
Knives, 110
Koch, Klaus-Friedrich, 112
Konner, Mel, vii, 179
Kroeber, Theodora, 166

Laird, Carobeth, 166
Lal, Krishnan, 174

Lancaster, Chet S., 150
Lance wounds, 178
Landes, Ruth, 160
Lasker, Gabriel, 72
Latrines, 56, 57
Laughlin, Bob, 174
Laurence University, 102
Leacock, Eleanor, 151
Leakey, Jonathan, 82
Leakey, Louis, 9, 72, 74, 84, 91, 98, 105, 118, 122, 145, 166, 174
Leakey, Mary, 72, 74, 82, 84, 86, 88, 91, 145, 166, 174, 177
Leakey, Richard, 69, 72, 82, 87, 89, 108
Lee, Alexander, 106, 174
Leeches, 79
Leishmaniasis, 119
Length of career, 40
Leslie, Charles, 107, 136
Lévi-Strauss, Claude, 6, 193
Levy, Robert, 123, 148
Lewis, Herb, 136
Liability of universities, 191
Library resources on field safety, 190
Lice, 86
Life insurance, 63
Lightning, 71
Lion attack, 87, 88
Littlewood, Robert A., 136
Living conditions in the field, 55
Loaiasis, 120
Local hospitals, 59
Local people, health, 157
Local transport services, 64
Locals, sexual relations, 169
Loneliness in the field, 152, 155, 156, 168
Loners, among respondents, 44
Loss of good judgment, 158
Lost, as a hazard of fieldwork, 69
Louchs, L. Jill, 102
Low "tech" transportation, 59
Lowie, Robert, 2
Loy, James, 87
Lubell, David, 136
Luggage, 90
Lung disease, ascariasis, 123; tuberculosis, 130; valley fever, 125, 126
Lyme disease, 137, 190
Lynch, B. Mark, 102

MacDougall, Bonnie G., 167
MacDougall, Robert, 150
Macinnes, Donald, 145
Macmillan, Mark T., 8
Malaria, 115, 158, 192; bladder complications, 118; blood tests, 117; cerebral complications, 118; course of illness, 116; and dehydration, 118; drug treatments, 116, 119; end of career, 118; geographic distribution, 116; and hepatitis, 119; and medical treatment, 116;

prevention, 116; side effects of drugs, 118; treatment of, 117
Malay, University of, 151
Malinowski, B., 157, 162
Mallowen, Max, 166
Malnutrition, 75, 76; in children, 76, 77; and mental health, 157
Malta fever (brucellosis), 139
Mammal bites and injuries, 87
Manic states, 153
Mapping unknown areas, 69
Marriage in the field, 158
Martin, Emily, 145
Mason, Richard, 8
Massachusetts, University of (Amherst), 136
Maybury-Lewis, David, 109, 154
Mayer, Enrique, 109
McCurdy, David, 177
Mead, Margaret, 2, 9, 77, 95, 112, 166, 188
Measles vaccine, 128
Meat-borne parasites, 124
Medical care in the field, 59; checkups, 62, 63; precautions taken, 62, 63; treatments practiced, 178
Medication, by mouth, 173
Melanoma, 150
Memorial University, Newfoundland, 156
Meningitis vaccine, 128
Mental, consequences of illness, 156–158; distress, denial, 163; health in the field, 44, 157; prevention of stress, 160; stress, 158
Merriam, Alan Parkhurst, 109
Messerschmidt, Donald, 175
Michigan State University, 126, 136
Michigan, University of, 109, 118, 142
Microfilariasis, 120
Military attacks, 97; transport, 109
Milk-borne infections, 139
Miller, Sheryl, 136
Milton, Katharine, 117, 136
Minnesota, University of, 71
Miscarriage, 143, 144, 145; result of accident, 103
Missionary societies, 187
Mixon, Donald, 102
Monkey bites, 87
Montezuma's revenge (giardiasis), 123
Moran, Emilio, 80
Mosquito, bites, 84; dengue fever, 137; and malaria, 115; nets, 85; prevention, 84, 85; and yellow fever, 138
Motion sickness, 75
Motor scooters, 106
Motor vehicle accidents, 192
Motorcycles, 106
Movius, Hal, 5
Mule accident, 88
Mumps vaccine, 128
Murder, 94, 95; attempt, 95
Myerhoff, Barbara, 150

Mysterious deaths, 94

Nader, Laura, 5, 55, 94, 136, 158
Nash, June, 98, 136
Nason, James, 72, 75
National Geographic Society, 69
National Institutes of Health, 53
National Science Foundation, 53
National University of Peru, 109
Native mistress, 157
Natural defenses, 128
Nebraska, University of, 126, 144
Netting, Robert, 121
Neurotoxins, 83, 84
New Hampshire, University of, 136
New Mexico, University of, 151
Newman, T. Stell, 102
Nimtz, Maxine Letcher, 150
Nimtz, Michael, 109
Nonrespondents, 29, 30
North America, field trips to, 51, 52
Northern Kentucky University, 111
Northwestern University, 112
Nourishment, 130; and stomach ulcers, 146

Obituaries, 102
Objections, to study of dangers, 6
O'Connell, Jim, 91
Occupational health and safety, 8
Oceanography, dangers of, 8
O'Laughlin, Bridgit, 100
Onchocerciasis, 120
Opler, Morris, 94
Opposition to safety policies, 193
Organization of respondents, 42
Origins of anthropology, 1
Ortner, Sherry, 142, 144
Otitis (ear infections), 140
Ototoxic drug reactions, 118
Outside experts, 189
Overgeneralizing, risk of, 5
Overweight, 41
Owen-Smith, Garth, 87
Owens, Delia, 72, 76, 82, 117, 119, 157
Owens, Mark, 68, 72, 76, 91, 157
Oxford University, 2

PABA creams and lotions, 67
Pacific area, field trips to, 51, 52
Parasitic diseases, defined, 115
Paratyphoid, 132
Pascon, Paul, 102
Passport, stolen, 90
Pasternak, Burton, 170
Patterson, Scott, 102
Payne, Kenneth W., 140
Peacock, Nadine, 120
Pedestrian accidents, 108
Penicillin, administered, 178
Pennsylvania, University of, 109

Perforated ulcer, 146
Person-months in the field, 53
Pets in the field, 172
Pharoah's curse (valley fever), 125, 126
Ph.D. granting departments, 3
Philippines, University of, 146
Photosensitivity, 66, 67
Physical fitness, 41
Physical violence, 91, 92
Piker, Steven, 124
Pitzer College, 136
Planes in the field, 59, 108, 109
Pneumonia, 123; and ascariasis, 123; as a
    complication, 131; drug hazards, 173;
    frequency, 131; prevention of, 131; vaccine,
    128, 131
Poison fish, 79
Poison ivy (or oak), 141
Poisoning in the field, 77
Poliomyelitis vaccine, 128
Political conflict, 98; instability, 34
Political crises, emergency, 99; evacuation
    plans, 64; hazards, 96; turmoil, 98
Powers, R., 108
Practicing medicine in the field, 177–181;
    consequences for fieldwork, 180; dangers
    180; distance to medical care, 177, 178;
    ethics, 181; frequency, 176; locals, 180;
    objections, 180
Precautions taken, 61
Pregnancy in the field, 143, 144; unwanted, 144
Preston, Samuel, 11
Primates and yellow fever, 138
Princeton University, 136
Private funding, 54
Professional association, 1; meetings, 9;
    policies, 192
Professors, and bad advice, 189; teaching
    safety, 189
Prophylactic treatment, malaria, 116
Protozoa, malaria, 115
Public transportation in the field, 59
Puleston, Dennis, 71
Pulmonary tuberculosis, 130

Questionnaire, 22, 186, 201–208
Quinine, 116, 118

Rabies, 87; vaccine, 128
Racoons, 87
Ramos, Rafael, 68
Rankin, Adrianne, 88
Rape, 93
Rappaport, R. A., 5
Rapport, 156, 159, 175
Rashes, 141, 148
Rationing of water, 69
Raybeck, Douglas, 150
Reciprocity, and robbery, 91
Reckless behavior, and suicide, 161, 163

Red Cross first aid courses, 186
Reducing fieldwork risks, 184, 193
Reduviid bugs, Chagas' disease, 119
Regional sharing of information, 190
Regional specialities of respondents, 61
Registering at a consulate, 63
Rehydration solution, 133
Relationship problems, 168, 169
Reo Fortune, 166
Repatriation stress, 160; thesis research, 161
Repeated fieldwork, 47
Respiratory infections, 129, 130
Respondents, activities of, 33; age and sex, 32; health, 39, 40; physical fitness, 41
Response rates, 28
Return to Laughter, 154
Rhesus monkeys, 87
Rhinoceros, 8, 88
Rhode Island, University of, 87
Richardson, Miles E., 136
Risk taking, 43, 56; to children in the field, 172; of fieldwork compared to home, 175
River blindness, 120
Road safety, 102
Robbery, 90–92
Rochester, University of, 122
Rockefeller, Michael, 74
Rockefeller, Foundation, 54
Rocky Mountain spotted fever, 137
Roghi, Gianni, 88
Rosaldo, Michelle Zimbalist, 112, 171
Rosaldo, Renato, 112, 159, 163, 171
Roughing it, 5
Roundworms (ascariasis), 123
Rubella vaccine, 128
Rubin, Vera, 150
Rules, of field safety, 87; of the road, 104

Sabbatical leaves, 3
Sabloff, Jeremy, 66
Sade, Donald, 137
Safety equipment carried, 60
Sallade (Brawn), Jane Katherine, 102
Salmonella (food poisoning), 131, 132
San Jose State College, 104
Sandfleas, 86
Sandfly fever (leishmaniasis), 119
Sanitary facilities in the field, 56
Sapir, Edward, 2
Satellite communications, 187
Satellite photos, 69
Saving lives, 179
Scheper-Hughes children, 173
Scheper-Hughes, Nancy, 172, 173
Schistosomiasis (bilharzia), 121
Schmerler, Henrietta, 94, 95
Schrire, Carmel, 82
Schroeder, Bruce, 97
Scorpion stings, 83
Seasickness, 75

Sea snakes, 80
Seat belts, 2, 101–103, 192
Secrecy about medical problems, 149
Self-funded research, 188
Self-limiting diseases, 128
Self-treatment in the field, 59
Separation from family, 156
Sept, Jeanne, 106
Serious first aid, 179
Serum hepatitis, 136
Sexton, Lorraine, 92
Sexual relations in the field, 136, 139, 158, 169, 170
Sexual transmission, of hepatitis B, 136; of veneral disease, 139, 140
Sharing information, 8, 185–190
Sheehan, Glynn W., 93
Shigellosis (bacillary dysentery), 133, 134
Shippe, David, 70
Shopping for food in the field, 57
Shostak, Marjorie, 159
Shots, *see* Inoculations
Sibley, Willis, 146
Singer, Alice, 106
Single parents in the field, 172
Size of field trips, 53
Skin cancer, and sun exposure, 150
Slavo, Ruth First, 99, 100
Sleeping conditions, 56
Sleeping pills, 155
Smith, Neil, 106
Smithsonian Institution, 136
Smoke of cooking fires, 129
Smoking of respondents, 42
Smuts, Barbara Boardman, 99, 100
Snails, and bilharzia, 121
Snakebite, 80, 82; kits, 60; prevention, 81; treatment, 82
Snakes, 80–82
Sociability of respondents, 44
Social isolation, 157
Social-cultural anthropology, 49
Sore throat, 129, 130
Sores (staphylococci), 141
Spouse in the field, 164, 165; both anthropologists, 167
Spradley, James P., 150
Stanford University, 99, 112
State University of New York, Buffalo, 148
Sticketon, Bobby, 82
Stingray, 80
Stitching or suturing wounds, 178
Stomach ulcers, 145
Stones, kidney or bladder, 146
Stonick, Susan, 136
Strains of fieldwork on marriages, 168; of separation, 169
Strep throat, 129, 130
Stress management, 163; on graduate students,

161; and heart disease, 150; interference with work, 163; on parents, 175
Strokes, 150
Students, safety in the field, 188; selecting field sites, 142; stresses of fieldwork, 161
Subdisciplines and fieldwork, 27, 49
Success in practicing medicine, 179
Success rates in survey, 28, 31
Suicide, 94; attempts and gestures, 160; in the field, 160–162
Summer Institute of Linguistics, 48
Sun exposure in archaeology, 68
Sun stroke, 68
Sunburn, 65, 66; of children, 67; chronic consequences, 66; prevention, 66, 67; and skin cancer, 66
Supervision of students, 142
Suppository medication, 173
Surgery, kidney stones, 146
Suspicion of spying, 97, 98
Swept away (in water), 74
Swimming accident, 112
Sympathy of spouse, 168
Syphilis, 139

Taking children to the field, 172
Taking people to hospital, 178
Tapeworms, 124
Teaching loads, 3; teaching, by respondents, 33; teaching students to do fieldwork, 35
Teleki, Geza, 120
Telephone, 60, 187
Tetanus vaccine, 128
Texas A. & M. University, 137
Theft, 89, 90, 91
Thiel, Barbara, 111
Thomas, R. Brooke, 120, 136
Tick bites, 86; and archaeology, 138
Tick-transmitted diseases, 137, 138
Tindall, B. Allan, 150
Tine test, for tuberculosis, 131
Tippett, Mike, 177
Toilets, 57
Tonsillitis, 129, 130
Toothache, 147
Toronto, University of, 105; safety policy, 191
Tourniquet application, 82, 178
Toxic foods, 77
Trachoma, 141
Training, first aid, 186; in medical care, 186; training students for fieldwork, 188, 189
Transmission of disease, 129
Transportation, 173; in the field, 58, 59
Traps, injuries from, 110
Traumatic injuries, 102, 114
Travel, and theft, 90
Traveler's diarrhea (giardiasis), 123
Trichinosis, 124
Tringham, Ruth, 7
Trinity College, Cambridge University, 157

Trips, *see* Field trips
Truck accidents, 103–105; prevention 104–106
Trypanosomiasis, American, 119; African, 119
Tsetse flies, 86; bites, 119
Tuberculosis, 130, 131
Tulane University, 68
Tullis, Julie, 70
Two-way radio, 60, 61, 187, 191
Typhoid fever, 132

Ulcers 145, 146; and drug complications, 146
Undergraduate students, 3
Underwood, Frances W., 105
Undulent fever (brucellosis), 138, 139
United Nations (U.N.), 186
Universities in sample, 24
University policies on safety, 191; responsibility for students, 187
Unsympathetic colleagues, 148
Urine, symptoms of dehydration, 69; disposal, 56, 57
U.S. Air Force, 69
U.S. Army, 187
U.S. Centers for Disease Control, 128, 199; health manual, 119; and malaria, 115
U.S. Peace Corps, 187
U.S. Postal Service, 88
Utah, University of, 91

Vaccines, 128
Valley fever (coccidioidomycosis) 125, 126, 127, 190
Value of anthropological work, 193
Valverdi, Victor, 70
Vampire bats, 87
van der Elst, Dirk, 126
Vaughan, James H., 150
Vehicle, accidents, 98; manuals, 63; spare parts, 60
Veneral disease, 89, 139
Vestibular neuronitis, 173
Violent attacks, 93, 94
Virus, 128
Visiting local physicians and scholars, 63; visiting students in the field, 35

Waivers of responsibility, 191, 192
Warsaw University, 109
Wartime spying, 98
Washington State University, 136, 174
Washington, University of, 92, 123, 148
Wasp stings, 83
Wassing, Rene, 74
Water consumption and kidney stones, 146
Water purification, 55; kits, 60
Water purity (giardiasis), 123
Water-borne infectious disease, 131, 132; parasitic disease, 120–124
Weapons, accidents, 110
Weight control, 41, 42

Weight loss, 76, 77, 173
Wellman, Klaus Friedrich, 150
Welsh, Robert, 92
Wenner-Gren Foundation, 54
Werner, David, 181
West Virginia, University of, 136
Where There Is No Doctor, 181
Whooping cough, 129
Wills, 63
Wilmott, Bobby, 81
Wimberly, Mark, 108
Wind burn, 73
Winslow, Deborah, 136
Wisconsin, University of, Madison, 136;
    Oshkosh, 112
Witchcraft accusations, 156
Wives in the field, 166, 167

Wolff, Kurt, 97
Women in the Field, 156
Woodbury, Nathalie, 166
World Health Organization, 128
Worst case, practicing medicine, 178, 179
Wright, Henry, 118
Wylie, Jonathan, 171–173

Years to completion of Ph.D., 37
Yeast infections (vaginal), 139
Yellow fever, 138; inoculations 138; jungle
    type, urban type, 138; vaccine, 128
Yengoyan, Aram, 77, 159
Young, S. James Clay, 74

Zoology, dangers of, 8
Zwicker, Thomas, 107

hANdbook on EThicAl issues in ANThropoloqy

Special Publication 23

edited by Joan Cassell
and Sue-Ellen Jacobs

To improve the ethical adequacy of anthropological practice, anthropologists must consider not only exceptional cases but everyday decisions, and reflect not only upon the conduct of others but also upon their own actions as researchers, teachers, students, and practitioners. Case studies offer a way to both heighten sensitivity and improve anthropological practice. Reading and thinking about situations faced by other anthropologists can help us to recognize our own ethical dilemmas and to make sensitive and informed decisions for resolving complex situations.

Handbook on Ethical Issues in Anthropology was designed to help social science faculty stimulate discussion and reflection on ethical issues in their courses—discussions that are an essential part of the teaching of anthropological theory and methods. Chapters in this valuable teaching aid include:

- an essay on issues and sources on ethics in anthropology by **Murray L. Wax**
- the background to the formation of the Committee on Ethics and the writing of the AAA's *Principles of Professional Responsibility* (PPR) by **James N. Hill** (PPR is included in the Appendix)
- a series of case studies compiled by **Joan Cassell** and **Sue-Ellen Jacobs,** presenting ethical dilemmas with anthropologists' solutions and additional commentary
- a description by Jacobs of how she used the *Principles of Professional Responsibility* and other materials to introduce issues of ethical responsibility in courses
- guidelines by Cassell on how to hold a workshop on ethical problems in fieldwork

Sponsored by the Committee on Ethics of the

American Anthropological Association

$6.00 ($4.50 for members)
Please enclose payment, in US funds, with all orders.

For information on bulk orders (10 or more copies) or to order individual copies, contact the **American Anthropological Association, 1703 New Hampshire Ave., N.W., Washington, D.C. 20009.**

culture, kin, and cognition in oceania:

essays in honor of ward h. goodenough

Mac Marshall and John L. Caughey, editors

Culture, Kin, and Cognition in Oceania demonstrates Ward H. Goodenough's influence on Pacific anthropology in eight original essays covering issues of continuing concern to anthropology. These include questions of informant reliability and ethnographic validity, the complexities of culture change, and the ways in which etic concepts obscure emic conceptualizations. Contributors address these issues via analyses of semantic categories and rules, gender, kinship and other aspects of social organization, describing and illustrating them with detailed ethnographic data from Melanesia, Micronesia, and Polynesia. The editors discuss Goodenough's approach to culture, identify influences important to the development of his anthropological thinking, and show how these essays build on his legacy and contribute to contemporary anthropological issues.

John J. Caughey and Mac Marshall / Introduction
Ann Chowning / Sex, Shit, and Shame: Changing Gender Relations among the Lakalai
Anna Meigs / The Cultural Construction of Reproduction and Its Relationship to Kinship and Gender
Jay Noricks / The Ethnographer as Detective: Solving the Puzzle of Niutao Land Tenure Rules
Anne Salmond / Tribal Words, Tribal Worlds: The Translatability of *tapu* and *mana*
William H. Alkire / Land, Sea, Gender, and Ghosts on Woleai-Lamotrek
Mac Marshall / Rashomon in Reverse: Ethnographic Agreement in Truk
Roger M. Keesing / Social Structure as Process: Longitudinal Perspectives on Kwaio Society

Special Publication No. 25.
$13 to members, $17 to all others.
Please enclose payment in U.S. funds, with all orders.

American Anthropological Association
1703 New Hampshire Avenue, N.W., Washington, D.C. 20009

ANThropoloqy for TOMORROW:

CREATiNq pRAcTiTiONER-ORiENTEd
Applied ANThropoloqy pROqRAMS

—Robert T. Trotter II, editor

Anthropology Practice is one of the hottest growth areas in anthropology today, and *Anthropology for Tomorrow* provides a model for developing practitioner-oriented applied anthropology programs.

This book, edited by Robert T. Trotter II, contains contributions from 15 authors who represent some of the most successful practitioners and some of the strongest academic leaders in the field of applied anthropology. It covers its subject thoroughly, from an exploration of program philosophies, through program development, to practical suggestions for creating and maintaining successfully tested innovations in training applied anthropologists.

The book provides models for applied programs at both the graduate and undergraduate levels, and discusses the essential core curriculum issues. It has several chapters that focus on the planning necessary for solid program development, and that point out the pitfalls to be avoided—from internal politics to departmental relationships university-wide. Other chapters illustrate successful applied program structures, relate university-industry linkages, and suggest ways to build solid ethics education into the program. It concludes with a provocative projection for the future of applied anthropology.

Anthropology for Tomorrow should prove useful for everyone interested in applied anthropology programs, from the development of a single applied course, to the creation of a well-articulated practitioner-oriented program involving an entire departmental faculty.

Special Publication No. 24.
$16 to members, $20 to all others.
Please enclose payment in US funds,
with all orders.

American Anthropological Association
1703 New Hampshire Ave., N.W., Washington, DC 20009